SOUTH CAROLINA PROVINCIAL TROOPS

Named in Papers of the
First Council of Safety of
The Revolutionary Party in South Carolina,
June - November, 1775

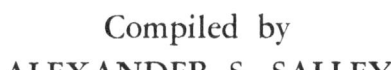

Compiled by
ALEXANDER S. SALLEY

With an Index by
ALIDA MOE

CLEARFIELD

Excerpted from
*The South Carolina Historical
and Genealogical Magazine,*
Volumes I-III, 1900-1902

Reprinted with an Added Index
Genealogical Publishing Co., Inc.
Baltimore, 1977

By permission of
The South Carolina Historical Society
Charleston, South Carolina

Copyright © 1977
Genealogical Publishing Company, Inc.
Baltimore, Maryland
All Rights Reserved.

Reprinted for
Clearfield Company, Inc. by
Genealogical Publishing Co., Inc.
Baltimore, Maryland
1999

Library of Congress Catalogue Card Number 76-57909
International Standard Book Number: 0-8063-0757-9

Made in the United States of America

PAPERS OF THE FIRST COUNCIL OF SAFETY OF THE REVOLUTIONARY PARTY IN SOUTH CAROLINA, JUNE–NOVEMBER, 1775.

[On January 11th, 1775, there met in Charleston the first Provincial Congress of South Carolina, and took under consideration the proceedings of the Continental Congress at Philadelphia at the close of the preceding year. This Congress was in session for several weeks. When it adjourned it selected a General Committee to look after the political affairs of the people of the Province until the Congress should again convene. The battle of Lexington, on the 19th of April, 1775, so excited the people of South Carolina that the General Committee re-convened the Provincial Congress on the first of June. In a few days after meeting, this Congress decided to place the Province in a position to resist British oppression, and so provided for three regiments of regular troops and selected a Council of Safety, consisting of thirteen members, to direct the affairs of the Province. This first Council of Safety consisted of Henry Laurens, President, Charles Pinckney, Sr., Rawlins Lowndes, Thomas Ferguson, Miles Brewton, Arthur Middleton, Thomas Heyward, Jr., Thomas Bee, John Huger, James Parsons, William Henry Drayton, Benjamin Elliott and William Williamson. Petei Timothy, the Secretary of the Provincial Congress, was selected to be secretary for the Council of Safety also. The first meeting of this Council was held on the 16th of June,

1775, and the journal of its proceedings from that day to the 26th of July, together with some correspondence and other papers, was published in the second volume of the "Collections" of this Society. The remainder of the journal of that first Council--was lost. The papers presented below form a part of the records of the first Council, and supplement those already published in the second volume of the "Collections" of this Society; in Drayton's Memoirs, Moultrie's Memoirs, Gibbes's Documents, 1764-1776, and Salley's History of Orangeburg County, 1704-1782. They are printed here from exact copies of the originals; all eccentricities of spelling and abbreviation being retained. Most of them are endorsed on the back by Henry Laurens. All words of explanation by the editor are put in *Italics*, and all editorial comments and numbers at the heads of papers are put in brackets.]

[1.]

ARTICLES OF AGREEMENT between the Council of Safety on behalf of the Colony of South Carolina of the one part and Andrew Williamson of Ninety Six Esqr of the other part[1] WHEREAS the Provincial Congress have agreed to raise two Regiments of Foot for the immediate Service of this Colony and have placed them under the direction of the said Council of Safety who have fixed the Ratio of each Man in the said Regiments at Three Shillings Currency Per Day. *NOW THESE PRESENT'S WITNESS* that the said Andrew Williamson for and in Consideration of the said Allowance of Three Shillings for each Man ⅌ Day to be paid Monthly *DOTH* hereby Covenant Promise and agree to Provide and Furnish to each Man in the said two Regiments of Foot the following articles—Viz!

,,One pound of good Beef ⅌ Day or One Pound of Fresh Pork or Twelve Ounces of Salt Pork—

---

[1] See Vol. 2 of "Collections," page 28, line 20 et seq.

,,One pound of Wheat Flour ℔ Day or One pound of Ship Bread or One Pint and a half of rice—
,,Half a pint of Vinegar ℔ Week when in Barracks or Stated Camps One Pint of Salt ℔ week when they are served with fresh Provisions &
,,One Pound of Black Pepper ℔ Year if it can be procured——

and the said Andrew Williamson doth also Covenant and agree that the said Provisions shall be good and Wholesome and regularly Supplied at such places within the said Colony as shall be directed by the said Council of Safety or by the Commanding Officer of the Troops and the Council of Safety do hereby agree to pay the full amount of all the provisions delivered in Manner aforesaid at the end of every Month as the same shall grow due Month by Month and also to allow the usual Carriage to Out Posts for such of the said Articles as the said Andrew Williamson shall be obliged to send from Charles Town and to pay for all Provisions which may be laid up in Store and for Cattle going to or delivered for the use of the Army by order of the said Council of Safety or of the Commanding Officer or Officers of the Troops, which may happen to be Burnt Taken or Destroyed by an Enemy and for the faithful Performance of these articles the said Parties do hereby bind themselves either to the other in the Penal Sum of Ten Thousand pounds Lawful Current money of the Province aforesaid   IN WITNESS whereof the President of the said Council of Safety on their Behalf and the said Andrew Williamson have hereunto set their hands and Seals this Twenty Seventh day of June in the Year of our Lord One Thousand Seven hundred and Seventy Five—

   Sealed & Delivered }
   In the Presence of } A. W^mSON [*Seal*]
         HENRY LAURENS, [*Seal*]
WILL^m VALENTINE‖.

 Endorsed : Contractors Agreement to supply the
     Troops———

[2.]

Addressed: To
   Col. HENRY LAURENS

Sir,

 As your Servant told me he was to wait for a Note from me to Mr Wiles, I have transcribed the Notification and sent it to Him.

 There was not a word that appeared necessary to be altered, nor one short or superfluous. I am
   Your most obed Ser
     PET.^r TIMOTHY
     7 July 1775

Endorsed: P. TIMOTHY
  7.th July 1775.

[3.]

Addressed : To
   WILLIAM THOMSON Esquire
   Lieu.^t Col.^o Commandant of the
   Rangers——
    Amelia——

   Glasgow near Ninety Six 18.th July 1775—

Sir

 In consequence of your Letter to me of the 1.st Ins.^t inclosing Orders from the Council of Safety,[2] directing me to Station Capt Purvis & his Company at Fort Charlotte, I wrote to him immedtly on the Subject and desired him to get his men ready for that Purpose, but not hearing from him untill the 10.th Ins.^t & then that he had inlisted only five men owing to a detention on the road of my Letter & Orders

---

[2] See Salley's History of Orangeburg County, 1704-1782, pp. 390-91.

SOUTH CAROLINA PROVINCIAL TROOPS   5

to him—I thought it best to wait no Longer but to go to Ninety Six where Captain Caldwell and Kirkland's Companies[3] were in Camp'd—the former having Twenty eight & the Latter Twenty three men, and to take with me both these Companies to Fort Charlotte; as I was informd Cap.t Whitefield[4] had knowledge of what was entended, by Some impruedent expressions of M.r Calhoun to the Serjant of the Fort.—we arrived there on the 12th and plac'd a Centinel at the Gate at noon, but had it been in the night we Should have had Some difficulty in taking it as a number of men slept there who was then out at their work. Captain Whitefield did everything an Officer could do without Power & he Submitted he did it with a grace that will do him honour—his Centiments seem to bee much in favour of the Congress and Council of Safety —I have Stationed Cap.t Caldwell at Fort Charlotte and gave him orders to defend it—I then took out the two Brass Pieces and Some ammunition & Sundry other Articles as Per a List inclosed—I returnd to Ninety Six on Friday the 14th with Captain Kirkland and his Company who incamp'd about Six miles to the Southwest of it on Saturday and on Sunday. Lieutenant Middleton deserted the Company & they all to a man desertd also, this you will see by Captain Kirklands Letter to me and by a Letter from M.r Middleton & the Report from his serjiant to him, Copies of which I now send you—Yesterday about noon a Party of about 200 disaffected People from Over the River headed by Rob.t & Patrick Cunningham, and Major Robinson of Col.o Neill's Regiment[5] came to Ninety Six all armd with Rifles &

---

[3] These companies formed a part of one (the 3rd) of the regiments already mentioned as having been authorized by the Provincial Congress, in June, 1775. (See Ramsay's Revolution in South Carolina, vol. 1., pp. 36-7. Collections of this Society, vol. 2, p. 24. Salley's History of Orangeburg County, 1704-1782, pp. 279-80.)

[4] The British officer at Ft. Charlotte, a nephew of Rev. George Whitefield.

[5] Provincial militia, as it existed before revolutionary measures were taken.

Capt Cunningham order'd them to halt as soon as they had got Round the Court house, he then demanded the Powder from us Rebells for the King & my orders for Robbing his Fort on my Refusing he had me apprehended as also Capt Kirkland who was Present from the beginning—I was Committed to Goal & was under the Power of the Constables; when they vouchsaf'd to admit me to Bail—they then Issued a warrant to Search for the Stories and took Every thing that Came from Fort Charlotte except they two field Pieces, & about Nine Oclock at Night they despersed, they declared them selves intirely in favour of Government & said they would ever oppose they measures of the Congress. all they Raingers that were Present at this trial which Last'd near eight hours, were Captain Kirkland Lieutenant Warley & myself—the Lieut: they were going to shew they Way to Charles Town.—I fear this Matter will spread on this side of the River if something is not spedily done in support of the resolves of Congress. & it will bee attended with every bad Consequence—many People from Savannah river have already come & subscribed Col? Fletchall & Captain Cunningham association & many others are daily expicted for the same Purpose, so that it will bee a Santuary for all such who opposes the measures of the Continentall & Provincial Congress.—the next thing that I have to mention to you is Provision—the Survice Cannot but bee attended with many inconveniences while the Rangers are not found therein— men seem very Backward in engaging for that very reason & should the People Refuse the money that they are to be paid with, as they say they will, they must starve, I hope you will use your influence with the Council of Safety that Provision may bee allow'd them—if the Pay of they man is not Punctually done at the end of one month from 26th Ulto it will dishearten them very much & many I expect will desert—I am afraid some Enemies to the Cause have fill'd the men belongiug to Captain Caldwell's Company with these notions the Cloathing is much wanted & I hope you have fallen on some Plan for that Purpose—I expect Captains Polk's Company daily as he wrote me the 7th Instant he would be in Camp in ten days—Capt Purve's Company I expect will bee Compleated in eight or ten days from this—Several of the men are sick when is the Doctor to visit us—I leave you to Judge of our Situation & hope both for your advice & assistance on this alarming Occasion—the Letter I have wrote to the Council of Safety I have Left unsealed for your Perusal & when you have read it Please to Seal it up & disbatch it by a fresh hand & horse to Town & keep the Ranger untill there is an answer from the Council of Safety[6]— Mr Cameron I understand will not except of his Commission on Account of his having an Estate in Scotland[7]—Lieutenant Middleton I think has Resign'd in a manner unbecoming an Officer & a Gentleman—both these Places are Vacant—Major Terry at Ninety six is appointed a Second Lieutenant in Captain Kirkland's Company. and I could wish if consistent with Millitary rule he could be appointed a first Lieutenant as Captain Kirkland informd me he intends to resign his Commission in his favour, but I told him that I could not see how that could be done & should bee very sorry for his Resignation—if he is harty in the Cause he would make an excellent Officer[8]—I shall bee Extremely happy if what I have done meets your approbation as I have endeavoured to Execute your Orders in every Perticular to the best of my Power and as near to Letter of them as Possible—we hope for more Companies being Ordered up I would be Glad in having the Pleasure to se you if Convenient—& Remain with Respect——

      Sir

     your Obdt humble Servant

(Copy)   (Sign'd) JAMES MAYSON

---

 [6] See Salley's History of Orangeburg County, 1704-1782, p. 400, line 10 et seq., and p. 404, line 11 et seq.

 [7] See Vol. 2 of "Collections," p. 67.

 [8] I have found no record of Terry ever receiving any commission at all, either as lieutenant or captain.—Ed.

Endorsed: Mr M{AYSON} to
Coll? T{HOMSON}—Copy—
16 July 1775 Recd 25th [9]

[4]

Fort Charlotte }
Ninety Six district }   Copy

Be it remembered that on Wednesday the Twelvth day of July in this present year One thousand seven hundred and Seventy five—between the hours of Eleven & Twelve OClock P. M. appeared before this Fort—Major James Mason—having under his Command Capt{ns} Kirkland & Caldwell with a party of Rangers consisting of Fifty Men—Major Mason sent a Messnage to Captn Whitefield—that he then in the Name of The Council of Safety took possession of Fort Charlotte. The Arms, Ammunition & Stores and immediately demanded the Keys—of the Magazine & Stores, to which Captn Whitefield as an Officer without power—was under the absolute necessity of acquiesing—at the same time—both Lieut{t} St Peirre & himself protesting and do hereby protest against the said proceedings—

GEO{r} WHITEFIELD.

Signed this 12th day of July } Mr LOUIS D. St PEIRRE
1775— }

Endorsed: Protest of
Capt W{HITFIELD} &
Leint{n} S{T} P{ERRE}—
the 12 of July 1775
Pr
Council of safety

Endorsed also: Capt W{HITEFIELD} &
Lt St P{IERRE}'s protest
Fort Charlotte
12 July 1775
Recd 25th [10]

---

[9] See Vol. 2 of "Collections," p 63, line 22 et seq.
[10] See Vol. 2 of "Collections," p. 63 line 22, et seq. Also Salley's History of Orangeburg County, 1704-1782, pp. 280-81-82, and pp. 390-91, 397-98-99-400-401-2-3-4-7.

[5.]

A return of Artillery, Ammunition & Stores at Fort Charlotte the 13th July 1775. by Capt. Caldwell

2 brass Cannon.
4 Iron six Pounders.
6 " four Pounders.
4 " two Pounders.
2 Swivels on Tryangles.
15 Muskets.
6 Ditto without Locks.
50 Cartouch Boxes.
11 Great Gun Worms.
8 " Pickers.
4 " Chargers.
123 lb Match.
717 lb Gun Powder in six Casks.
338 Do damaged in 4 Casks & Cags.
83 Cartridges in a Cask.
4619 Gun Flints.
343 Iron Balls.
2521 lb Musket Balls.
2 Iron Eyes for Swivels.
6 Iron bolts for Carriages.
3 large Iron Crows.
3 Tackle Blocks.
good and bad
15 Quires Cartridge Paper.
3 Smiths Vices.
1 Smiths Anvil.

2 Sledge & hand Hammers.
1 Screw Plate.
1 Coopers Crow Stock & Iron.
30 Copper Hoops.
1 Spade.
68 Shovels.
38 Grubbing Hoes.
34 Pick Axes.
10 Bill Hooks.
2 Broad Axes.
1 Lathing Hammer.
9 Old Chisels.
1 Smoothing Plane.
1 Rabbit Plane.
2 Guttering Planes.
2 Foot Adzes.
4 Augres.
3 Old Files.
5 Old Hand Saws.
4 Old Cross cut Saws.
1 Whip Saw.
3 Tennant Saws.
2 paring Gouges.
20 Cartridge Pins.

The above is a true Copy from the Original which is in my possession.

Ninety Six 18th July 1775.
JAs MAYSON

10 SOUTH CAROLINA PROVINCIAL TROOPS

Copy of a return of Artillery, Ammunition and Stores at Fort Charlotte the 20th May last, which Capt Whitcfield said he then sent to the Governor in Charles Town, out of which He has since Lent 500 lb Gun Powder for which he promises to be answerable—This Powder I understand was lent to some Merchants in Augusta who are to return it as soon as Capt Maitland—arrives in Georgia.—

13 Copper Hoops.
.2 Froes.
.3 Spades.
.71 Shovels.
.59 Grubbing Hoes.
.37 Pick Axes.
9 Bill Hooks.
4 Iron Wedges.
4 broad Hoes.
8 falling Axes Old.
4 broad Axes.
1 large Hammer.
10 Carpenter's Firmers.
1 broad Chizel.
3 broken Ditto.
5 treading Ditto.
3 large Compasses
1 Jointer.
2 long Planes
4 Jack Planes
3 Smoothing Ditto.
2 Rabbit Planes.
5 broad Ditto.
4 foot Adzes.
8 Augres.
14 Augres without handles.
15 Gimblets.
4 Iron Squares.
10 Hand Saws.

2 brass Cannon.
4 Iron six Pounders.
6 " four Pounders.
4 " two Pounders.
2 Swivels on Tryangles.
16 Muskets.
6 Muskets without Locks.
66 Bayonets.
11 Scabbards very Old.
20 Cartouch Boxes.
23 Do without Straps.
11 Great Gun Worms.
10 " Pickers.
6 " Scoops.
3 Rammers.
192 lb Match.
1500 lb Gun Powder.
500 Do damaged.
3000 Gun Flints.
272 Iron Balls.
96 Swivel Balls.
330 lb Trading Balls.
2 Iron Eyes for Swivels.
.29 Iron Bolts for Carriages.
3 large Iron Crows.
2 Tackle Blocks Iron bound.
1 Ditto not bound.
2 Colours old.

SOUTH CAROLINA PROVINCIAL TROOPS

10 Cross cut Saws.
2 Whip Saws.
2 Saw Setts.
.3 Hand Saw Files Old.
1 Cross cut File D?
7 Whip Saw Files D?
1 Crow Stock & Iron.
11 Quires Cartridge Paper.
9 Quires damaged D?
3 Smiths Vices.
2 " Anvils.
5 " Sledge Hammers.
2 " Screw Plates.
1 Coopers Adze.
3056 Musket Balls.

The above is a true Copy from the Return delivered to me by Capt Whitefield—

Ninety Six 18th July 1775.
JAs MAYSON.

N. B.—I find upon comparing Capt Caldwell's Return with Capt Whitefield's, a deficiency of 695 lb ct Wt Powder & a few other Articles, which Capt. Whitefield has promised upon his honour to make good—Captain Cunningham and Major Robinson with their party took away from this place the following articles which were not included in Capt Caldwell's Return above.—Vizt

250 lb ctWt Gun Powder in three barrels.
500. Lead in Trading & Musket Balls.
69. Bayonets.
1. X cut saw } which I took out of the Fort in order to
2. Old Axes } make Camps for to keep the Rangers from bad weather—

Ninety Six 18th July 1775.—
JAs MAYSON

Endorsed: Inventory of Stores at
Fort Charlotte & Copy of
a return made to the
Governor————
signed Mjr MAYSON 18 July
1775. Recd 25th [11]

---

[11] See vol. 2 of "Collections," p. 63, line 22 et seq.

12 SOUTH CAROLINA PROVINCIAL TROOPS

[6.]

Pay Bill of the first Regiment of Provincial troops, commanded by Colonel Christopher Gadsden—

Capt CHARLES C PINCKNEYS, Pay bill

1775—					
16 June to 1s July. both days inclusive	Hugh Milling: Serjeant....	16 days 10/	£ 8	"	—
	Saml Hunter ditto........	do	— 8	"	—
	Solo Proby, Corporal......	do 8/9	— 7	"	—
	Ferdinand Fisher. Private.	do 7/6	— 6	"	—
	Archibald Love...........	do — —	— 6	"	—
	Alexander Murray........	do	— 6	"	—
	Thomas McLain..........	do	— 6	"	—
19th to 1st July ..	John Fitzpatrick..........	13 days	— 4	17	6
21st to 1st do.....	Daniel Fowler	11 do	— 4	2	6
24th to 1st do.....	Henry Fry................	8 do	— 3	"	"
24th to 1st oo.....	James Barlow............	8 do	— 3	"	"
28th to 1st do.....	James Gill.	4 do	— 1	10	—
			£63	10	

Captn Wm CATTELL'S Pay Bill

16th to 1st July ...	Hugh Irvine Serjeant......	16 days 10/	£ 8	"	—
	David Piggot ditto	16 do do	— 8	"	—
	Chas Hansbury, Corporal..	16 do 8/9	— 7	"	"
	Brian McDonald Privt ...	16 do 7/6	— 6	"	"
	Thomas Gillmore..........	16 do	— 6	"	"
	John Niess................	16 do	— 6	"	"
	Michael Buckman.........	16 do	— 6	"	"
17th to 1st July ...	George Hensy.............	15 do	— 5	12	6
	John James Noble........	15 do	— 5	12	6
19th to 1st July ...	Henry Evans..............	13 do	— 4	17	6.
25th to do ...	Elisha House..............	7 do	— 2	12	6
			£65	15	

Captn ADAM McDONALD'S pay bill

16th June to 1st July	Thomas Malcom : Serjeant	16 d 10/	£ 8	"	—
	Amos Buck, Corporal. ...	16 d 8/9	— 7	"	—
	Esprit Solis.. Private......	16 d 7/6	— 6	"	—
	John Nash....d...........	16—	— 6	"	"
	William Morgan..........	16—	— 6	"	"
	Andrew Smith............	16—	— 6	"	"
[July	Jehu Gamble.............	16—	— 6	"	"
20th June to 1st	Patrick Kelly.............	11—	— 4	2	6
22 to do	James Sherwood..........	9—	— 3	7	6
25th to do	Theophilus Thorpe........	6—	— 2	5	—
			£54	15	—

SOUTH CAROLINA PROVINCIAL TROOPS

Captn Thomas Lynch's Pay Bill

Dates	Name	Time	£	s	d
16 June to 1st July	Michael Hubbard Serjt.	16 days 10/	8	"	—
22d to do	James Barron-ditto	10 do	— 5	"	—
17th to do	Samuel Peters, Corporal	15 d 8/9	6	11	3
16th to do	Richard Trimble ditto	16—	— 7	"	"
	Charles Moshill, Private	16 7/6	— 6	"	—
	David Mc Crady	16—	— 6	"	"
	John Hamilton	16—	— 6	"	"
	James Mc Kinley	16—	6	"	"
	Thomas Harvey	16	6	"	"
19th to 1st July	John Riley	13	4	17	6
21st to do	James Lyons	11	4	2	6
			£65	11	3

Captn William Scott's Pay Bill

Dates	Name	Time	£	s	d
16th June to 1st July	Wm Robinson, Serjeant	—16	£ 8	"	—
	Jas Mc Gowan, Ditto	—do	— 8	"	"
	William Miller do	—do	— 8	"	—
	Wm Hughes, Corporal	—do	7	"	"
	Dennis Sexton, ditto	—do	— 7	"	"
	John Hamilton, Private	—do	— 6	"	"
	Mathias Mc Carthy	—do	— 6	"	"
	John Ryan	—do	— 6	"	"
	Daniel Caulfield	—do	— 6	"	"
	Joseph Roberts	—do	— 6	"	"
17th to 1s July	William West	15 days	5	12	6
21st to ditto	Nathan Miller	11 do	— 4	2	6
22 to ditto	James Scott	10 do	— 3	15	—
30th to ditto	James Geoghagen	2 do	"	15	—
			£82	5	

Captn John Barnwell's Pay Bill

Dates	Name	Time	£	s	d
16th June to 1st July	John Reed Serjeant	16 days	£ 8	"	"
	Robt Mc Cleave Corporal	16 do	— 7	"	—
	Robert Campbell, Private	16 do	— 6	"	—
	William Kirk	do —	— 6	—	—
	George Colson	do	— 6	—	—
	Henry Fuguey	do	— 6	—	—
	William Evans	do	— 6	—	—
24th to 1st July	Thomas Conely	8 do	— 3	—	—
25th to do	James Thomas	7 do	— 2	12	6
27th to do	Simon Long	5 do	— 1	17	6
			£ 52	10	"

14 SOUTH CAROLINA PROVINCIAL TROOPS

Captⁿ Thomas Pinckneys Pay Bill

			£	s	d
16th June to 1st July	An: Redmond, Serjeant...	16 days	8	—	—
	John Hutchison, ditto.....	16 do	— 8	—	—
	Thos Chaddock, Corporal..	16 do 8/9	— 7	"	"
	John Sandwick, ditto.....	—do	— 7	"	—
	Thomas Langley. Private..	16 do @7/6	— 6	"	—
	Joseph Pettitt.............	16 do	— 6	—	—
	Thomas Turner...........	do	— 6	—	—
	John Mc Gill.............	—do	— 6	—	—
	William Cook.............	—do	— 6	—	—
20th to 1st July...	Hugh German.............	12 days	4	10	
24th to do ...	William Orr..............	-8 do	— 3	—	—
26th to do ...	Samuel Marchant.........	6 do	— 2	5	—
			£69	15	

Captⁿ Edmond Hyrne's Pay Bill

[July]			£	s	d
20th June to 1st June 16th to do	Richd Doggett, Serjeant..	12 days @ 10/	£ 6	—	—
	Roger Cannon, Corporal..	16 do @ 8/9	— 7	"	—
	Matthew Lamb : Private..	16 do @ 7/6	— 6	"	—
	An: Omensetter..........	:6 do — —	— 6	"	—
	Jacob Rian...............	16 du	— 6	"	—
	John Washon.............	16 do	— 6	"	—
	William Hoit.............	16 do	— 6	"	—
	Hugh Jones..............	16 do	— 6	.'	—
23d to 1st July...	John Dodds..............	9 do	— 3	7	6
30th to do	James Berriman..........	2 do	— "	15	
			£53	"2	6

Captⁿ Roger Sanders's Pay Bill

[July]			£	s	d
17th June to 1st 16d to 1st do	Wm Buck, Serjeant.......	15 days 10/	£—7	10	—
	John Goddard, Ditto......	16 do —	—8	—	—
	Philip Gruber Corporal....	16 do @ 8/9	—7	—	—
	Anty Murque, Private.....	16 do 7/6	—6	—	—
	William Roth, do	16 do	—6	—	—
	Anthony Gillmore.........	16 do	—6	—	—
19th to 1st July	Thomas Minar............	13 do	—4	17	6
	John Claera..............	13 do	—4	17	6
	James Hare..............	13 do	—4	17	6
25th to do	Joseph Jackson	7 do	—2	12	6
			£57	15	"

SOUTH CAROLINA PROVINCIAL TROOPS 15

Captⁿ BENJⁿ CATTELL'S Pay Bill

22d June to 1s July	Willm Landy, Serjeant....	10 days 10/	£ 5. 00.	0
29th to do.......	Robert Forshaw, Ditto....	3do 10/	—1 10.	0
16th to do.......	Chris^r Byrne's Corporal...	16 do 8/9	—7 00	0
	John Morrow, Private.....	16 do 7/6	—6 00.	0
22d to do........	Robert Roberts...........	10 do	—3 15.	0
16th to do.......	Wm Congdon Smith......	16 do	—6 00.	0
	Garrat Byrnes............	16 do	—6 00.	0
17th to do......	Frederick Aney...........	15 do	—5 12"	6
21st to do........	Joseph Barnes............	11 do	—4 2"	6
22d to do........	John Stiley..............	10 do	—3 15"	0
29th to do.......	Michael Huntsinger......	3 do	—1 2"	6
			£ 49 : 17	.6

Amdt Capt C C Pinckney............................£ 63	10	-
Capt Wm Cattell................................ .65	15	
Capt A Mc Donald............................. .54	15.	
Capt Thos Lynch............................... .65	11	3
Capt Wm Scott................................ .82	5	0
Capt Jno Barnwell............................. .52	10	0
Capt Th^s Pinckney .... .69	15	
Capt Ed: Hyrne........................ .... .53	2	6
Capt R: Sanders.. .... .57	15	
Capt Ben: Cattell................................. .49	17.	6
£ 614.	16	3
Serjeant Major Milling......................... 12	"	-
£ 626	16	3

16 SOUTH CAROLINA PROVINCIAL TROOPS

Pay Bill of the first Regiment of Provincial troops commanded by Colonel Christopher Gadsden from 2nd to 17th days July instant, both days inclusive—

Captn Chas C. Pinckney's Compy

1775			£		
2d to 17th July....	Hugh Milling. (Serjeant).	16 days 10/	£ 8	00	0
	Saml Hunter — — ditto...	d^o	.8	00	0
	Solo Proby, Corporal......	d^o 8/9	.7	00	0
	Jno Fitzpatrick ditto.......	-d^o	.7	00	0
	Ferdd Fisher. Private....	d^o @ 7/6	.6	00	0
	Thomas Mc Cann, ditto....	d^o	.6	00	0
	Alex^r Murray.....ditto.....	d^o	.6	00	0
	Archibald Love..........	d^o	.6	00	0
	Daniel Fowler,............	d^o	.6	00	0
	Henry Fry................	d^o	.6	00	0
[July	James Barlow............	d^o	.6	00	0
26th June to 17th	Philip Maguire............	22 days	8	5	0
22d June to d^o	Thomas Mains............	26 d^o	.9	15	0
[July	Charles Mc Alister........	ditto	.9	15	0
27th June to 17th	Jeremiah Mc Carty.......	21 days	.7	17	6
1st to 17th July....	John Davis................	17 ditto	6	7	6
	John Mc Gilton..........	ditto	.6	7	6
6th to 17th July...	David Jones...............	12 days	4	10	0
8th to 17th d^o	Josiah Simmons..........	10 d^o	.3	15	0
1st to 17th July...	Tinson Chesson............	10 d^o	.3	15	0
	John Riley................	17 days	6	7	6
			£ 138	15	..

Captn Wm Cattell's Company

			£		
2d to 17th July....	Hugh Irwin, Serjeant.....	16 days 10/	£ 8	00	0
	David Pigott,—ditto	ditto	.8	00	0
	Chars Hanbury, Corporal..	16 d^s 8/9	.7	00	0
	John Niess—Private.......	16 d^s 7/6	.6	00	0
	John James Noble ditto....	ditto	.6	00	0
	George Hensy—ditto	ditto	.6	00	0
	Michael Buckman, ditto...	ditto	.6	00	0
	Brian Mc Donald..........	ditto	.6	00	0
	Thomas Gillmore..........	ditto	.6	00	0
	Henry Evans..............	ditto	.6	00	0
[July	Elisha House.............	ditto	.6	00	0
29th June to 17th	Arch^d Knox	19 days	.7	2	6
30th to ditto.....	Burril Hill..	18 d^s	.6	15	0
Came to Barracks } 6th to 17th July }	William Elzey.............	12 d^o	.4	10	0
7th to 17th ditto.	Lawrence Murray..........	11 d^o	.4	2	6
29 June to 17th July	Josiah Little	19 d^o	.7	2	6
4th to 17th d^o	Thomas Smith...........	14 d^o	.5	5	0
26 June to 17th July	Samuel Bowman.........	22 d^o	.8	5	0
6th to 17th July..	Thomas Gibson	12 d^o	.4	10	0
4th to ditto......	Henry Cordal............	14 d^o	.5	5	0
7th to 17 ditto	Nicholas Irwin............	11 d^o	.4	2	6
			£ 128	00	..

SOUTH CAROLINA PROVINCIAL TROOPS

Captⁿ ADAM M^c DONALD'S Company

2d to 17th July....	Thomas Malcom, Serjeant	16 ds 10/	8	00	0
22d June to 17 July	William Rhodes ditto......	26 ds	13	00	0
2d to 17th July ...	Amos Buck, Corporal	16 ds 8/9	7	00	0
	Esprit Solis, Private.......	16 ds 7/6	6	00	0
	Andrew Smith, ditto......	.do	6	00	0
	John Nash..ditto.........	.do	6	00	0
	James Sheerwood, ditto...	.do	6	00	0
	Theophilus Thorpe........	do	6	00	0
	Patrick O'Kelly..........	do	6	00	0
[July	Michael Huntsinger.......	.do	6	00	0
22d June to 17th	George Richardson........	26 ds	9	15	0
[July	John Duvoux.............	26 ds	9	15	0
30th June to 17	John Harlow.............	18 ds	6	15	0
	James Farnell	18 ds	6	15	0
5th to 17th July...	John Hill Senr	13 ds	4	17	6
	John McNanamara........	13 ds	4	17	6
4th to 17th July..	John Leinard.............	14 ds	5	5	0
7th to 17th do.....	James Cooper.............	11 ds	4	2	6
	Martin Glass.............	11 ds	4	2	6
9th to 17th do....	Thomas Russell...........	9 ds	3	7	6
4th to 17th do....	Thomas Conelly..........	14 ds	5	5	0
			£ 134	17	6

Captⁿ THOMAS LYNCH'S Compy

2d to 17th July ..	Michael Hubard, Serjeant.	16 ds 10/	8	00	0
	James Barron..Ditto.....	ditto	8	00	0
	Saml Peters..Corporal....	16 ds 8/9	7	00	0
	Richard Trimble.ditto....	ditto	7	00	0
	Charles Monchell, Private.	16 ds 7/6	6	00	0
	David Mc Cready-ditto....	do	6	00	0
	John Hamilton............		6	00	0
	James Mc Kinley..........		6	00	0
	John Riley...............	do	6	00	0
	James Lyons..............		6	00	0
[July	Thomas Haresey...........		6	00	0
29th June to 17th	William Skilling	19 ds	7	2	0
	Abijah Winds.............	do	7	2	0
24th to 17th July..	Hugh Mc Guire.........	24 ds	9	00	0
25th to 17th July .	Philip Stapleton..........	23 ds	8	12	6
3d to 17th do......	William Williams.........	15 ds	5	12	6
7th to 17th do....	Charles Loughrea.........	11 ds	4	2	6
4th to 17th do....	Edward Barrett...........	14 ds	5	5	0
6th to 17th do....	William Smith............	12 ds	4	10	0
8th to 17th do....	Christopher Brett.........	10 ds	3	15	0
	Wm Summersett..........	10 ds	3	15	0
			£ 130	17	6

18 SOUTH CAROLINA PROVINCIAL TROOPS

Captⁿ WILLIAM SCOTT'S Company

1775			£	s	d	
2d to 17th July....	William Robinson, Serjeant	16 days 10/	£ 8	00	0	
	William Millen,—ditto....	ditto	— 8	00	0	
	James Mc Gowen,—ditto...	ditto	— 8	00	0	
	John Hamilton—Corporal.	16 days 8/9	— 7	00	0	
	William Hughes, ditto....	ditto	— 7	00	0	
	Dennis Sexton—ditto......	ditto	— 7	00	0	
	William West. Pri ato...	16 days 7/6	6	00	0	
	Mathias Mc Carty ditto....	— — —	— 6	00	0	
	Nathan Miller............	— — —	— 6	00	0	
	James Scott..............	— — —	— 6	00	0	
	John Ryan................	— — —	— 6	00	0	
[July	James Gill...............	— — —	— 6	00	0	
25th June to 17th	William Strain...........	23 days	— 8	12	6	
30 do to 17th July.	John Brown..............	18 do	— 6	15	0	
3rd to 17th July..	Joseph Harvey...........	15 do	— 5	12	6	
	Matthew Canady..........	15 do	— 5	12	6	
	John Flin...............	15 do	— 5	12	6	
9th to 17th July..	Jeremiah Deadman........	9 do	— 3	7	6	
27 June to17th July	Thomas Larimore.........	21 do	— 7	17	6	
4th to 17th July.	John Burke.............	14 do	— 5	5	0	
30th June to17th do	Isham Craie............	18 do	— 6	15	0	
	George Page...........	18 do	— 6	15	0	
4th to 17th do....	Thomas Scurry..........	14 do	— 5	5	0	
2nd to 17th July..	John Gordon...........	16 do	6	00	0	
			£ 154	10		

Captn. JOHN BARNWELL'S Company

			£	s	d	
2d to 17th July....	John Reed - - Serjeant.....	16 days 10/	£ 8	00	0	
	Robert Mc Cleave, Corporal	16 do 8/9	— 7	00	0	
	Robert Campbell, Private..	16 do 7/6	— 6	00	0	
	William Kirke, ditto.....	ditto	— 6	00	0	
	Henry Fuguey............	— —	— 6	00	0	
	Thomas Conaly...........	— —	— 6	00	0	
	George Colson...........	— —	— 6	00	0	
	William Evans...........	— —	— 6	00	0	
	James Thomas............	— —	— 6	00	0	
[July	Simon Long..............		— 6	00	0	
30th June to 17th	William Gunter..........	18 days	— 6	15	0	
29th do to ditto...	James Wisdom...........	19 ditto	— 7	2	6	
4th to 17th July..	Thomas Gillmore........	14 ditto	5	5	0	
7th to 17th ditto..	Nathaniel Watson.......	11 do	4	2	6	
8th to 17th ditto..	George Ferguson........	10 do	3	15	0	
13th to 17th do....	Richard Reily...........	-5 do	— 1	17	6	
	James Reed............	-5 do	— 1	17	6	
14th to 17th ditto..	Andrew Touchstone......	-4 do	— 1	10	0	
	Jacob Frost............	-4 do	— 1	10	0	
8th to 17th July..	Samuel Scott	-10 do	— 8	15	0	
1st to 17th ditto..	Michael Moor...........	-17 do	6	7	6	
			£ 106	17	6	

SOUTH CAROLINA PROVINCIAL TROOPS 19

Captain Thomas Pinckney's Company

Period	Name	Days	£ s d
2d to 17th July	Andrew Redmond, Serjeant	16 days 10/	£—8 00 0
	John Hutchison, - ditto....	ditto	—8 00 0
	Thomas Chaddock, Corporal	16 days 8/9	7 00 0
	John Sandwick, - ditto.....	-ditto-	—7 00 0
	Joseph Pettitt, --Private..	16 days 7/6	6 00 0
	Thomas Turner - -ditto...	....	6 00 0
	John McGill.................	....	6 00 0
	Samuel Marchant...........	....	6 00 0
	William Cook................	....	6 00 0
	Hugh German...............	....	6 00 0
	William Orr.................	....	—6 00 0
	James Berriman............	....	—6 00 0
3d to 17th July...	William Ross.............	15 days.	—5 12 6
27th June to 17th do	Francis Cullian...........	21 ditto—	—7 17 6
1st to 17th July...	John Hill, jun............	17 ditto	6 7 6
29 June to 7th July	John Cook................	19 ditto.	—7 2 6
4th to 17th July...	Cornelius Heynes.........	14 ditto	5 5 0
	Daniel Sullivan..........	ditto	—5 5 0
9th to 17th July...	John Smith................	9 days	—3 7 6
7th to 17th July...	Francis Archer............	11 ditto	—4 2 6
8th to 17th ditto..	Lazarus Wooley	10 ditto	3 15 0
			£ 126 15 0

Captain Edmond Hyrne's Company

Period	Name	Days	£ s d
1775 [July] 27th June to 17th	James Stafford, Corporal..	21 days 8/9	£ 9 3 9
2d to 13th July...	Roger Cannon, ditto.......	12 do	5 5 0
2d to 17th ditto..	Andrew Omensetter, Private	16 do 7/6	6 00 0
	Jacob Rian.................	— —	— 6 00 0
	William Hoyt..............	— —	— 6 00 0
	Matthew Lamb	— —	— 6 00 0
	John Washon..............	— —	— 6 00 0
	Jehu Gamble...............	— —	— 6 00 0
	Hugh Jones................	— —	— 6 00 0
	John Dodds...............	— —	— 6 00 0
4th to 17th July..	Charles Wood.............	14 days	5 5 0
29th June to 17 do .	William Pring.............	19 ditto	— 7 2 6
3d to 17th July...	Bartholomew MacDonald..	15 ditto	5 12 6
4th to ditto......	William Johnston.........	14 ditto	5 5 0
30 June to 17th July	John Williams............	18 ditto	6 15 0
29th to 17th July.	John Corker	19 ditto	— 7 2 6
14th to 17th July..	Roger Cannon............	4 ditto	— 1 10 0
29 June to 17th July	Thomas Manning.........	19 ditto	— 7 2 6
30th do to ditto....	William Edwards.........	18 ditto	6 15 0
14th to 17th July..	James Parsons	4 do	— 1 10 —
2d to 18th do	Richard Doggett (Serjeant)	12 do 10/	6 00 0
			£ 122 ,,8 9

20 SOUTH CAROLINA PROVINCIAL TROOPS

Captⁿ Roger Sanders's Compy

1775			£ s d
2d to 17th July....	William Buck, Serjeant...	16 days 10/	£ 8 00 0
	John Goddard, Ditto......	ditto	8 00 0
	Philip Gruber, Corporal...	16 ds 8/9	—7 00 0
	Thomas Minar, ditto......	ditto	—7 00 0
	Anthony Marque, Private	16 ds 7/6	—6 00 0
	William Roth.............	ditto	—6 00 0
	Anthony Gillmore.........	ditto	—6 00 0
	John Claera.............	ditto	—6 00 0
	James Heir..............	ditto	—6 00 0
	Joseph Jackson..........	ditto	—6 00 0
[July	James Geohagen..........	ditto	—6 00 0
22d June to 17th	Robert Brice.............	26 days	—9 15 0
2d to 17th do.....	Joseph Roberts...........	16 ditto	—6 00 0
8th to 17th do....	Daniel Brient............	10 ditto	—3 15 0
3rd to 17th do....	John Danniles...........	15 ditto	—5 12 6
6th to 17th do....	William Huggins.........	12 ditto	—4 10 0
4th to 17th do....	James Boswood...........	14 do	—5 5 0
5th to 17th do....	Peter Crosbee............	14 do	—5 5 0
5th to 17th do	Moses Baker.............	13 do	4 17 6
10th to 17th do	Robert Bonds............	8 do	—3 00 0
29 June to 17th July	John Budding............	19 do	—7 2 6
1st to 17th July...	Thomas Burt.............	17 do	6 7 6
			£ 133 10 "

Capt Benj. Cattell's Company

2d to 17th July...	William Landy, Serjeant.	16 days 10/	£ 8 00 0
	Robert Forshaw, ditto....	ditto	— 8 00 0
	Chrisr Byrne, Corporal...	16 das 8/9	— 7 00 0
	William Congdon Smith, Private..................	16 ds 7/6	— 6 00 0
	Gerald Byrne............	ditto	— 6 00 0
	Frederick Aney	ditto	— 6 00 0
	John Morrow............	ditto	— 6 00 0
	Robert Roberts..........	ditto	— 6 00 0
	John Stiley.............	ditto	— 6 00 0
[July	Joseph Barnes...........	ditto	— 6 00 0
25th June to 17th	William Johnston Campbell	23 days	— 8 12 6
[July	William Nangle..........	23 days	— 8 12 6
30th June to 17th	Needon Lamb............	18 ditto	— 6 15 0
27th to 17th do...	Gabriel Scott...........	21 do	— 7 17 6
28th to 17th do...	Richard Stinson.........	20 do	— 7 10 0
8th to 17th July..	James Carigon..........	10 do	— 3 15 0
4th to 17th do....	Peter Lewis	14 do	— 5 5 0
7th to 17th do....	Arthur Rogers..........	11 do	— 4 2 6
4th to 17th do....	Peter Larey............	14 do	— 5 5 0
3d to 17th do.....	James Mc Kutchon.......	15 do	— 5 12 6
			£ 128 7 6

SOUTH CAROLINA PROVINCIAL TROOPS

Capt C C Pinckneys Compy	£138,,	15:	0
Captn Wm Cattell's ditto	128,,	00.	0
Capn Adam Mc Donald, ditto	134:	17:	6
Capt Thos Lynch, junr	130:	17:	6
Capt William Scott	154:	10.	0
Capt John Barnwell	106:	17:	6
Capt Thos Pinckney	126:	15:	0
Capt Edmond Hyrne	122:	8:	9
Capt Roger Sanders	133:	10.	0
Capt Benj Cattell	128:	7:	6
Serjeant Major Milling	12:	00.	0
	£1316:	18:	9
Amot Pay Bill from 16th June to 1st July both days inclusive	£ 626,,	16,.	3
	£1943,,	15,,	

Endorsed: Two Pay Bills for the
   1st Regiment of foot
   up to the 17 July 1775.
     total £1943 15—
☞ Cash advanced
 the 16 July £2000
 Balance in Pay-Master's
 hand 17 July £57—

[7.]

Addressed: To
    Henry Laurens Esqr
 ℔ Mr Adinger.[12] Charles Town

           Beaufort 18th July 1775.
Sir
 about Nine O Clock this morning your favour of 16th & 17th Instant were delivered to me by Mr Adinger, and should have Complyed with the Council of safetys order in deleivering the Letter directed to Mr Tebout,[13] but he set out yester-

---

[12] See vol. 2, "Collections," pp. 44, 47. [13] Ibid, p. 53, line 27.

day morning for Charles Town with Capt. Joyner and others to convey down about 5000!ᵇ Gunn powder taken out of Maitlahds ship, so that he will be with you earlier than if he were here now; I took the liberty of opening the Letter directed to him, thinking that probably there was some order to be executed, if the Vessel you mention came here & which perhaps I coud have complied with, but I find that is not the case. I Return the Letter & hope it will not be taken amiss of me you may depend I shall keep this matter as it is Intrusted to me.—many Gentlemen were present at the delivery of the Lettr & ask'd what was the Express, to which I Replyed it was a private one. & that put an end to their Enquirys—we have sent off this morning 5000 ᵇ Gunn powder which came here yesterday under care of Lieutn Doharty, from Savannah, he is to deliver it, a Guard is sent with it from hence. I wish the first and this parcell safe to Chs Town, where I make no doubt it will meet with a hearty Reception—I am with Respect

       Sir
     Your Hble servant
      D.·.DeSAUSSURE

Endorsed : D DeSaussure
    18 July 1775
     Reported
    & paid Adinger—
Endorsed also : No 26-24 papers

[8.]

St Pauls Parish ye 18th July 1775——

Personally appeared before Andrew Leitch Esquire one of his majesties Justice of the Peace for Charlestown District & The Committee for St Pauls Parish, Allen Miles, Robert Miles, & Melcher Garner be:ng Present————

Agreeable to a summons by us to Cause Charles Webb to

Clear himself of some Malicious Expressions said against His Honour the Lieutenant Governour & the Committee's of the Said Province—Messrs John Jackson, William & James Rugge & Jn.o Humphreys being Witnesses to what They Heard the said Charles Webb Say in Public Company ——The affidavits of the Said Gentlemen are as follows——

That on monday ye 8th May Last, Jn.o Jackson in Company with the aforesaid witnesses, went from ye quarter house to Charlestown to the house of Valuntine Lynn, their in the Evenning of the same day Charles Webb ask'd the Deponant to Walk with him to Francis Bremars, accordling he went with the said Charles & found Mr Bremar at Mr Ramages Tavern, when on that very Day the news was brought that Hostilities had commenc'd against Boston, & the Bostonians were Success,full & there was Mrs Ramage & Mr Bremar Present when Charles Webb Declared he woud go to England take a Commission & come Against the Americans——

Mr William Rugge on Oath saith That on the Precedeing 8th Day May, he heard the said Charles Declare he woud Stand to what he said at Mr Ramages Tavern, then the Deponant asked him what he said; he Answer'd, That he wou'd go home & get a Commission & come Out & fight against the Americans—Shortly after That, at Mr Edwards Tavern on the Bay, the Deponant with Jno Jackson heard the said Charles Call the Lieutanant Governor, a Damd Fool for not Hoisting the King's Standard——

Mr. James Rugge on Oath saith That some time in April last that the said Charles Inform'd the Deponant, that his Father—in=Law Thomas Harcombe was then Just return'd from Charlestown, Charlestown, during the time he was Their, one Mrs Pendergrass Dun'd his Father (meaning Mr Harcombe) for an Accot Due Mr. Long). Publicly in the Street, & had Threaten'd him that she woud apply to The Committee, Provided he woud not settle the Account with her, the said Charles Replyd, a Pretty Joke indeed, to apply to such a Sett of Mechanical, Ignorant Rascals, & that they consisted of Butchers, Taylers & Coblers & Hop'd that his Father wou'd not obey ancy Summons from Them, wch If it was his Own Case he wou'd not—sometime after, the Deponant came from Charlestown & the said Charles ask'd him whether the Delegates were Sail'd for the N^o Ward, in Answer, he told him he Believ'd they were; he then reply'd, that he wish'd the men of War woud meet with 'em & take them Pris'oners & carry them to England, Their to be Treated as Rebels, for he thought them more so then Ever the Scotch were, & he was not Surpriz'd at the Scotch, being such Loyal Subjects, for a Burnt Child wou'd Dread the Fire & how Pretty the Foolish, Rascals of Property wou'd Look when their Lands & Negroes comes to be for=feited to the King that he cou'd take the whole Province, if he had a Regement of the Kings Soldiers, for he well knew that the Americans wou'd not fight, The Deponant Further heard the Said Webb say that he Blam'd the Lieutanant Governor for his being so Inactive & that the People wou'd not been so Rebelious had it not been for his Foolish Proceedings, that he wonder'd he Did not Put up the King's Standard, that he mout be able to know who was Friends to the Government or who Not———

Mr Jno Humphreys on Oath, saith That In may last Their was some Gentlemen at Mr Thomas Harcombe's Talking about the Affairs of the Country, & after those Gentlemen went away he heard Mr Webb say he thought it was a Pit'y their was not a Gallows in charlestown to hang all the Americans in a String, & as for the Committee They were a Lousey Sett. Blackgards, such as Butchers, & Taylers——& Further Saithe Not——

Sworn ye 18th July 1775 before me

       AND^w LEITCH
       JOHN JACKSON
       Wm RUGGE
       JAMES RUGGE

S^t. Pauls Parish ye 18 July 1775—

Whereas Charles Webb being brought before the Committee for saying many disrespectfull words against the Lieutenant Governor (of this Province) & the Committees in general,—it has appeared to us, by several Affidavits that the said Charles Stands Guilty of the Accusation——Wee Therefore Look on him as an Enemy to This Province & America in General And an Object of the Resentment of the Public— by Order of the Committee

MELCHER GARNER Chairman

Endorsed: Proceedings & Sentence
against Charles Webb
St Paul's Parish
July 1775

[9.]

Gentlemen   Charles Towne 20th of July 1775

Give me Leave to Assure you, Nothing Can Give Me Greater Concern than being an Idle Spectator att A time When Every Lover of Liberty, Should be In Some Manner Assisting to the Preservation of that Invaluable Blessing, With a heart full of Zeal, I most humbly Offer my Poore Service, Voluntary to Goe on any Expedition, Where your Honours think I Can be of Any service, and Should I be Thought Worthy of Any Trust, I Shall Deemd It The most Happy moment of my Life

I Am allways ready to Goe Where your Honors Please To Send me, and hope With the Blessing of God To Prove My self Deserving The Tittle of a Lover of this Country And Not Unworthy of your Commands

I have only To Say With Greatest Truth I am
Gentlemen Your Most Obedient
Most humble servant
JOHN COPITHORN[14]

To The Honble Councill of Satfty

Endorsed: JOHN COPITHORN
20 July 1775

---

[14] See Vol. 2 "Collections," p. 53, line 28.

[10.]

Addressed: M?̱ Charcman & To
The Gentelmen
of
the Comity of Saifty

Gentelmen of the Commity of Saiftey

I have inclosed the bill of Expince in gowing On the Secret Sarvcce to North Edesstoe, the Expince would not have so greait had I not Supplied the boat with Nessessarey that I thought it Prudent to Send Back to Georgiea

from Gentelmin your humble
Sarvant
JOSEPH VERREE[15]

Charlestown July 27th 1775

Endorsed: Jo^s VERREE
Endorsed also: £64 10/ to
M Jos VERREE
for Expences
going to North
Edisto for the
Gun powder

[11.]

Addressed: CLEMENT LEMPRIERE Esq?̱ Beaufort
Port Royal

Charles Town 27th July 1775—[16]
past midnight ——

Dear Sir——

Notwithstanding the inclosed Letter, or I Should Say the Letter in which this is inclosed, is Signed by order of the

---

[15] See vol 2 "Collections," pp. 54 and 55.

[16] The only preserved journal of the first Council of Safety ends with the 26th July, 1775. The journals containing subsequent proceedings of that body were lost—See Vol. 2, "Collections," pp. 63 and 64 and 74

Council of Safety—I do not like it—it was written late in the Evening when Gentlemen Seemed desirous of retiring to their Beds & disinclined to reconsider or even fully consider—I therefore, now they are all probably on their pillows, take the liberty of recommending, & desiring, you will, in the first Instance, if you meet the Brig^t, offer to purchase the Gun powder at Six or even Seven pounds Sterling ⅌ C^t & Muskets & Ball, if any, at prices in proportion & for the amount you may draw on me as President of the Council of Safety & depend upon it such draughts to the amount of Fifteen Hundred pounds Sterling if needful shall be paid, if the Council will not justify this act—I must for their & my own Sake so far this request of mine cannot work any contradiction to the Councils orders which must be obeyed if there is a necessity for it, in Case the Captain of the Brigt. will not sell—if he will then certainly we shall be all much better pleased by a purchase than we shall be to obtain the articles by force & violence.—I wish you success in all your enterprizes & beg you to add my Compliments & good wishes to the Gentlemen your Companions & I remain with great regard &co—

Endorsed : Copy[17] 27. July 1775—
   Clem. Lempriere.

[12.]

Addressed : To
   Henry Laurens Esqr
   Charles Town.

Sir   Beaufort 29th July 1775.

I Received your favour ⅌ the Express Adinger and in Compliance with your order, I deleiverd the Letter to Capt Lampriere (who arrived here yesterday) he is Busied in geting

---

The journal of the second Council of Safety begins on November 30th, 1775, and ends February 26th, 1776. The remainder of these papers are practically the only further record of the proceedings of the first Council of Safety.

[17] Letter by Henry Laurens.

the Vessel Ready, which prevents his writing, but he has Requested me to acquaint you that he will Comply with the order you sent him—and hopes to get away tomorrow:—I shall dispatch the Letter for Savannah today, and Inclose it to Joseph Clay & Joseph Habersham Esq^{rs} in case one should be absent, the other may deliver it without Loss of time   I beg leave to assure you that I shall be particularly pleased whenever the Council of Safety shall lay their Commands on me for the Countrys Service & shall endeavour to execute them the best in my power.

I am much obliged to you for the Information of the arrivals from Urope.   I am with Esteem
     Sir
      Your most ob^t d
       Hble Servant
        D : D<small>E</small>SAUSSURE

Endorsed : D<small>AN</small> D<small>ESAUSSURE</small>
    29 July 1775——

[13.]

Addressed : On the Colonys Service
    To
    Col^o H<small>ENRY</small> L<small>AURENS</small>.
      Chas Town

     Camp near Granby 29th July 1775—
Honour'd Sir

I have this moment been inform'd by a Traveling Man, that Capt Polk Cross'd Saluda River with a Compleat Company of very Likely Men on Sunday Last, on his way to Ninety Six—[18]   I am with Regard
     Honourd Sir
      Your Most Obed^t Servt
       Wm THOMSON

Endorsed : W^m T<small>HOMSON</small> 29 July
    1775 Rec^d 1st Aug^t

---

[18] See Mayson's letter, ante p. 47. Salley's History of Orangeburg County, 1704-1782, p. 406, line 19, et seq.

[14.]

Addressed : WILLIAM THOMSON Esquire
Lieut: Colonel Commandant of the Regiment
of Rangers—
⅌ Express   at
M.ʳ Cochran   Amelia

Col.º WILLIAM THOMSON.
Camp near Ninety Six 30.ᵗʰJuly 1775.

Sir

Inclosed you will receive M.ʳ Kirkland's Letter to me of the 28.ᵗʰ by which you will see his reasons for resigning his Commission & that they correspond with the hints given you in a former Letter; He has hurted the Cause very much by telling his Company that it was bad & that they had all better return home than remain & fare worse — I am informed that he was with them a few days ago, when they all seemed willing to come to Camp with him, but he possitively refused & discharged them—I have ordered Lieut. Martin to get them together & take the Command but have very little expectation of his success or of ever seeing them in Camp—Cap.ᵗ Kirkland came here last Thursday Morning & immediately had a long private Talk with Cap.ᵗ Polk, which I am a stranger to—but I am certain his coming was of very little service—The next morning I gave Cap.ᵗ Polk Orders to sett off with a Command of men to Fort Charlotte for to conduct the ammunition which you ordered me to send for in your Last Letter ⅌ M.ʳ Forbes, when I was told, that he had discharged both the Grass & Quarter Guards from their duty—that he was their Officer & would not sacrifice their Healths for no Council of Safety's Parading notions, that it was contrary to the rules of the Congress to march them towards Town & a great deal of such like inflamatory Language—I must confess that this sudden conduct of Cap.ᵗ Polks surprised me very much as well as his behaviour since—His men were very impudent to me after his telling them that he would not order them below without their consent & as for his own part he would not go without there was an absolute occasion—so that his jaunt to Fort Charlotte was not complied with—I am very certain it would be impossible for Capt Polk ever to carry any Command over his Company, from what I have seen since his arrival here which was last Sunday Evening—The Morning preceeding that day I received a Letter from him by an Express, informing me, that he would be glad to see me immediately, as he was likely to be ambuscaded by some of Capt Cunningham's party—accordingly I went & met him & his Company about eight miles over Saludy river & Conducted them hither—This party consisting of about sixty men had actually stopp'd them on the road. but Capt Cunningham Ordered them to Disperse as soon as he came up with them—When I found Capt Polk was determined to march his Company back again, I entreated him to reflect seriously on what he was going to do, as his honor was at stake—He said he had already done it and that he would not take the Tour which was Ordered by the Council of Safety at this season of the year, that he allways understood the Rangers were raised to protect the Frontiers & not their Plantations, that he & all his Company were ready & willing to go, if there was a necessity for so doing; but at present in his opinion there was none, that they were now inlisted near a month, that neither he or his men expected any pay from the Province, & that he would not charge them a single farthing for the Expence he had been at in providing for them during that time—directly after this conversation Capt Polk Ordered his Company to get ready for marching & left the Camp about 10 ºClock yesterday afternoon—I found myself all this time in a very disagreeable situation, having only 20 of Capt Purves's men, who tho' obedient were not sufficient to execute my Orders, if I had given any, I thought it most prudent to let them depart in Peace, as they were all ripe to commit the most daring Enterprise—You will find under this cover from Capt Polk a Letter for you together with another to me, which I received just before he quitted the Camp—I do not think it safe just now to send for any Ammunition from Fort Charlotte as there are so few Rangers here to protect it in case of need & the People still seem to be in as great a ferment as ever, if not greater several Gentlemen of Fortune I learn have come from Savannah & Georgia & signed Fletchall & Cunningham's Association & I am of opinion many others will join them—I shall be glad to know by the return of the Bearer whether you expect I will conduct Capt Purves's Company down to Amelia as you ordered in your las.^t[19]

> I remain with respect
> Sir
> your obed.^t hum.^l Servt
> Ja.^s. MAYSON.

Endorsed: Maj.^r, MAYSON to Coll.^o
THOMSON 30. July 1775
Read in Council
11th August

[15.]

Addressed: To
The Honour.^{le} HENRY LAWRENCE

S.^r /

That Happy period in ye Earley Time of Life when youth in us Knew Nothing of ye Cabinett or ye field and which gave birth to An Acquaintance, made me Apply to you Last Even. & in ye manner that I Did Hopeing that ye Kind Benevolent Monitor which Allways Appeared in you for me in former Cases of wich shall Ever be Retaind with ye moast greatfull Remembrance would have Assisted my weak Indevours in ye Address befour you ye Common Cause Demanded this as

---

[19] See Salley's History of Orangeburg County, 1704-1782, p. 290, line 2 et seq., p. 295, line 20 et seq., pp. 294-95, p. 307, p. 414, p. 417.

I Realey thought and wether it was A principall Inspired by
God or that of Nature from my fore fathers Loins who have
Marked there way in blood in former days for this province
—*I know not]* but One of ye two is ye Acting principali
Moveing me by this first Address to ye Counsell where I see
you so far advance^d, and Honoured in Such a Emenent
Distincktion whose Capassity I Admired while I Lament
ye Loss—but I wisper you Something that ye Hardships of
Life has Qualified there Nerves for Labour in ye field this
Glorious field that I would wish all my Heart and Soul Con-
tend in till Every Spring of Life Lost its powers there I
never had An Opperuunity because it was not in my power
And from ye Expressions I heard fall from A gent^n I See my
first Attempt all Vanisht in Air where my prayers Accom-
panyes them to Heaven for ye publick safety in more Abler
Hands while I Seek Other Methods if I am Obliged to seek
At Boston its self in this Glorious Cause Adue I am done
God Bless you in Every Indevore forgive my Ignorance pitty
ye Capassity In ye Sentiments of your Ever Affection^{te}
      Herty Well Wisher
         J. COACHMAN

 Endorsed: JAMES COACHMAN
    30 July 1775, Answered
    immediately as within—

[16.]

         Ansonburgh 30 July 1775—
Dear Sir—
 I had flattered my self as well as my friends with the hopes
of a Company of Men upon your plan which would have
been truly serviceable in the common cause if occasion should
have required their appearance in the Field, therefore believe
me, your secession[20] is no little mortification to me & that in
my opinion the Council of Safety in general will be sorry for

---

[20] A very early use of that term.

it—the expression from Capt. Elliott which seems to have affected you was not intended to offend, & I beg you will not, from that or from any other attempt in the Council to explain our meaning in order if possible to accommodate our Duty with your patriotic proposition, take hasty exceptions—consider, we have a part to act as well as other Men—the most difficult part too—we have to please all Men—every Man thinks he has a right to arraign those whose task it is to *direct*—but I will say no more on this Head—M? Withers is anxious to go, therefore I shall only add that I hope you will not wholly abandon your laudable impulse, think farther of the subject & be assured the Council of Safety will be glad to concur with you in every thing consistent with the line of their Duty & the public good & none more cordially than Dear Sir

Your most obed! Serv!

JAMES COACHMAN Esq! —

Endorsed : Answer to JA COACHMAN
30 July 1775.

[17.]

Addressed : To
HENRY LAURENS Esq!
Charles Town.

Beaufort 2ᵈ August 1775.
Sir

In consequence of your directions, I sent Express to Savannah & the Letter for the Council of Safety was deliv ered, and the Inclosed sent me to be forwarded, I Received it yesterday morning, and as I dout whether its Contents are of such a Consequence as to need an Express, I declined sending one in hopes an opportunity woud offer soon, which does this day: I have to Inform you Capt. Lampriere set sail from here on Monday forenoon, and in all probability

got over the Barr that afternoon, Cap! Joyner with a few Volunteers from here, went with him—Inclosed is an acco! due me which you will please to order payment to my partner M! Josiah Smith, there is another acco! due me for Sundrys Supplyed Cap! Joyner & Capt. Barnwell on the first Expedition, but the acco! is given in to Cap! Joyner who will Render it amongst the others——I am with Esteem
Sir
Your most obed!
and most Hble servant
D.: DeSAUSSURE

Sir
Your favour of the 2^d Ins! came duly to hand & was presented immediately to the Council of Safety who return you their thanks—the Account which came Inclosed in it was also immediately endorsed by an Order on the Treasurers for Payment I signed it by order & desired the Secretary to deliver it to M! Josiah Smith.——

I am Sir
Charles Town, 10th August 1775—   your most obed! Servt
H L. Presid! of C S—
P S
Inclosed you will receive a Letter
from M! Delagayé——

Endorsed: DAN DeSAUSSURR 2^d Aug!
1775. Rec^d & Read in Council
the 5th Ans^d 10th
as within

[18.]

In the Council of Safety. 6th August 1775
Sir—
We have fully considered the Contents of your Letter of the 4th Ins! but we cannot, from any thing you have alledged or referred to perceive the Smallest ground for a misunder-

standing between the Council of Safety & the Army—nor do we find any point so obstruse as to render a foreign enquiry necessary on our part

We do not think it needful at present to define your duty nor to mark the extent of your authority, but, without quoting precedents in justification of our proceedings, we trust it will be sufficient to say, that in vertue of certain Resolutions of the Provincial Congress—"that the Council of Safety shall have the supreme direction regulation maintenance & ordering of the Army & of all Military establishment & arrangements." & that the said Council shall have "power & authority to do all such matters & things relative to the strengthning securing & defending the Colony as shall by them be judged & deemed expedient & necessary" We Issued our Order of the 1st Curr! which you are pleased to call a paper, "for leave of absence to Lieutenant John Blake from duty in the 2d Regiment of Foot till further orders" —an act which we deemed to be both expedient & necessary for the public service. We assure you this was not done either in matter or manner with any design to give you offence nor to intrench upon those Rights which in the absence of the Colonel of the first Regiment, reside in you & which we shall aways be ready to support. We have therefore no doubt but that upon reconsidering this matter you will pay that regard to our Order which is due & which ought not to have been delayed.

By order of the Council of Safety.

Endorsed: Copy. 6th Augst 1775 [21]

---

[21] This letter was written by Henry Laurens, and must have been written to Col. William Moultrie, of the 2nd South Carolina Regiment. It does look a little strange to see the three Regiments of South Carolina Regulars spoken of as "the Army."

PAPERS OF THE FIRST COUNCIL OF SAFETY OF THE REVOLUTIONARY PARTY IN SOUTH CAROLINA, JUNE-NOVEMBER, 1775.

[19.]

A return of the officers, non=commissioned Officers, & Privates, of the Company of Capt: Kershaw. now in Camp at the Mineral Springs, near the Congrees [22]
1st: Lieu^t : Francis Boykin }
2^d ·· Thomas Charlton [23] } .
Serj:^{ts} Alexander Smith }
        Augustine Prestwood }
Drummer Thomas Wood
Privates. Robert Martin 1
        Newill Barefoot........................ 2
        James Saxon......................... 3
        Uriah Goodwyn......................... 4
        Jacob Cherry............................. 5

---

[22] See Salley's History of Orangeburg County, 1704-1782, p. 414. The roll of Capt. Goodwyn's company is missing.
[23], Ibid, p. 283, line 17 et seq.

James Cook............................. 6
Peregrine Magness....................... 7
Thomas Pemble.......................... 8
Joseph Ferguson 9
Mordicai Mc Kinny 10
William French......................... 11
Richard Nichols.........................12
Jeremiah Simmons.......................13
Thomas Howell 14
Thomas Coweson.......................15
John Payne 16
John Wright 17
Hugh Garton............................18
Robert Garton..........................19
Alexander Garton 20
George Grey..............................21
John Grey 22
John Steel 23
John Swilla 24
Aaron Alexander.........................25
William Wetherford 26
Robert White...........................27
Henry Harmon 28
Samuel Sessions.........................29
Benjamin Ferguson.......................30

The above is a true Copy of the officers; Non Commissioned officers & Privates. belonging to the fourth Company[24] of the Regimt. of Rangers commanded by Collonel Wm Thomson

Given under my Hand
7th Augt 1775.
ELY KERSHAW

Endorsed : Return of Capt ELY
KERSHAW's Company
of Rangers
7 Augt 1775.
Recd 11th

---
[24] Wise (1), Polk (2), and Caldwell (3).

38 SOUTH CAROLINA PROVINCIAL TROOPS

[20.]

A return of the officers, non commissioned officers & Privates of the Company of Captain Richardson, now in Camp at the Mineral Springs near the Congrees.[25]

1st Lieut: Lewis Dutarque ⎫
2n ·· Richard Brown ⎭
Serjeants Reuben Bromfield ⎫
        Joseph Fox ⎭ James Bachhannan Drummer.

Privates. Andrew Hanåh 1
    Charles Mc Ginney 2
    Robert Spurlock 3
    Benjamin Franklin 4
    David Brunston 5
    Ezekiel White 6
    Zeth. Poole 7
    Abraham Poole 8
    Wm Poole 9
    Dennis Henston 10
    Wm Rogers 11
    Johnston Parish 12
    Edwin Ferril 13
    John Mattison 14
    Richard Singleton 15
    Micajor Wallis 16
    Isaac Hilton 17
    Wm Hilton 18
    Isaac Brunston 19
    Wm Griffin 20
    Josiah Brunston 21
    Michael Morgan 22
    Wm Wood 23
    Joseph Smith 24
    Ben: Mc Kinney 25
    John Bronnaugh 26

---

[25] See note 22.

John Hilton........................... 27
William Sloan.............................28
Patrick Sloan............................29
John Belsher 30

The above is a true List of the officers. non commission'd officers & Privates belonging to the seventh company[26] of Rangers commanded by Collonel Wm Thomson.

Given under my
Hand this 7th—
Augt. 1775./.
E. RICHARDSON.

Endorsed : Return of Capt E.
RICHARDSON's Comp. of
Rangers 7 Augt 1775
Recd 11th

[21.]

A return of the officers, non==commissioned officers & Privates of the Company of Capt. Woodward, now in Camp at the Mineral SPrings, near the Congrees.

1st. Lieut. . Richd Wynne }
2^d · · John Woodward }
Serjeants John Smith }
        William Boyd }
Drummer William Wilson........................... 1
    John Owens 2
    James Pickett........................... 3
    James Owens 4
    John Carr................................ 5
    John Carson 6
    John Henderson........................ .. 7
    Daniel Oaks 8
    Francis Henderson...................... 9
    William Henderson 10

---

[26] Goodwyn (5), Kirkland (6).

Jacob Frazier 11
Henry Wimpey 12
Benjamin May 13
Charnal Durham 14
James Anderson 15
William Rayford 16
Matthew Rayford 17
Benj: M̊ Graw 18
Augustine Hancock 19
William Owens 20
John M̊ Donald 21
Francis M̊ Donald 22
Thomas Gather 23
Pritchard Stone 24
John Jacobs 25
John Bull 26
Joseph Owens 27
Thomas Winningham 28
Edward M̊ Graw 29
Benjamin Mitchell 30
William Duggans 31

The above is a true List of officers Non commissioned officers, & Privates belonging to the Eighth Company of Rangers commanded by Collonel W̊ Thomson

Given under my Hand
7th Aug̊ 1775./
THOMAS WOODWARD

Endorsed: Return of Capt Tho?
Woodward's Company
of Rangers—7 Aug̊ 1775
Recd. 11th

[22.]

Gentlemen

I received your esteemd favour with a talk Inclosed for the Indians. I sent for Mr Hammond & Mr Zubly & shew'd it to them—as we were appointed by the Gen[t]. of the Committee in Charlestown to be a Committee of correspondence for the Creeks,—as what amunition you have promised woud be but little to every one we thought if we coud git as much from Charlestown it might stop their mouthes for some time 'till more could be got for them, but we receivd for answer that they had settled that point with you, and you were to take the Creeks under your care, & they were to take the Cherokees & Catawbas under theirs—M[r] Rae was down here & says he has receiv'd no order from you yet how the Amunition is to be disposed of I shew[d] him the Talk & the letter I had from you, he says he does not know the man that is to see it deliverd in the Nation—if it is not equally Shared it will do more hurt than good. I told M[r] Rae I thought the best way would be one half to be carried to the Parachukclass in the lower Town which is near the Center & have the Head men Call'd from every Town & delever it to them with the Talk & let them Share it ammongst there People the oak frieshes & oak Joiese in the Same manner in the uper Towns. I told M[r] Rae if he woud go up him self David Holmes & my Indian Son shoud go up with him which he agreed to—but since that Holmes receiv[d] a Letter from M[r] Pooler that you woud not let there Goods be sent up—for the last Indians that went from here I told them when the went home to tell the Indians that there was so much Amunition going up to be given them from the beloved Men of Georgia and it was all that coud be spared now but that there was other Goods enuff come in & they woud go up at the same time for I did not think in the least that them Goods woud be Stoped. I always take care to avoid telling the Indians a Lie & that is the reason they put so much Cofidence in me for once they find a person tells them lies they never put more Confidence in him afterwards any Person that advised the Stoping the Goods from the Indians knows nothing of Indians and are not your friends for once the find the trade is Stoped from them it will not be in the power of any Man to keep them peaceable Longer Mr Rae told me their was an Indian at his House Just come from the Nation & Says Mr Tate is returned from Pancecola and gave out a Talk amongst the Indians but the Indians woud not take his talk but went of disatisfied. but the ffellow will not tell what the Talk was. he says he did not hear it if you will ask Mr Mc Gilverry's opinion what he may think the Consequences will be of Stoping the Goods from the Indians, if any person has a design of setting the Indians upon us it will be a fair opportunity for them to gain their point. the Gentlemen of the Committee of Charlestown has appointed Stephen Forster for Lingester there is none so good gose to the Nation, he is very much liked by the Indians in the Lower Towns & if you shoud want one for the upper Towns. Jack Cornel is the best their—The Gen^t of the Committee wrote me you woud send up Instructions to Foster how to Act in the Nation You will please send them by first oppy. as Mr Rae will send of the Amunition in four or Five Days I will do all in my power to keep them peaceable but it is hard for a Man to Work without Tools—the expence of carrying up the Amunition might have been saved for the people in trade woud have carried it up for nothing but as that is Settled it will make no great ods, I suppose the Gentlemen of Augusta has acquainted you of the danger they are in from one Fletcher they say he is coming against thim with Seven or Eight Hundred men and is reported that afterwards he is to come here. please God I am going to Augusta in the morning to know the Certainty of it. if so we must praper to receve thim, I am Gent^n with respect &C^o

(Signed. GEORGE GALPHIN)
(Coppy)   Augt 9th 1775—
To The Councill of Safety
  Savannah—

Endorsed : Copy of GEO GALPHIN's
  Letter 9th August 1775
  to Council of Safety in
  Savanna—

[23.]

Charles Town 11. August 1775

Sir

Inclosed you will find Copies of three Letters the Contents of which are very alarming.—one dated 6th Inst from the Committee at Augusta to the Council of Safety at Savanna — one from that Council dated the 8th to the Council of Safety in Charles Town & the third from Capt Moses Kirkland to to his late Lieutent Middleton, which are recommended by the Council of Safety to your particular attention.

I have by order of the Council & by the bearer of this written to Collo Thomson & inclosed to him Copies of the abovementioned Letters.[27]

Collo Thomson is enjoined to exert his utmost endeavours for the Interest of the general Cause in this dangerous conjuncture & to avail himself if possible of your advice—If you are in the neighborhood of his Camp he will lay before you his Instructions, which from necessity are general, & the Council of Safety being perfectly satisfied that you will leave nothing undone that shall appear to be necessary have not charged me with any particular direction to trouble you with.

I flatter my self with hopes that your success in the main business of your journey will be found to have anticipated our wishes & that the intelligence from Augusta will prove unbottomed.—I am with great regard

Sir

by Order——

P. S.

you know what ought to be done
  when practicable with Safety in the
   Case of Kirkland——
 this Instant a Letter returned from Capt. Lempriere

---

[27] See Salley's History of Orangeburg County, 1704—1782, p. 417.

arrived with Success beyond expectation—Six Tons—collected at Sea.—

Honble M.r Drayton

Endorsed : Copy 11.th August 1775.

To W.m HENRY DRAYTON

[24.]

Charles Town 12th August 1775.

Gentlemen—

Capt Clement Lempriere arrived a few days ago at your Port in a small Vessel having on board a quantity of Gun powder for the service of this Colony which we are informed is landed in Beaufort. We think it expedient to lodge twenty Barrels of the said Powder in a safe Magazine or Store in or near Beaufort to be in readiness for removal if necessary to Georgia. We therefore request you to take the trouble of receiving & Storing that quantity observing that none of it is Cannon powder which is easily distinguished by marks on the Barrels,—the inclosed Letter to Capt Lempriere directs the delivery—If you shall think it necessary to keep a Guard upon the Store House your Bill on us for the charges which will be thereby incurred shall be paid.

If the Council of Safety at Savanna at any time shall send for said powder you will deliver it to their Order being first well assured of the authenticity of the application.

By order of the Council of Safety

—H L

The Committee at Beaufort Port Royal—
by Ph. Will under Cover to D. Desaussure Esq

Sir

In Reviewing the transactions which by order of the Council of Safety employed me till near 1 oClock this morning, I discovered the omission of those Copies of Letters which you were referred to in the Letter which I had the honour of writing to you by the hands of Philip Will.

You will receive them under this Cover & in so short a time after the delivery of the former Papers as to remove any apprehension of damage to the public service from my Error.—I have the honour to be

your most obed! Serv!

Charles Town 13th August 1775—
Recommended for dispatch
to the particular care of Mr Tibout—

Endorsed: Copies to Col? BULL & Comm͞e͞e of
Beaufort—

[25.]

Addressed: To
THE COUNCIL OF SAFETY
In Charles Town

℘ favour Post }.

Pee Dee Prince Fredricks Parish,[28]
July 21st 1775

Worthy Gentle Men/

This to Inform you I live in A District on the south wst side of pee dee River, and on the north Es! side of Linches Crick, from the mouth of s^d Linches Crick up to willow Crick, all Inclusive, which s^d District has not bin Desciplened this fifteen years past, and as I think the present state of this provence, as well as the Rest of the Colonies, is an Object that Requires Every Mans attention, and Exertion, to put him self in a proper position of defence against his Enemies. Both forreign and Domestick, I therefore have summonsed the male inhabitants of s^d District to Assemble together to Choose there officers to teach them the Military Discipline and make them usefull if Called on to March Against Our Enimies, They Cheerfully Obayed my sommons, and Assembled together and Did me the Honnour

---

[28] From the private collection of A. S. Salley, Jr. See *The Sunday News*, Charleston, S. C., March 19, 1899.

unanemously to Choos me for there Capt., Mr Hugh Giles, first Leut., Mr Thos Potts second Leut.—we therefore Requier Commissions from you to impower us to Act as you may Direct, But we Humbly Begg your Indulgence to give us Liberty to Devide the Above District in two Companies as it is very Ill Convenient for the hole to Assemble together once A fortnight to dwo duty, the District being thirty Miles in Length, And A hundred men in sd District—Gentle Men if it is your pleasure to grant this Request I wood Requier Our Commissions or the Lower part of sd District, and when officers Are Chosen for the upper part, I will make them known to you—I also make application in Behalf of Another District Destetute of officers, Above Ours Agasent in sd parish from the Above sd willow Crick up to black Crick, which on My Request has assembled together and Choose there officers, viz—James Gregg: Capt Robert Scott and John Gregg Junr there Leut. these Gentle Men Also Requier Commissions of you, your Complyance by the Post will much oblige An Onfeigned friend to America And Am Gentle men your Humble Sert

THOs POST

NB/
I have the pleasure to inform
you that Every man of the above Districts
that has Assembled together has signd
the Assotiation without one Desenting Voice—

Endorsed: THOs POST 21st July 1775.
Recd 1st August
Answd 13th

[26.]

Charles Town 13th August
Sir—— 1775[29]
Inclosed under this Cover you will receive Commissions

---

[29] From the private collection of A. S. Salley, Jr., See *The Sunday News*, Charleston, S. C., March 19, 1899.

for two of the Volunteer Companies applied for in your Letter of the 21st July, which did not reach us till the 1st Inst, Viz! that to be commanded by your self & that which is to be commanded by Capt. Gregg——in describing the district we have conformed as nearly as we could understand that part of your Letter which we hope will prove to be exact —if there shall appear to be any material Error—New Commissions shall be made out.

You may undoubtedly raise an additional Company in your district as you say there are a sufficient number of Men for that purpose & when you transmit the names of Officers poperly chosen We shall Certify their appointment & send you the Commissions—

By order &c

H L.

|+ We highly Commend your Zeal & public Spirit on this occasion—

Endorsed: Copy to Capt Post
13 Augst
Ad with Commission
to Capt G Cogdell
☞ for G C Lieut!
Paul Lepeir—

[27.]

Charles Town 13th August 1775.

Sir.

We have received a Letter dated the 7th [30] Inst signed by your self & M! Tennant also yours of the 9th [31] & have taken both under our consideration.

We are truly sensible of your Zeal & diligence in the

---

[30] See Drayton's Memoirs, Vol. I. p. 331. Salley's Hist. Orangeburg County, 1704—1782, p. 284 et seq. Gibbes's Documentary History, 1764—1776, p. 128 et seq.

[31] Ibid, p. 134. Salley's Hist. Orangeburg, 1704—1782, p. 291 et seq.

public service & rejoice to learn that your endeavours have been so far crowned with success. Yourself & your fellow Labourers in the present arduous task are intitled to the highest acknowledgements from your Country.

The General Committee are to meet to Morrow Morning at an early hour for the express purpose of considering the Case of Messrs Dunn & Boote

We think it best to postpone the consideration of a Military appointment for Mr Sumpter until your return or till we more clearly understand what Duty he proposes to take upon himself & upon what consideration. You were probably misinformed of Capt Kirkland's intention of coming to Charles Town—the Copy of an intercepted Letter which you will receive in a packet with this shews that he was to have attended an Election at Cuffee Town on the very date of your Letter—such a Watch is set as will not suffer him to pass unnoticed if he appears here in day light. but as we much doubt his venturing We desire you will spare no expence to secure & have him brought hither if that can be done with safety. We have signed Eight Commissions for Officers in the Regiment of Rangers—these go to Collo Thomson by this conveyance, he will explain to you the particulars—We do not understand whether you mean to ask for a Commission as Surgeons Mate for Lieut Charlton in lieu of or in addition to his Lieutenancy, if the former, although we are not expressly authorized yet for the good of the service we might find means to accommodate him—but you know that a double Commission would be directly contrary to a Resolution of the provincial Congress—this article therefore must unavoidably wait for explanation.—[32]

It well becomes us to be frugal of the public Treasure & we are sorry to find that you have been obliged to draw upon us for the purchase of more Horses, but we do not recollect any service for which we have paid with more

---

[32] See Salley's History of Orangeburg County, 1704—1782, pp. 290—91, 294 and 423. Ante p. 1.

cheerfullness than we shall honour draught upon this occasion. Your putting off the Election for Delegates at Congaree appears from the reason you have assigned to have been a step necessary & judicious & we hope there will be no objection made against it in Congress—no doubt but that through the Contrivances of Mr Kirkland & his confederates Elections have been interrupted & even prevented in several other places; wherever you discover such Instances we recommend to you to animate the people to appoint a proper Day & give the most public notice of their intention to choose & then proceed to the choice of deputies to Represent them in Congress in December.

Neufer went into the Country with Summer at our special request & as we believe upon public expence, if those Men should carry double forces we must find out means for reducing them to order—

We shall lay before the General Committee to Morrow the necessity, for appointing proper persons to deprive Non associates from enjoying the benefits of a free intercourse with the Inhabitants of this Town & we are persuaded that hereafter such persons will not find it so easy to dispose of their Flour & other Merchandize here as Mr Summer was pleased to intimate—he had no reason to boast from his own experience—

You will receive by this conveyance Commissions properly signed for Officers to form six Volunteer Companies, Blanks left for names dates & district to be filled by you, which you will dispose of as you shall judge for the service & Interest of the Colony whenever the names of fifty Subcribers for Rank & File are produced to you together with the names of Officers chosen by such fifty for forming one Company to be restricted to 75 Men—the names of Officers & Men of each Company so formed to be duly returned to us with the dates of Commissions these Companies should be informed how far they are exempted from the orders of their former Field Officers & that if these should attempt to thwart & vex them in revenge for their associating in Volunteer Companies the Council of Safety will certainly remove such Field Officers—the people should also be made sensible of the illegality of granting Warrants & processes for recovering Debts contrary to the Resolution of the provincial Congress—

Although we are sensible of the benefit which this board would receive from our personal attendance yet we cannot help expressing our opinion that your continuance in prossecution of the present plan will redound greatly to public advantage therefore we wish it may consist with your own inclinations & Interest to persevere for some weeks longer in the work which you have in hand & that you may meet with uninterrupted success.

Capt Lempriere returned 4 or 5 days ago to Beaufort with about six Tons Gun powder of the very best quality 20 Barrels of which we have ordered to rest where it is subject to the order of the Council of safety at Savanna & the remainder we have sent for under a proper guard :|. We pray God to protect you———

By order of &c———
In Mr Drayton's Packet
A Packet to Mr Tennant
a Lr to him from P T—
the above from the Council & their Lr
of the 11th

24 Commissions
⅌ Mc Ginney & Demer.

Endorsed : Copy 13th August 1775
To Wm H. DRAYTON

[28.]

Charlestown 16th Augt 1775.[33]

We whose Names are hereunto subscribed do mutually agree to unite, and form a Company of Foot; to be commanded by

That the said Company shall consist of One Captain three Lieutenants one ensign a Serjeant Major, four serjeants, four Corporals, and One hundred privates or whatever other number the Council of Safety will allow.——

That the officers be chosen by Ballot from among the subscribers

That as soon as fifty have subscribed a Meeting be called to appoint a Committee to apply for Commissions, to determine on a proper Uniform, to choose the Officers and to consider of Rules proper to be observed by the Company.

That it is strongly recommended, that the Uniform be; Scarlet French Frock Coats—with white Lappels Collars & Cuffs with white Buttons & white waistcoat & Breeches; to wear Buskins & Black Garters .... The officers by way of Distinction to wear Silver Epaulets—a Silver Girdle & Loop & Button in their hats—to have Silver Gorgets on which to be engraved in a Circle an armed hand holding a drawn sword—round which a Motto "Et Deus omnipotens"—The privates to wear military cocked hats with Cockades.

1 Charles Drayton
2 Jno Gilbank
3 Geo: Grey
4 Geo: Jno: Fardo
5 Wm H. Roberts:/:
6 Ed North
7 Wm Rudhall
8 Wm Day
9 Daniel Wilson
10 Joseph B. Hollier
11 Jas G,, Williams
12 Joseph Jennings
13 Thomas Storkiff
14 Jno Maromet.
15 James West
16 Andw Thomson
17 Henry Kennan
18 Samuel Hutchins
19 Wm Jordan—
20 Thos Fenwick

---

[33] From the private collection of A. S. Salley, Jr. See *The Sunday News*, Charleston, S. C., March 19, 1899.

21 Jacob Michau
22 John Ewing Colhone [34]
23 Harry Michie
24 Ripley Singleton
25 Erskine Kennedy
26 Peter Bremar
27 Thomas Theonin
28 William Greenage
29 Abram Maddock
30 Richd Morgan
31 John Griggs
32 Wm Hamilton Cole
33 Thomas Conn
34 Robert Leavengston
35 Ja^s Leeson
36 James Stobo
37 John Moore
38 Mat^w Murphy

39 Fran^s Morelli
40 John Johnson
41 John Raphel
42 James Holmes
43 Jacob Tobias
44 Robt Testard
45 Joseph Day
46 Daniel Keeffy
47 Patrick Dougherty
48 Nich^s Smith
49 John Davis
50 Edm^d Fitzpatrick
51 Bracy Singleton
52 John Mills—
53 Lewis Linder
54 Alexander Fitzpatrick
55 Thos Capers
56 Peter T: F Gee
57 John Howard
58 Jos. Glover Junr [35]
59 Alexander Horn

60 Joshua Eden
61 William Mc Kinnon
62 John Hybart

63 Samson Clarke
64 Tho's Middleton Junr

Endorsed: List of Capt DRAYTON's
Volunteer Comp^y

---

[34] Undoubtedly this is John Ewing Calhoun, subsequently United States Senator from South Carolina from March 4, 1801 to the date of his death, Nov. 3, 1802. The signature is his own and his spelling of his name at that date, being then a young lawyer in Charleston, is striking.

[35] Scratched out.

PAPERS OF THE FIRST COUNCIL OF SAFETY OF THE REVOLUTIONARY PARTY IN SOUTH CAROLINA, JUNE–NOVEMBER, 1775.

[29.]

[HENRY LAURENS TO CLEMENT LEMPRIERE.]

Sir

The Council of safety are desirous of consulting you upon a subject of great importance in the American Cause & by their order I request you to meet them in the State House to Morrow Morning——the Council will sit from 9 to 11 oClock—[36]

I am with great regard Sir—

Thursday
Night
13 July 1775
On Colony service

CLEM^t LEMPRIERE Esqr

Endorsed: 13 July 1776—
CAPT LEMPRIERE

---

[36] See Journal Council of Safety, July 14, 1775, (Collections S. C. H. S. Vol. 2, p. 40); July 15, (Ibid p. 43); July 17, (Ibid, p. 47); July 21, (Ibid, pp. 53, 54); July 22, (Ibid, p. 57); July 24, (Ibid, p. 59); July 25, (Ibid, p. 62); S. C. Hist. and Gen. Mag., Jan., 1900, pp. 66, 73-4; April, 1900, pp. 126-7, 127, 133.

[30.]

Rec.d 21st August 1775. of Daniel DeSaussure the sum of Ten pounds Currency for going Express to Captains Stephen Bull and Ulysses Mc Pherson I say Rec.d by me——William Heilsall

[31.]

[FROM BASIL JACKSON.]

Addressed : To ———
  The Councel of Safety

Gentlemen

at a time when all America, is in danger of loosing her Freedom, I think it the indisputable duty of every individual to exert himself, in the defence of liberty, especially those that are young. This with my having served as an Officer before in one of the neighbouring provinces imboldens me to make application for a commission in the service of this Province, I do not expect a high commission, as I am almost a stranger in this place, unless upon tryal, you find I Have Merit deserving your confidence——I am

  Gentlemen, with the greatest
August 24th 1775   respect your Hble servt
     BASIL JACKSON

Endorsed : BASIL JACKSON
   24 Augt 1775—
   Read in Council same day
   to Apply to Officers
   of the Regiment

[32.]

We The Subscribers Whose Names Are here Under Writen do Volluntarely list & In roll Our Selves In A Vallanteer Company of Horse to be Commanded by Capt Mathew Singleton Isham Moore John Singleton In the Parrish of St Marks subject to the resolves of the General Provinsial Congress & the Counsell of Safety for the service of the

SOUTH CAROLINA PROVINCIAL TROOPS

Collinies Purely to Acct. within this Collony & to be ready Upon Any & Every Emergency when thereunto Cauled by the Counsell of Safety and do hereby bind Our Selves in A band by all the Ties of religion & honour to be furm in Our duty to Our Officers and Agree Willingly And Uanumasly to be Subject to the Acct. for Mutiny & desursion As Other Companies in like Surcomstances are so far to be Tried by Our Own Officers of ridgment & Companies to Which We belong In Witness Whereof We have hereunto set Our hands this 26th day of August 1775

William Williams	Joseph Rodgers	Matt.w Singleton
Charles Brunson	Ja.s M.c Cormick	John James[37]
George Brunson	Zachariah Howell[37]	Isham Moore
Mathew Brunson	— — — —[37]	Joseph Hill—
John Malone	Isaac Jackson	Tho.s Moffett
Edward Lane	Henry Wheeler	William Brunson
John foster	Willis Ramsey	Jacob Chambers ×
Joseph Singleton	Billinton taylor ×	Daniel ×his Jinnings× mark
William O Harrow	Robert Fleming	
francis Martin	Thomas Jackson	Peter Matthewes
Thomas Wells	Drury ×his fletcher mark	Jn.o Singleton
	Josiah Gayle Jun.r	james farmer ×
	Edward Hill	Jesse temple
	Samuel D witt	Caleb Gayle
	Sabe Stom—	Sam.l Tynes
		Rich Wills
		Elliott Holaday
		Richard harvin
		Epheram petty pool Jun.r
		Jacob brigman
		James Brunson
		Charles Goodwin
		Hope Ridgway
		Henry Hannsworth[37]
		James Allen[37]
		— — — —[37]

---

[37] These names are scratched out.

56 SOUTH CAROLINA PROVINCIAL TROOPS

Endorsed : CAPT MATH. SINGLETON'S
Volunteer Company.[38]
Memorandum : Capt Singleton John Singleton Isham Moore

[33.]

South Carolina, To Charles Pinckney Esquire Colonel of the Militia for the District of Charlestown in the Province aforesaid.

The Petition of Charles Drayton Esquire on behalf of himself and the several persons whose names are mentioned in the list or Schedule hereunto annexed.

Sheweth, That your Petitioner, at the request of and, with the several persons mentioned in the said list or Schedule, having associated to the Number of Fifty and upwards, are desirous of uniting and forming a Company of Foot for the service of the Province aforesaid

That Your Petitioner at a Meeting held for that purpose was unanimously elected and appointed to be the Captain, William Roberts Esquire Thomas Middleton Esquire and M! George Grey Lieutenants and M! Thomas Fenwicke Ensign of the said Company Which several and respective Ranks Your petitioner and the several other persons have agreed to accept.

That in order to the training and forming the said Company as soon as possible Your petitioner and the said several other persons are desirous of receiving Commissions according to their several appointments.

Your petitioner therefore on behalf of himself and the rest of the persons whose names are mentioned in the list or schedule hereunto annexed, prays You, Sir, that you would be pleased to use your influence with the Governour in their favour

---

[38] From the private collection of A. S. Salley, Jr. See *The Sunday News*, Charleston, S. C., March 12, 1899.

SOUTH CAROLINA PROVINCIAL TROOPS

for the purpose of obtaining Commissions as above-mentioned

And Your Petitioner &c.

CHARLES DRAYTON

The List or Schedule within referred to

Charles Drayton
Jn:o Gillbank
W:m H. Roberts
Edward North
George Grey
W:m Day
Daniel Wilson
Joseph B. Hollier
Ja:s G: Williams
Joseph Jennings
Thomas Roche
John Maromet
John Raphel
James Holmes
Jacob Tobias
Robert Testard
Joseph Day
Daniel Keefy
Patrick Dougherty
Nicholas Smith
John Davis
Edmund Fitzpatrick
Bracy Singleton
John Mills
James West
And:w Thomson
Henry Kennan
Samuel Hutchins
W:m Jordan
Thomas Fenwicke
Jacob Michau

John Ewing Calhone
Henry Michie
Ripley Singleton
Erskine Kennedy
Peter Bremar
Thomas Keowin
W:m Greenage
Abraham Maddock
Richard Morgan
John Griggs
W:m Hamilton Cole
Thomas Connor
Robert Lavender
James Leeson
James Stobo
John Moore
Matthew Murphy
Fran:s Morelli
John Johnson
Lewis Lindor
Alexander Fitzpatrick
Thomas Capers
Peter T. F: Gee
John Howard
Alexander Horn
Joshua Eden
William M:c Kinnon
Jn:o Hybart
Sampson Clark.
Thomas Middleton

Endorsed: Charles Drayton's application for a Volunteer Company—no date—produced in Council by Coll? Pinckney 28 Aug. 1775[39]

[34.]

[DR. ALEXANDER ROGERS TO DR. ROBERT WILSON.]

Addressed: To

Doct. ROBERT WILSON
on the Bay Near
Robert Wells——
Charlestown

Sr Please send the Medicenes by the first oppertunity and you shall be paid by the public the are for the Use of Col. Thomsons Regement of Rangers pray Dont Disapoint us if you cannot let us have them Give the Memorandum to some other of the faculty person, but I Expect you can Let us have them your Compliance will much oblige your humble sevt ALEXANDER ROGERS[40]
Amelia August 28 1775

---

[39] From the private collection of A. S. Salley, Jr. See *The Sunday News*, Charleston, S. C., March 12, 1899. Also the South Carolina Historical and Genealogical Magazine for April, pp. 134-5.

[40] Alexander Rogers was the Surgeon of the 3rd South Carolina Regiment. See "Collections" of this Society, Vol. 2., p. 39. The memorandum referred to by him is a list of medicines he desired. This paper is in the Society's collection, but it was deemed unnecessary to publish it here.

SOUTH CAROLINA PROVINCIAL TROOPS 59

[35.]

Addressed : To
Col? Henry Laurens Esq?
Charles Town.

Beaufort 22ᵈ June 1775

Sir

Capt Lampriere Spared me a barrel of Pork & a Barrel of ship Bread, for the use of the Melitia when Cal'd here to Guard the powder, but the former not being used, was omited to be put on board the scooner that carried the powder, have therefore put it on board a Scooner of Mr Josiah Smith's & Requested of him to Receive it for you—I am with Esteem

Sir
Your obt Hble servt
D: DeSAUSSURE

Endorsed : Dan Desaussure
22ᵈ June 1775—supposed to
mean August Recᵈ 29ᵗʰ Augt

[36.]

A Return of the First Company of Rangers with the Dates of Enlisting[41]

Captain Saml Wise Esq? ....Commissioned June 18ᵗʰ 1775.
1ˢᵗ Lieutenant John Donaldson....ditto.....d? 18.
2ᵈ Lieutenant Joseph Pledger. Chosen.   July 1ˢᵗ
1ˢᵗ Sergeant Trustum Thomas Appointed ..July. 1ˢᵗ
2ᵈ Sergeant Benjamin Hicks   ditto.....d? .. 1ˢᵗ
    Drum   Ditto ....d? .. 1ˢᵗ

---

[41] See Salley's History of Orangeburg County, 1704-1782, p. 414.

60 SOUTH CAROLINA PROVINCIAL TROOPS

PRIVATES.

1. Burgess Williams........Enlisted 1st July,
2. Thomas Dean..............d?..1st d?
3. Thomas Cochran............d?..1st d?
4. Isham Gardner............d?..1 d?
5. Edm? Hodge..............d?..1..d?
6. John Hodge..............d?..1 d?
7. Alexd? Johnakin..........d?.1. d?
8. Bently Fearson...........d?..1. d?
9. John Heard..............d?..1. d?
10. Benj? Fathern............d?..3? d? ⎫
11. John Booth..............d?..3? d? ⎭
12. Daniel Welch............d?..8th d?
13. Dixon Pearce............d?..8th d?
14. Peter Hubbard...........d?..8th d?
15. Isham Hodge............d?..8th d?
16th John Stubs..............Enlisted July 8th
17. Thomas Conner...........d? d? 8th
18. Lewis Conner............d? d? 8th
19. Silvanus Cooper..........d? d? 8th
20,, W? Morris..............d? d? 8th
21. Sam. Desurrencey........d? d? 12th
22. D? M? Donald...........d? d? 12th
23, Moses Mace..............d? d?.12th
24,, Isaac Lockhart..........d? d? 12th
25,, John Jones..............d? d? 12th
26. Henry Wyly.............d? d? 15th
27. W? Covinton............d? d? 15th
28. Jesse Smith.............d? d? 22?.
29. Thomas Pearce...:........d? d? 22?
30. Daniel Young. Aug? 10th

Endorsed: A Return of the First
CAPT WISE's Company of
Rangers—not dated nor
signd Rec? 30 Aug? 1775.

SOUTH CAROLINA PROVINCIAL TROOPS 61

[37.]

[HENRY LAURENS TO LT. COL. WM. THOMSON.]

Charles Town 31st August 1775

Sir—

We have before us your Letter of the 25th Inst & inten.d the following as the present needful answer.

Your Zeal in dismissing several disaffected Captains from service in your Regiment of Militia[42] merits commendation, the vacancies occasioned thereby ought to be forthwith filled up but as Commissions are not now to be obtained in the usual way we recommend to you to encourage volunteer Companies of about 68 Men, who, or the first collected 50 may chuse their own Officers, one Captain, two Lieutenants & one Ensign to whom we will give Commissions when we are informed of their names, the Mens Names & local situation of each Company—

You judged well in giving a Blank Commission to Capt Inhoff for a Second Lieutenant—but if you will recur to our former Instructions you will see that the distinction of first & second is now unnecessary—The Return of your whole Regiment is much wanted & we desire you will make it as soon as possible, that of Capt Wise's particular Company is neither dated nor signed, an Omission which you will guard against hereafter by Issuing proper Orders for that purpose.

We have found it necessary to grant the Honble. Mr Drayton enlarged powers hoping thereby to promote peace & good order in those parts where you are at present threatened with distraction; We therefore enjoin you to Cooperate with that Gentleman in such measures as he may recommend & to add all the Military aid in your power when he may think proper to demand it.

---

[42] Although Col. Thomson was commanding the regiment of Rangers under control of the Council of Safety he still retained the colonelcy of the Orangeburgh District regiment of militia. See Salley's History of Orangeburg County, 1704-1782, p. 468.

In order to avoid repetitions we recommend a careful review of all our former Instructions & especially to keep the important Post of Fort Charlotte & the safety of our Associated friends at Augusta objects always in sight.

Submitting to your own discretion at the proper time to determine on the propriety of your leaving the Camp we consent to your coming to Charles Town about the 10th Septem according to your request, but we desire you will in such Case leave the Regiment under the Command of the Major.

For good & sufficient reasons we have confirmed the Reappointment of Capt. Ezek. Polk to a Command by Mr Drayton & Mr Tennent but not to be incorporated with your Regiment, although Mr Drayton may order him to be under your Command, for particulars in this Case we refer you to Mr. Drayton—We have a right to expect that Capt. Polk's future behaviour will at ne for his past misconduct; if he does not again disappoint us, a reunion with a Man of his influence & connexions will prove beneficial to our Cause.

We refer great confidence in you, & expect that upon every occasion you will transmit all necessary intelligence to us & that without delay. It affords us satisfaction to learn that your Regiment is advancing in the knowledge of Military discipline in which no doubt you mean to comprehend that most essential branch, readiness to obey orders without questioning propriety or necessity.

By order of the Council of Safety
Coll? Thomson———

[38.]

[HENRY LAURENS TO WILLIAM HENRY DRAYTON.]

Charles Town 1st September 1775—

Dear Sir—

After the Council of Safety had retired from the Room where I had been laying before them the Letter to you which comes inclosed with this, a packet arrived from Augusta in

SOUTH CAROLINA PROVINCIAL TROOPS 63

which was contained Copy of a Talk which had been sent from thence to the Lower Cherokees, a duplicate, of which I here inclose you the perusal of it may be of some use to you in your intended interview with the Six Head Men—inclosed also you will find Mr Loocock's Account for certain Indian presents now delivered to Thomas Dean & Thomas Pierce who have promised to convey the whole safely to you— which when done you will Certify in order to entitle them to Five pounds Curr.^{t} Money for the safe Carriage—I am with great regard—

Sir

Your most obed.^{t} Servt

You will also receive under
Cover with this three small
Packets from Mr Middleton

WILLIAM HENRY DRAYTON Esquire

Endorsed: Copy 31st August 1775
To Wm H. DRAYTON

[39.]

[HENRY LAURENS TO DANIEL DESAUSSURE.]

sent by Capt Joiner—
& Mr Thebout—

Dear Sir—

I request your care of the inclosed packet for the Council of Safety at Savanna—if no very safe opportunity immediately presents send it by a cheap express Messenger & your draught for the expense will be paid—it has been too long delayed—your Committees Letter on Mr Stuart's affairs was referred to the General Committee who have ordered their Committee of Intelligence to answer it—I know there are some other of your Letters which remain unanswered, these have been presented to the Council & shall be again on Saturday—a multiplicity of business has occasioned the present want of punctuality.—

Charles Town 1st Septemb.r I am Sir
1775— Your most obed.t Serv.t

DANIEL DeSAUSSURE Esquire

Endorsed: Copy 1st Septem 1775
To D. DeSAUSSURE

[40.]

[FROM ALEX. INNES.]

Addressed: COLL: LAURENS Chairman
of the Gen.l Committee[43]

Charles Town 2d Jan.ry 1775

Sir—

I beg leave by your means to acquaint the Committee that as I have submitted to be their prisoner to avoid all possibility of giving them offence I have order'd those few arms I possess (which are only such as Gentlemen generally have to protect them from insult) on board the Tamar.— ——

If I have acted in this matter differently from any other Gentleman it does not proceed from the least wish to appear singular but from a persuasion that our bases are totally different.

I will not detain you any longer Sir on this very trifling subject, I shall only add that concessions which cannot be submitted to with honor, the Committee will I dare say think it below them to insist on.

I am Sir
Your Most Obed.t
& Most Hb.le Serv.t
ALEX: INNES.—

COLL: LAURENS—

---

[43] Laurens was not Chairman of the General Committee, but was President of the Council of Safety.

Endorsed : ALEX^r INNES 2ᵈ Janry
intended for September 1775.
Rec̊ᵈ 2ᵈ Septem—Read
in Committ & deter-
mined that A I.
have leave of absence
from this Colony &
that tis expected he will
avail himself &c°

[41.]

Addressed : To
M! ROBERT ELLISON
between Wateree & Congaree Rivers
on Simpson's Creek.——

South Carolina ⎰   We the Subscribers sensible of the Dan-
Camden Dis! ⎱ ger to Which all the Rights and Libertys of
this Colony are Reduced to by the Violence with which all
America is Threatned By a Wicked Ministry do freely unite
our selves into a Volunteer Company of Rangers as soon as
our number amounts to thirty to Chuse and submit to the
Comm of such officers as the Majority shall agree to Hereby
Engaging to obey such officers punctually in subordination;
the Commanding officer of the Regt in this District and
Und! the Direction of the Counsell of Safety: muster and
Exercise Under Arms as often as necessary and to hold our
selves in readiness to march to any part of the Province to
defend it against the Enemies of its Libertys at an hours
Warning. Given Under our hands this 2ᵈ Sep! 1775

R! Ellison Capt!
James Sanders 1 Lieut,
John Ellison 2d Lieut,
Alexander Boyes
Eleazar Gore
John Ashford Gore
David Hamilton
Sam! X Armstrong (his/mark)
James T. Kennedy
W!" X Martin (his/mark)
John X Martin (his/mark)

Cato West
Edward Bland
Alex! X M° Dowle (his/mark)
William Penny
James M° Dowell
David M° Crieght
James M° Creight
Robert Gray
Samuel Dods
James Dods
Will!" Willson
Alex M° quarters
John Askew
An!, M° Dole

Wil!" mcCalester
Rob! Potts
William M° Lvey
James Morison
Aexd! X Robinson (his/mark)
James Mcquoin
John agnew
James MCmullen
W!" Young
James hanin
Thomas saint

We the Within Subscribers Most Earnestly Beg the Council of Safety to Grant Commissions to the Within Mentioned Gentlemen (Viz) Rob! Ellison: James Saunders & John Ellison With Proper Instructions how to Proceed in Raising And Training Our said Company and Petitioners as in Duty Bound Will Ever Pray[44]

[42.]

[HENRY LAURENS TO WILLIAM ERVEN.]

Sir.—

When I wrote by order of the Council of Safety to your Council the 25th Ult? your favour of the 17th happened to be mislaid & I had not time then to go or send for it at the State House, therefore I beg you will pardon the delay of an answer.

agreeable to your advice, this, which will inclose a packet for the Council of Safety at Savanna, Shall be covered by a direction to Joseph Clay Esq! & as a further guard

---

[44] From the private collection of A. S. Salley, Jr. See *The Sunday News*, March 19, 1899.

against its falling into improper hands I shall commit it to the care of the Post Rider after the Mail is made up—who for a small gratuity will deliver it directly to M[r].Clay—if you approve of this mode you will no doubt adopt it & then your Letters for our Council of Safety may be covered by a Simple direction to

      Sir—
       Your most obed[t] hum Serv[t]
Charles Town So Carolina 5th September 1775—

Yesterday our Grenadier Company Commanded by Capt. B. Elliott were detached into Rebellion Road in order to take certain deserters from on board a Sloop lying under protection of the Tamar Man of War—the deserters it seems had fled on board the Man of War but Capt Elliott brought the Sloop up to Charles Town this is the vessel which took in part of Capt Maitland's Cargo for S[t] Augustine & put in here in distress—

WILLIAM ERVEN Esquire

Endorsed: Copy 5th Septem 1775
    W[m] EVEN

[43.]

[HENRY LAURENS TO WILLIAM HENRY DRAYTON.]

       Charles Town 5th Septem. 1775--
Sir—

The powers contained in our last Letter of the 31st Ult[o] which went by Tho[s] Dean & Thomas Pierce who carried the Indian presents will have shewn the confidence which we have reposed in you & we assure our selves that you will make such use of your authority & of the means which are in your hands as will be productive of great advantages to the Colony & give general satisfaction.

But we perceive by yours of the 30th Aug[t] which came to

hand this Morning that you had from the Contents of our Letter of the 11th assumed all the powers which we intended to vest you with by our last therefore we cannot avoid remarking that if the former was adequate & sufficient a further application was altogether unnecessary, however we make due allowances for the necessity of the times—We are not under the least doubt of your ability to defeat any Plots which Kirkland may have concerted against Fort Charlotte or Augusta, & since you have thus seriously entered upon a contest with him, it will be absolutely necessary to subdue him, or drive him out of the Country. but we strongly recommend to you to discharge the Militia as soon as you can possibly do it with safety such additional expence will be very heavy on our treasury—

We informed you in our last that we had supplied Collo Neyle with certain quantities of Gun powder & Lead—we shall now send two Barrels of Powder & about 400lb Lead to Mr Kershaw's Store at the disposal of that Gentleman & Collo Richardson, for the use of Collo Richardson's Regiment we should have sent this directly to himself if we had precisely known his station—

As we are come to a Resolution to distribute Powder throughout the Colony among our friends we beg you will consider what will be proper proportions for the several districts in which you have & will have been in the course of your tours—

We are now also to acknowledge the Rect of a Letter from you & Mr Tennent dated at Ford's upon Enoree[45] by the hands of Mr Downs, for carriage of which he demanded, as he said by agreement with you, £35,—& we have paid him although you have mentioned nothing of the agreement nor did it appear to us that he came expressly for that purpose—We hope Mr Tennent will be assured that we have a proper sense of his services & excuse our not writing particularly to him for the reason mentioned in our last our daily expectation of seeing him happily returned to Charles Town—

---

[45] See Gibbes's Documentary History, 1764-1776, p. 156.

We have sent Copies of Cameron's interrupted Letter & of Clark's affidavit to the Council of Safety at Savanna & to Mr Galphin, no doubt you have made Andrew Williamson fully acquainted with the Contents of both but to guard against the contrary as possibly you may in your hurry have omitted to take Copies we send one of each under this Cover these will do no harm even if they should prove superfluous.

We have Resolved to equip three Schooners to be mounted with two Nine pounders each, for defence of this Harbour & have named Commissioners for the purpose—Captains. Blake Lempriere & Tucker—We have also Ordered the Militia throughout the Colony to be held in readiness as in time of Alarm & you will herewith receive 4 Copies of our Declaration on that head which we desire you will distribute to Coll^o Savage Coll^o Richardson, Coll^o Fletchall & Coll^o Neyle—we shall now send one to Coll^o Thomson—

We shall wait with anxiety for further intelligence from you in the mean time be assured of our continued good wishes for your success.——

By order of the Council of Safety

WILLIAM HENRY DRAYTON

Endorsed : Copy 5.th Septem 1775—
Wm HENRY DRAYTON

[44.]

[HENRY LAURENS TO LT. COL. WILLIAM THOMSON.]

Charles Town. 6.th Septem 1775[46]

Sir—

In Answer to your Letter of the 2.^d Inst we refer to our last by Deans & Pierce, by which you will see that although Mr Drayton may from necessity have inticipated he has not exceeded the powers vested in him by calling forth the

---

[46] See Salley's History of Orangeburg County, 1704-1782, p. 430.

Rangers & Militia in order to prevent or defeat the Plots of our Enemies—We have great doubts of Kirkland's boldness in the face of danger & consequently no sanguine hopes of your taking hold of his Body—this is a serious matter & of the utmost moment therefore we shall wait in great anxiety for your further accounts.—Inclosed you will receive a Copy of our Declaration concerning the Militia to which we particularly refer for your Government as Colonel of one of the Regiments—

By order of the Council of Safety.

COLL? WILLIAM THOMSON.

Endorsed: Copy 6th Septem 1775.
COLL? THOMSON

[45.]

[CAPT. ARTHUR CLARKE TO HENRY LAURENS.]

Chas Town Septr 9th 1775

Sir

As you gave me to understand the intention of my summons before the Genel Committee, was to know wether I chose to subscribe to the Association agreed to by this Province; I hope the following reasons will shew the impossibility of such a measure, without giving any offence, which would be farthest from my wishes.

The first & principle consideration before the making a solemn Engagement like this, is how far we can in honor & conscience comply with it, & how far it may be compatible or interfere with any previous obligations. These considerations duely taken. I find myself under such obligations to my King, whose servant I have been for these 20 years, whose gratuity I now receive, & who I have allways found a kind & benevolent Master; the solemn oath I took upon receiving the Commission I am now honor'd with & under which I act; render it impossible for me to subscribe to this

Association, without fixing the most indelible stain upon my character, & being guilty of the most heinous of crimes, Ingratitude.

Further, sir, I beg leave to represent that having no property in the Province & my duty calling me another way, induc'd me to flatter myself the Gentlemen wou'd have consider'd me as a Transient Person, and not have thought it necessary to make such a request : in order to which I have actually given up the House I possess'd & had determin'd to proceed in the line of my Duty; had not the greatest of misfortunes, the loss of a true Friend & Parent alter'd my intention, & made me desirous of continuing in the Province, to be of all the service & comfort in my power to his Family under so heavy an affliction.

I therefore hope, sir, the General Committee will be satisfyed with these reasons, & not consider them as proceeding from any disregard to this Province, which to the contrary, I ever respected; & so far from wishing that any part of his Maj:s Dominions may be depriv'd of the blessing of the British Constitution; I sincerely hope every member of them may enjoy it in its fullest plenitude, and that the present unhappy situation of affairs may be speedily brought to a reconciliation that shall establish harmony among all his Maj:s subjects; and restore that mutual confidence between Great Britain & her Colonies that before subsisted.

As the Packet is under sailing orders, & my future Conduct depends upon the determination of the General Committee on these sentiments, I request your earliest representation of them, & am with respect
     Sir
     Y:r
       Most Obed:t
       Hum:le Ser:t
       ARTHUR CLARKE

Endorsed: CAPT ARTHUR CLARKE
9th Septem 1775—
Read in Gen Commee
the 13th—agreed that
Capt Clarke shall be
deemed a transient person

[46.]

[HENRY LAURENS TO CAPT. ARTHUR CLARKE.]

Ansonburgh 13 Septr 1775

Sir

At the Meeting of the Gen Committe this Morning I presented your Letter of the 9th Ins! & the Commee were pleased to resolve that you should be considered as a transient person

I am &c

H L

CAPT. ARTHUR CLARKE

[47.]

[HENRY LAURENS TO COL. WM. MOULTRIE.]

Sir

In answer to your Letter of this date we acquaint you that the business relative to the No Carolina Prisoners has been conducted altogether by the General Committee & does not lie before this Board.

With respect to the removal of Artillery Stores from the Magazine we have appointed a Commee. to enquire for a proper place to receve them—when that is effected we hope the apprehensions of danger from too free & too frequent access of people to the Gun powder & at the same time the Evil of quarrels & misunderstandings between the Inhabitants & Soldiery will also be removed—having these in view we do not think it needful to make an investigation into the particular case which you have mentioned especially as we find the Sentinels at the Magazine have sometimes been faulty—we have been informed by a Member of this Council of very improper behaviour on their part—Nothing shall be wanting in us for the public service & safety & for attaining these great ends we shall particularly endeavor to prevent bickering between people who ought to be held in the strictest Union——By order of the Council of Safety

H L
Presdt.

Charles Town 12 Sept! 1775
W M—Esquire
Coll? of the 2^d Regt.

Endorsed : Copy to Col? Moultrie
12 Septem 1775—

[48.]
[HENRY LAURENS TO CAPT. JOHN HARLESTON.]
Sir

You will learn from the Inclosed order by the Council of Safety, what was their determination upon the Complaint brought before them against the Officers of the Militia Company under your Command—You will carry the said Order into Execution & make a proper Report as soon as possible to the Council of Safety in order that Commissions may be filled up—

I am
Sir
Your most obed! humble servt
HENRY LAURENS.

Charles Town 12th September 1775— President of
the Council of Safety
Capt John Harleston——

Endorsed : Copy 12 Septb 1775
to Capt John Harleston

[49.]

[HENRY LAURENS TO COL. STEPHEN BULL.]

Charles Town 12. Septem. 1775

Sir.— —

Until this day I have not been in any degree blameable for the delay of an answer to your several Letters directed to me as president of the Council of Safety, the last of which dated so long since as 24th August came to hand but yesterday.

I had devoted this Morning for writing to you by the post in answer to the whole agreeable to the orders which I have received, but a variety of affairs have crowded in & one which renders it necessary to call the Council very early. I am therefore reduced to this necessity of apologizing lest you should charge the Council with neglect & to beg you to be assured of hearing fully by the next opportunity, from Sir
your most

STEPHEN BULL Esquire.— —

Endorsed : Copy to COLL? BULL
12 Sept? 1775—

[50.]

[FROM COMMITTEE FOR LITTLE RIVER.]

Addressed : To
The Committee of Intelligence
In
Chas Town

Little River South Carolina Sept? 13th 1775

Gentlemen

We the Committee for this place in Conformity to the Duty of our office, and pursuant to the Directions of the Continental Congress, find ourselves under the Necessity of exposing to the Publick, the Conduct and behaviour of Daniel

Robins Coaster and Trader of this place who after signing the Association might have lain in his native Obscurity, had not the Contemptliness of his principles and his Enmity to the rights and Liberties of this Colony as well as America in General, *did openly in the presence of two of the Committee Violate the resolves entre'd into by the General Committee of Charles Town on the fourteenth of August last with respect to trading with persons who had not signed the Association* and allso employing a Certain James Hamilton who positively refused signing the Association and refused to shew a Certificate of signing a Similar one in North Carolina or Georgia and being called upon by Us did not appear to shew reason why He did so behave and further is now loading his Vessel to Charles Town which we now particularly recommend to You how he disposes of ! We desire that the said Daniel Robins for his despicable Behaviour in the above mentioned should be publickly Advertised

     We are Gentlemen
    Your most Obedient humble servants
     SAM^l DWIGHT
     JOSIAS ALLSTON
     WILLIAM PIERCE   } Committee for Little River.
     ALEX^r DUNN
     JOHN ALLSTON JUN^r.
     SAMUEL PRICE

To
 The Committee of Intelligence
  In
   Chas Town

Endorsed: Committee of Little River
    13 Septem 1775
    to Commee of Intelligence
    Concerning Dan Robin
    Read 23^d Sepr G C—

PAPERS OF THE FIRST COUNCIL OF SAFETY OF THE REVOLUTIONARY PARTY IN SOUTH CAROLINA, JUNE–NOVEMBER, 1775.

[51.]

To the Hoṅble Council of Safety

The Petition of a number of the inhabitants of St Johns Parish Berkley County

Sheweth,

That your Petitioners are willing to hazard their lives in defence of the liberties of this Colony, and would gladly have observed the recommendation of the Congress in learning the use of Arms and being properly prepared for the purpose aforesaid: But that they lie under the disadvantage of not having officers who give proper attendance and instruction.——

We therefore request the Councel of Safety would indulge us by granting Commissions to the following Gentlemen upon whose Conduct, courage, and abilities we have the utmost reliance Viz. Job Marion, Richd Gough, and Elias Ball Junr.———

SOUTH CAROLINA PROVINCIAL TROOPS 77

S! Johns parish Sept 2ᵈ 1775

John proost	David Campbell	Elishe Tamplett
Lewis Farill	John Geor Bird	Peter Campbell
	John Mc Cullogh	Thos. Wesberry
	Thomas Butler	Thoᵝ Hoocks---
	Andw Campbell	Isaac Osborn--
	Thoᵝ Broughton	Nathˡ Brantley
	Walter Welsh	Alexʳ Broughton
	Thomas Commander	Daniel Ross
	Thoᵝ Rivers	Luis David Brindly
	Robert	Samˡ Richardson
	Kennedy	Benj Lewis—
	Isaac Ball	Josʰ Bossly
	John Smith—	

Endorsed: Petition from Militia
S! John's Berkley
County Considered
12 Septʳ 1775[17]

[52.]

[HENRY LAURENS TO LT. COL. ISAAC MOTTE.]

Sir.—

We have already written to you this Evening to which we refer observing that instead of 150. mentioned in our Letter the reinforcement is to be 250 Rank & File—

Lieut! Walter has just delivered us your Letter of this date ½ past 6 oClock—in consequence of which we have hastened Capt Cochran, & applied to Collº Moultrie, to embark the intended reinforcement together with provisions & other necessary articles as Speedily as possible & we flatter our selves with hopes that the whole will reach you before Midnight & that you will be able to Mount some of the heaviest

---

[17] From the private collection of A. S. Salley, Jr. See *The Sunday News* March 12, 1899.

Cannon before Daylight—We have such confidence in you as to leave us no room to doubt your making a brave defence in case of an attack, & we are persuaded that you will do every thing that prudence will warrant to repel any force which may be brought against you.

We refer to Coll? Moultrie more particular direction & heartily wish you success.

By order of the Council of Safety

Charles Town
15. Septem 1775—
Friday Night 9 oClock P.
Coll? Motte

Endorsed: 2ᵈ Answer to Coll? Motte
15 Septem 1775.

[53.]

[HENRY LAURENS TO WILLIAM HENRY DRAYTON.]

Charles Town 15. Septem. 1775.

Sir.—

Moses Kirkland came into Charles Town on Monday late in the Evening & disguised, repaired immediately to the Governor at whose House he was accomodated with a Bed & from whence he embarked on Tuesday Morning in the Tamar's Boat & got safe on board, that Man of War—these facts the General Committee were informed of on Wednesday—the Committee Examined a young Man one Bailey Chaney who was said to have accompanied Kirkland & amidst heaps of shuffling & prevarica'ion they collected enough to confirm not only their belief of Kirkland's being actually on board the Man of War but also that His Excellency held a correspondence with our Enemies of a very different nature from that which he had endeavoured by various arts to represent to us as the true motive of his writing to Fletchal & others of that party, in order however to obtain more satisfactory proofs some of the Gentlemen of the Army by a stratagem which succeeded to their wish procured such from his own Mouth as were indubitable, the particulars of which we shall inclose & refer you to—hence-forward we can depend upon this Gentleman only as upon one who under the guise of neutrality & even pretended friendship is devoted to work our destruction—tis not improbable he will of his own Accord soon leave the Colony, if he has any feelings he must do so in preference to being looked in the Face by Gentlemen whom he has deceived & by whom he has been so clearly detected—be that as it may we judged it proper to send a party of men under the Command of Coll? Motte to take possession of Fort Johnson which was effected before day light this morning & the Garrison consisting of the impudent Gunner Walker & four other men made prisoners—but Coll? Motte reports that the Governor who was at the Fort yesterday had ordered a party of sailors on shore from the Tamar & by their means thrown the Cannon off the lower Battery & destroyed many of the Carriages

This moment your Packet dated 11th Inst by the hands of Fields Pardue was delivered to us—We approve of the measures you have taken & you may clearly perceive that even in instances where you have not been altogether clear & explicit in your advices we have imputed the deficiency to the right Cause & put the most favourable construction on all your Acts. Kirkland has eluded all your schemes, but we will not yet think him out of our Reach tis possible we may still bring him to answer for his misdeeds—his Companions Robinson, Brown & Cuningham's we hope will be taken or driven out of the Colony by you.

16th Septem. last night a packet arrived from Capt Pearis who was at Congaree with four Cherokees who were waiting for you—Mr Pearis laments your delay, represents the anxiety of the Indians & fears bad consequences will follow if they should return without seeing you or some person to Talk to them in your stead—this appears to be a matter of great moment & will require your immediate attention —we need not inform you of the contempt in which Indians hold the man who deceives them & they scarcely know a difference & never will make the distinction when their friendship is Courted, between, disappointment & deceipt—Cameron too will exult & repeat his slanders, we therefore recommend this business to your most serious attention.

last night also the Governor who was on board the man of War sent Capt Innes to demand at Fort Johnson—

What Troops are in the Fort?

Ans? American Troops.

who Commands them?

Ans. By what Authority do you ask it?

By the Governors.
the Governor desires to know by what Authority you took possession of this Fort?

Ans. By the express Command of the Council of Safety?——

The man of War & Cherokee Guard ship are nevertheless still at Anchor in the Road We have reinforced the Garrison by an addition of 250 Rank & File--some volunteers are gone down & we have hopes that by this hour Coll? Motte has remounted his Cannon, Carriages & other necessary articles having been sent for that purpose before midnight—

the Swallow Packet arrived three days ago the Letters were long detained & we learn in general that the King & Administration are determined to reinforce Gen. Gage & also to throw Troops into all the Colonies—

We repeat our good wishes for your health & continued success— By order of the Council of Safety

H L
Presid!

P· S.

I have paid the express £25.
send by him 12 Association papers
two Quires of writing paper
a letter from M! Middleton
this will be sealed first by a Wafer
the cover by a Wafer & Wax & my Cypher
plainly impressed on both— H L
☞ a Letter from M! C Drayton
ad with the above but not inclosed
it came after that was sealed—

Endorsed: Copy of a Letter 15 & 16
Septem 1775 to W H
Drayton—by

[54.]

[DANIEL DE SAUSSURE TO HENRY LAURENS.]

Addressed: To
Colonel Henry Laurens Esquire
⅌ favour M! ⎞   Charles Town
Tebout— ⎠

Beaufort 17th Septem^r 1775.

Sir

Inclosed you have a Return of the Subscribers to the Association, there are a few that have not yet signed owing to their Residence on Remote Islands in the Parish & have not been at either places when sent about to be signed, but we know their Chearfullness in the Common Cause—M! Leechmer, our Collector, is the only person that has Refused to sign, but he has given the Committee proper assurances—they coud wish to have a Line from the Committee of Enteligeance Respecting M! Shaw.—

I am with Esteem. Sir

Your obed! servant
D. : DeSaussure

Endorsed: Dan Desaussure
17 Sept 1775.
Rec'd 25th Report'd same day—

[55.]

[HENRY LAURENS TO THE SOUTH CAROLINA DELEGATES TO CONGRESS.]

Charles Town So Carolina
18 Septem 1775

Gentlemen—

As we have business of very great importance to lay before you, which we think will merit the consideration of the Representatives of the United Colonies we are fortunate in meeting with the present opportunity for its conveyance by Mr Hindson who has promised not only to deliver our dispatches into your own hands but also to communicate a verbal message which cannot be so well imparted in any other manner.

Recent transactions of a most dangerous tendency in the interior parts of this Colony, the treachery of our Governor who has been pursuing the Steps of Mr Martin nearly as his situation would allow him, our late intelligence respecting the Indians & the unhappy differences which now subsist among the Inhabitants of Charles Town render this application for your advice & assistance absolutely indispensable. We had for some time entertained suspicions of the conduct of L. W^m. Campbell, but a late circumstance has furnished us with positive proof of his disengenuity & intention to undo us by stealth. His Lordship had not only shown a fair face when waited upon, but had in the most condescending terms invited Gentlemen to call on him in order to give him opportunity for expressing his good wishes to the Colony while he was at the same time privately spiriting up the people on our Frontiers to oppose our Association & to hold themselves in readiness to act in Arms against the Colony.—

SOUTH CAROLINA PROVINCIAL TROOPS 83

after having received reiterated accounts of the increasing discontents of those people, together with assurances that they were instigated by the Emissaries of the British Administration & supported by the promises of Royal favour, this Council judged it expedient to send proper persons to explain to them, the causes & nature of the dispute subsisting between Great Britain & the Colonies to endeavour to reconcile their minds to an Union in defence of their common rights; for these good purposes The Honble. Mr Drayton & the Reverend Mr Tennent were sent into those parts where the disaffected were most powerful & most numerous & although their progress has been attended with many salutary effects yet particular characters and their abettors continued so irrectionable that it was found necessary to abandon the mild modes of persuasion & to have recourse to the use of Arms which they had first taken up—we have now 1200. men of the Regiment of Rangers & Militia under the direction of Mr Drayton at Ninety Six we hope he will be able to suppress all opposition or at least to drive away the ring leaders of it.—among the head of our opponents was Capt Moses Kirkland who may with great justice be denominated a Traitor.—he had actually taken a Commission in the service of the Colony, & had enlisted a Company of Rangers whom he afterward incited to Mutiny & Desert. this Man after having threatened the destruction of Augusta & Recapture of Fort Charlotte in vain attempted to make a stand with his adherents & being closely pursued fled in disguises to Charles Town, which he entered by night took sanctuary in the Governor's House & was by His Lordship's means conveyed on board the Tamar Sloop of War.—a report of this fact was soon brought to the Gen Committee which happened to be sitting & a discovery was made of a person who had been one of Kirkland's Company of Rangers & had attended him in his flight, this person being Committed to the Guard was made use of by some of the Officers of our Troops to carry on a stratagem the result of which you will learn from one of the inclosed papers marked "Minutes of a Conversation." The Committee upon this discovery demanded a sight of the Letters which the Governor had just received from Administration by the Swallow Packet, His Lordship peremptorily refused to comply but in the course of conversation acknowledged that Ships & Troops were to be sent from England to all the Colonies & might be shortly expected; the next Evening he gave orders for dismantling Fort Johnson which was in part performed by men from on board the Tamar who dismounted all the Guns on the lower Battery & broke many of the Carriages, after which His Excellency dissolved the Assembly & without assigning any reason in public, retired on board that Man of War where he has ever since remained & from certain circumstances we believe he means to remove his family to the same place.—fortunately the Seamen neglected to spike the Cannon, we have therefore taken possession of the Fort & remounted them—the Garrison now consists of about 400. of our new raised Troops commanded there by Coll? Motte we intend to persevere in repairing the Fort & will put it in the best posture of defence. we also intend to fortify the Harbour as effectually as our circumstances will admit of—tis possible the Man of War may interrupt our proceedings, in such Case we shall be under a necessity of attempting to take or destroy her.—here we are at a loss to know to what lengths each Colony will be warranted by the Voice of America in opposing & resisting the King's Officers in general & the British Marine, tho' such opposition should be necessary for the very existence of a Colony & support of the Common Cause.—

Our Provincial Congress in June last Resolved that Officers in the two Regiments of Foot in Colony Pay should when acting in Conjunction with Officers of the Militia of equal Commissions take Rank & precedence of these without regard to dates of Commissions—this Regulation gave no Umbrage till lately, when we judged it necessary to Issue an Order for compelling many delinquents to do equal duty with their fellow Citizens in the Militia *then* a general Clamour was *raised*, petitions & Remonstrances from the "12 United Companies" of Volunteers were sent in, to this Board & to the General Committee & the dispute was carried to so great a height as to threaten an overthrow of our Association, temperate measures have however pacified many of the well meaning honest people who had been misled by the contrivances of false friends, nevertheless there remains no inconsiderable degree of ferment & dissatisfaction—to this untoward circumstance add, the unfavorable accounts which we have received from the Indians, the danger which we are always exposed to & more especially at this time from domestic Insurrection the expectation of British Troops & Ships of War with other incidents hereafter to be mentioned & you will agree that we have before us a very unpleasant prospect. We have been informed that you have granted 1000. Men to North Carolina on Acco! of the disturbances in that Colony, be that as it may surely we in this weaker part stand more in need of an Army of Observation & General Officers to Command all our forces; at the general charge of the Colonies; we would if time had permitted have applied to North Carolina & Georgia to have joined us in an application for such an Army, & we now recommend it to your serious consideration & enjoin you to Address the General Congress upon this subject & to use your endeavors for obtaining such defence for us, without which Carolina & Georgia will be involved in such difficulties as may & probably will greatly injure the common Interests of America. We particularly request you to consider of proper measures for Regulating the Militia & to procure a strong recommendation on this head from the Congress.—

the Judges have refused to do business in their department, hence the Courts are shut up, the Custom House may soon follow the example & we rather suspect it from an application which M! Haliday has made for leave to retire from the province altho' he has assured us that he will leave a Deputy. We have used our utmost endeavours & gone to very great expence for procuring ammunition, we were stimulated to the Act upon Lofthouse's Vessel at Agustine Bar by our hearty desire to supply the common Stock on your side, we rejoice to learn that you now have abundance we have also in our Magazines enough to serve our present purposes & no bad prospect of receiving additional quantities very speedily— *but none to spare*—Nothing would be more acceptable to us than two or three thousand stand of good Arms is it possible to obtain such & so many from Philadelphia? if it is, we recommend it as a most essential service—

Your letter of the 3ᵈ August with Resolutions of the 1ˢᵗ came duly to hand, perhaps after a Post Office is established, the Congress will find it necessary to open the American ports to Foreigners & to pursue the most vigorous measures in our Infant state, by Sea as well as Land neither of which in our opinion can be effected if the Doctrine of abandoning our Sea Coasts should prevail.—& We

We must not concluded without intreating you to consider of proper measures for keeping the Militia in due subordination & procuring a strong recommendation, on this head from the Congress.⁴⁸——By order of the Council of Safety.

Henry Middleton   Henry Laurens.
Thomas Lynch   President.
Chris. Gadsden
John Rutledge
Ed. Rutledge Esquires, Delegates for So Carolina
         in General Congress Philad.

✕ We have just received a private information that Moses Kirkland is to be put on board this Sloop after she is over the Bar—he is to proceed to General Gage & apply for Men & Ammunition to enable him to recover his ground & to distress us in the back Country—We have laid a plan for having him safely landed at George Town if that should fail,

---

⁴⁸ This last sentence is scratched out.

the Committee or Council of Safety at New York will be informed of his arrival & of his intended Schemes we hope in such case they will detain him for your directions & that you will give such as shall put it out of his power to do us any further mischief—to return him to Carolina in order to be tried by a Court Martial will be best.—Inclosed you will find a Copy of our late Order concerning the Militia

Endorsed: Copy 18th Septem 1775
  To The Delegates of S?
    Carolina

[56.]

[HENRY LAURENS TO THE COMMITTEE FOR SAXE GOTHA TOWNSHIP.]

Charles Town. 19 Septem. 1775.

Gentlemen,

The business contained in your Letter of the 29th Ult? which reached me 17 days ago came properly before the General Committee to whom I presented it at their first meeting after it came to hand, when it was to have been taken under consideration some affairs of great importance happened to intervene & their attention was diverted which occasioned another whole Weeks delay—at a late meeting the Committee ordered a proper number of Printed Advertisements to be sent to you & the day for the intended Election was ordered to be left blank in order that you might insert a Day most convenient to the public but the printer has by his own authority or by mistake inserted Saturday the 7th October as you will see by the Inclosed Resolution 24 Copies of which will be under cover with this—if that will be an improper time you may easily alter the Date with a pen.—

The public have taken Fort Johnson into their hands & Garrisoned it with 400 men—the Governor without assigning any public reason is gone on board the Tamar man of War, the General Committee have recommend to the Council of Safety the immediate fortifying of the Harbour of Charles Town—tis more than possible that Moses Kirkland will be in the hands of his Country men within forty days—We have room to expect pacific propositions suddenly from Great Britain on the contrary Ships of War & Troops are destined for the Harbours & Towns all along the Continent & no doubt we shall receive a due proportion—if the number should be proportioned to our own provocations we shall not have the fewest.—I am with great regard

      Gentlemen

        Your most obedient serv^t

Committee for Saxe Gotha

Endorsed: Answer to the Saxe Gotha
    Commee. 19 Septem 1775.

[57.]

[HENRY LAURENS TO CAPT. HINDSON.]

      Charles Town. 19th Septem. 1775

Sir—

Inclosed is the Packet for the Delegates from South Carolina at Philadelphia which we mentioned to you yesterday we recommend it to your special care to be delivered into the hands of one of those Gentlemen—

Touching Moses Kirkland we refer to our late conversation on that subject generally & have now to add that we will indemnify Capt Little if you shall find it necessary to go into George Town to deliver him to the Committee there with special orders to hold him in safe Custody till delivered to us—we will pay any reasonable sum for loss of time & Insure the sloop together with such reward as you may agree to give & as this is a matter which almost equally concerns all the Colonies we hope Capt Little will not hesitate, We

heartily wish you a good voyage & thank you for your good disposition towards us—By order of the Council
of Safety
Capt Hindson

Endorsed: Copy 19 Septem 1775
to Capt Hindson

[58.]

[Copy of a letter written by John Stuart, Indian Agent for the Southern Provinces of America, to Messrs Mc Kay & Mc Lean. The letter was intercepted by the Georgia Council of Safety and a copy thereof forwarded to the South Carolina Council of Safety.]

St Augustine 30th August 1775.

Messrs Mc Kay & Mc Lean,
Gentlemen,

I wrote Mr Andrew Mc Lean by post the 12th Inst acknowledging the receipt of his Letters from Savannah, & acquainting him that I had written to Mr John Inglis concerning the small sum in Carolina paper which I had left in his hands, vizt £89—Caro^a Curr^y and 40/ Georgia, to be exchanged for Gold—but Mr Inglis writes me that Mr Mc Lean had forgot to mention it to him.—As the seizure of your Gun powder must be a great disappointment, & might be attended with bad consequences. as the jealousies of the Indians must be greatly excited by being cut off from their usual supplies of Ammunition—to prevent which, as far as in my power, I have prevailed with Governor Tonyn to lend me some, which I wish to divide equally between the Creeks & the Cherokees, but horses are wanting—the quantity is 3000^{lb} & Bullets in proportion, which will require 30 Horses for each Nation—this may be of some service to you, as your Traders are not supplied, so I wish to hear from you immediately—& I think this supply, with what I am informed the Committee has sent will be sufficient for the purposes of hunting, &

defence against their Enemies, and convince them that we have nothing hostile in meditation against them.

Thomas Carr arrived here three days ago, by whom I received M! M͡c Leans Letter, & those inclosed in it. I have enabled M! Penman to supply Carr with 150 lb of Gun powder & 300 lb Ball.—The Cusseta King's Brother came with him, & brought me a Talk, to which I send an answer, so I hope to keep the Indians quiet.

The new Superintendants have been sending Talks to the Nation, & have acquainted the Indians that my death was determined upon—They are ungrateful, but I shall endeavor to return good for evil. I have not time to enlarge being hurried, so I conclude with assurances of my being sincerely,

Gentlemen,

Yr, M! ob! h! Sev!

Signed—John Stuart.

The foregoing is a true Copy of an original intercepted Letter lodged in the Council of Safety.—

Certified by

Seth Jn͡o Cuthbert, Sec.ry

Endorsed by Cuthbert: Copy of Letter to Messrs M͡c Kay and M͡c Lean—at Augusta

Endorsed by Henry Laurens: John Stuart 30 Aug!
1775—to M͡c Kay &
M͡c Lean
Read in Council & Gen
Commee—19 Septem

SOUTH CAROLINA PROVINCIAL TROOPS

[59.]

Pay Bill of Capt Heatley's Company in The Regiment of Rangers commanded by William Thomson Esqr up to the 20th of Sept 1775. Inclusive[49]

Names of Officers, nonCom=mission officers & Privates	Dates of Commisions & Attestations	Time in Service—	Amount
Capt Chs Heatley	12 August 1775	39 days @ £3, 10/	£136 10 0
1st Lieut Richd Brown	13 Sept 1775	7 Days @ 45/	15 15 0
2 Lieut Fras Taylor	12 Do Do	8 Days @ 45	18 00 0
Edward Leger } Sergts	15th Augst 1775	1 Month & 5 days @ £25 ℔ Month	£29 3 4
Alexr McKensey } Sergts	" Do	Do & Do a Do	29 3 4
John Surginor	15" Do	Do & Do a £ 20 ℔ Do	23 4 8
John Siders	15" Do	Do & Do a	23 4 8
Thos Burdell	15" Do	Do & Do a	23 4 8
Daniel Wooton	18" Do	Do & 2 Days a	21 6 8
John Roctin	20" Do	Do a	20 " "
John Wootan	20" Do	Do a	20 " "
William Lucus	20" Do	Do a	20 " "
George Coband	20" Do	Do a	20 " "
Petr Burns	20" Do	Do a	20 " "
William Parler	22" Do	Do a	20 " "
Isaac Vaughn	22" Do	28 Days	18 — —
Joseph Williams	25" Do	25 Do a	16 13 4
Jno Killingsworth	25" Do	25 Do a	16 13 4
Soloman Floid	26" Do	24 Do a	16 " "
Dennis McCarty	26" Do	24 Do a	16 " "
Chs Boiles	26" Do	24 Do a	16 " "
Wm McGraw	28" Do	22 Do a	14 13 4
Wm Runnalds	28" Do	22 Do a	14 13 4

[49] See Salley's History Orangeburg County, 1704-1782, pp. 418-19.

92 SOUTH CAROLINA PROVINCIAL TROOPS

Name	Date		£	s	d
Andrew Mc Kelvy	29"	Do a	21	14	"
Rich'd Person	29"	Do a	21	14	"
Ormand Morgan	31"	Do a	19	13	4
Benj'a Waide	31"	D'o a	19	13	4
William Thomas	1st Sepr 1775	D'o a	18	12	"
Jn'o Mc Lain	1"	Do a	18	12	"
Rob't Crocket	2"	Do a	17	12	"
James Hawkins	4"	Do a	**15**	11	6
Joseph Trotter	4"	D'o a	**15**	10	"
Jn'o Glass	4"	Do a	**15**	10	"
Joshua Glass	4"	Do a	**15**	10	"
Jn'o Miller	1st July 1775	Do a		10	"
James Crawford	1st July 1775	From Polks Comp'y,[50] 2 months & 20 days at £20.	50	50	

Carried Over £797,, 12s 4d

Brought Over £797,,12, 4

Charles Heatley maketh oath that the above
is a Just & true Bill of his Company to the
20th September 1775—
Sworn before me . .
        Rich Brown

Endorsed: Cap: Charles Heatleys
    Pay Bill £797. 12. 4.

---

[50] See page 70 January issue of this Magazine. Salley's History Orangeburg County, 1704-1782, p. 414. Ibid, pp. 418-19.

SOUTH CAROLINA PROVINCIAL TROOPS

[60.]

To Daniel Desausure Esq.
Pay to M.r Tunes Tebout the sum
of thirteen Pounds 5 shillns for ferrege
of the Cumpeney under My Command[51]
Aug.t 18 : 1775   John Jenkins

Endorsed: Voucher for £147. 3
        Paid D. Desaussure
        20 Septem 1775.

[61.]

S.o Carolina
Ninety Six District.   Whereas by A Resolution of the provincial Congress such persons as incline are encouraged to form volunteer Company's, and allowed as soon as they are Collected to the number of thirty persons to Choose their own officers. We Subscribers have enterd into and united ourselves in one volunteer Company, and for our Officers have Chosen David Hunter for Captain Andrew Miller first Lieutenant James Stevenson Second Lieutenant to be Commissioned by the Honourable the Council of Safety as they shall see Cause. We therefore Humbly Recommend these Gentlemen to the Honourable William Henry Drayton in order to obtain Commissions, so as we may be ready for service when called upon. Sign'd this 18.th Sept.r 1775
Near Little River that Runs into Seveney

That the above named Gentlemen   Robert Miller
were Chosen officers for the foresaid
Company in our presence Day Date
and place as above is attested by us   John Lawrence

---

[51] This was a company of volunteer militia from St. Helena See *The Sunday News*, Charleston, S. C., March 12, 1899.

I do believe m^r Hunter an honest man and that he may be chosen a Capt by the People as I would as a Lt Col on first vacancy
                                                              Ja^s Mayson
To the Honourable
William Henry Drayton

The Company being of a sittlement upon little River between Savannah & Saluda Rivers.

                          Commisions dated Sepr 20. 1775

South Carolina   ⎫   Persnolaly apeareed before me
Ninety Six District ⎭   Esqr one of his
                           majestes Justices of the peace for
said District. Jered liddell and being duly sworn on the holey Evanglest of almighty God—Deposeeth and Sayeth that he the said Jerad is one of the volanteers Entered in the Compney wherein David Hunter was Chosen Capten And^w Miller first Leu^{tt} and James Stevenson Second and that he was at the Election when dun, and that the Soldears signing the obligation Entered into by them Dateed the 12th Day of Septem^r 1775 was the persons that Elected them, and that the Certefecat Dated the 18th Day of the same month the day on which they were Elected wherein Robert miller and John Lawrance atestes the same Bears Refearance the one with the other, and was writen to answer one and the seam End and furder sayeth not, Sworn and Subscribed before me this 20th day of Septem^r 1775

Sworn before me   ⎫
this 20th Septr 1775 ⎭   John Purves J P.

Endorsed : Capt D. Hunter's
              Volunteer Company[52]
              W H D—

---

[52] From the private collection of A. S. Salley, Jr. See *The Sunday News,* Charleston, S. C., March 19, 1899.

[62.]

[EDMUND EGAN TO HENRY LAURENS.]

Addressed: To
Henry Laurens Esqr.

Sir

I am Just returnd from Town where I heard enough of this day. they don't do me Justice Trayton I was a poor One, tho' I have not done no duty as a delegate, nor Could not, for untill it was I suspected no deceit, except in that of a General forgive me one word this day (I Care for nobody) have made an apology to Mr Cannon which I you will see, the intent of this my usual imprudence is to acquaint you that I was Confused at sight of your General Committee, I this day addressed Mr Weyman Mr Lockwood Trezevant and Mr Laurens as Mr Laurens, but I was at sight of the Assembly there was something Uncommon in their faces, tho all my friends; Confused, the last Motion I made in Our Military Meeting was that we should pray Council of Safety and General Committee to meet in a Collective body, and that the whole of us go wait on you in full body to have the prayer of petition Granted, Mr Logan Over ruled it sir if you think proper to order the whole officers from each Company to wait on your body in full assembly, You I believe have their names or I can Send them to you and the Characters of most of them regard must have awed me, a little must strike them, except two Barkers, Harris the Silver Smith & Byron a Clerk to Stoll & Co.(Byron is honest the alarm only frightens him) Logan & Jamieson will only trouble you, Never forgive me if guilty of imprudence in this Cause except in Case of insult, and I beg you will now forgive one who retires Guiltless and free

Tuesday Night Your humble Servant
19th Septr 1775 Edm^d Egan

If any thing I have Confusedly advanced this day should be denied, I beg the substance from you and shall produce an answer in Writing (I am no Orator) and I hope Witnesses ———

Endorsed: Edm^d Egan 19 Septr 1775. Read in Council the 20th [53]

[64.]

[HENRY LAURENS TO WILLIAM HENRY DRAYTON.]

Charles Town 21st Septem. 1775

Sir—

We refer to our last dated the 15th by your messenger from Ninety Six which we hope has reached you & that you are now on your way to meet those Indians who led by Capt Pearis came from the Cherokees at your Command & who have in the utmost anxiety & impatience been many days waiting for you.—

We have Several Copies of interupted Letters from the Superintendant at St Augustine to his Agents in the Nation they look so much like design to amuse us that we hold it unnecessary to trouble you with them but since you have entered upon that branch a Caution against every stratagem may not be unnecessary Pearis applies for a Commission to the Good Warrior if one is granted it must be special & you will be the best judge of the necessary terms we have therefore referred him to you.

Coll^o Wofford has likewise applied for Commissions in order to erect a whole Regiment in the Colony's service from Fletchall's district—for that purpose we send you 34

---

[53] From the private collection of A. S. Salley, Jr. See *The Sunday News*, Charleston, S C., March 19, 1899. Egan had evidently not recovered from his confusion at the time he wrote this letter, and omitted certain words that were essential to the sense of the letter.

signed by us & blanks left for you to fill up you will keep a Copy of the names of Officers &c° as formerly directed—

We are called together by an alarming account which threatens the destruction of this Town by three Frigates & a Bomb Ketch we hope it may prove a groundless report— but it becomes us to act instantly as if was real—We shall be glad to hear that you have established peace & quietness on our backs & of your outset for Charles Town as soon after as you please   By order of the Council

The Honble W H. Drayton

Endorsed: Copy to W H Drayton
           21st should have been
           the 20th.

[65.]

Pay Bill of Captain Purvis's Company in the Regiment of Rangers commanded by William Thomson Esq.r up to the 22d Sept.r 1775 inclusive

Names of Officers Non Commission officers and Privates	dates of new officers Com:missions & Attestations	Time of Pay being due	Amount
John Purves Captain	21st June 1775	31 days—a £3.10*l*	£ 105—10
William Martin Lieutenant	1st Sept.r	9⅗ days—a 2.5*l*	209.— 5
John Carraway Smith—ditto	19 August	22 ditto—a 2.5*l*	49,—10
George Liddle—Serjeant		1 Mo. 3 days a £25 p. M.o	27,,—10
David Bucks— ditto		1 Mo.	25,—
William Skinner		1 M.o	20,—
Samuel Norwood Junior		ditto	20,—
James Sexton		d.o	20,—
Fl.nd Mitchell		d.o	20,—
William Mosely		d.o	20,—
Theophilus Nawood		d.o	20,—
John Jackson		d.o	20,—
Peter M.c Mahan		d.o	20,—
John Russel		d.o	20,—
Thomas Hallum		d.o	20,—
James Robinson		d.o	20,—
John Warnock		d.o	20,—
Michael Warnock		d.o	20,—
Samuel Nelson		d.o	20,—

SOUTH CAROLINA PROVINCIAL TROOPS

Name	Date	Days	£	s	d
John Pretter	do			20	—
James Mc Elwee	do			20	—
James Russel	do			20	—
John Jordan	do			20	—
Patrick Smillie	do			20	—
Arthur Sharburrow	19 Aug^t	d: 1 Mo 3 days		22	—
Thomas Moore	25 Aug^t	28—days	13	18	4
Thomas Jackson	26—do	27—days		18	—
Robert Johnston	26—do	27— do		8	—
Patrick Morris	30—do	23— do		15	—
James Davelin	1 Sept^r	22— do	6	14	8
John Anderson	— do	22— do	13	14	4
James Martin	— do	17— do	13	11	4
Edward Mc Kay	5— do	16— do	6	10	8
William Harbison	6— do	16— do	13	10	4
William Colter	— do		13	10	4
		£	948	8	4

John Purves maketh oath That the above is a just and true Bill of his company to the 22^d Sept. 1775

Sworn to before me

  Rich Brown

              John Purves

Endorsed : Cap^n John Purves's
    Pay bill

[66.]

[HENRY LAURENS TO THE COMMITTEE AT BEAUFORT.]

Charles Town. 23. Septem. 1775—

Gentlemen

The delay of an answer to yours of the 18th U!to has been occasioned by our waiting for a plan & Estimate of the repairs necessary for your Fort Lyttleton which we requested Capt. Joiner to procure, but we have not yet received it, when we receive them we shall give that subject the consideration which is due to it.—

The present circumstances of this Colony renders it absolutely indispensable that we should detain the two Thousand Weight of Gun Powder which we had lodged under your protection for the order of the Council of Safety in Georgia & we desire you will not part with it until you hear further from us—we shall write to that Board at Savanna by the next mail & we flatter ourselves with hopes that no order will appear on you for said powder before we have obtained their concurrence be that as it may we request you not to part with it before we have interchanged another Letter on the subject—

As to the 400! Powder which you detained pr your Chairman's Rec! —we can only say that it added to 600! formerly detained by Coll? Bull, the amount by far exceeds a due proportion of the whole Colony Magazine compared with other parts of the Colony, but we make no doubt of your economy & strict watchfulness to prevent misapplication of any part of an article upon which our safety from attacks even by our domestic foes may so immediately depend, &co

Committee at Beaufort

Endorsed: Copy 23d Septem 1775
    To The Comee at Beaufort.

SOUTH CAROLINA PROVINCIAL TROOPS 101

[67.]

[COL. STEPHEN BULL TO HENRY LAURENS.]

Beaufort. 19th of August 1775 —

Sir

Yesterday I did myself the honor of writing to you as President of the Council of Safety, by Captain Lampriere who commanded the Schooner which has the Gun Powder on board, and in that Letter I would have been more full, had not the wind and tide suited for Captain Lampriere to sail immediately; but soon after they got under sail a thunder squal came up the River by which means the tide was lost; which has given me an opportunity of writing again by Captain Lampriere; in my last I mentioned that I should keep a sufficient number of men in this Town, untill the Powder was safely out of this River, which would have been in a few hours, had not the squal happend; as soon as the Vessels were under sail, I discharged a detachment from two Companies of Prince Williams Parish, where there were the fewest white men in proportion to the Domestics, with orders to proceed to their own homes or districts; but as soon as I found that Captain Lampriere had lost the tide and could not proceed I detain'd a number of other men so as to have one hundred & sixty of my Regiment, which added to the detachment of Provincials under Captain Cattles command, with the detachment of Grenadiers and Artillery from Charles Town amounting in all to two Hundred and fifty, a force which I thought would be sufficient for the intended service— these men I shall detain untill the Vessell with the Powder is out of this River, which I expect will be by one O'Clock, when I will discharge the men untill farther Orders—

With regard to your Recommendation of establishing a Company of Volunteers on Purysburg or Wrights neck, I could have no objection if there were a sufficient number of men, which matter was mention'd sometime ago by a Mr Brisbane to the Lieut! Governor, who wrote me on the subject, and the reasons I gave him are still of force, for upon enquirey I found that there were not over five & twenty men in the boundaries they described, which were too far agreeable to the Resolution of the Congress—As to the Argument of their domestics being left without white men, they certainly are in the predicament with every other Parish or District on field or muster days; and you certainly, will allow that when they are in a body they are more safe and ready to march to Purysburg Neck or any other part where an Insurrection may be apprehended—

I do assure you I would by no means discourage Volunteer Companies as I know it excites an Emulation to excell, which must have a good effect, and induces them to put themselves into our Uniform, and provide themselves with the best Arms they can—

I wrote to each Captain in my Regiment acquainting them with resolution of the Congress, promoting Volunteer Companies, and order them to make it known to the Men under their Command—which has in some measure been complied with, as a very good Volunteer Company is nearly compleated on S! Helena Island, in a few days I expect to receive their List, when I shall review them, and apply for Commission agreeable to the resolution of the Congress—

I can with pleasure inform you that our troubles will at least have one good effect in the lower part of this County as the men are in constant training they are at present upon a footing with any Militia in the Province, and I have procured them an exceeding good Drill, and you may be assured that nothing on my part shall be left undone to have them as compleat as possible—

In your favor of the 3rd Inst! ; you are pleased to say, that the Report of my being censured by the Council of Safety, was groundless—give me leave to say, I do think 'twas sufficient to make any man of feeling uneasy, and I was not singular in my opinion, as people here in general thought me ill used, which I make no doubt proceeded from misrepresentation, and although I would not condescend to tax Captain Joyner, (the Person who was suspected) before I had related to you the manner of the Powder being left here, and requesting the favor of you to acquaint me, who the ungenerous Person was that presumed to make so free with my Conduct, but as Captain Joyner has declared to one of my Officers who spoke to him on the subject that he was innocent of the matter—give me occasion once more to repeat my requisition, and I shall take it as a singular favor if you will let me know as much as you conveniently can, being fully convinced I have been unfairly dealt with in some representation. if not with regard to the Powder, or I flatter myself the Council of Safety would not have encouraged Joyner or Teabout to raise an Artillery Company on this Island which must be taken from the Militia, and their view or expectation is to have that Company under their command entirely exclusive of me—

As the Council of Safety is so far distant from this County, cannot know its circumstances and scituation so well as I do, immagine they would not take a step of that sort without knowing my opinion as they must be fully convinced that I am actuated by no other motive than the good of my Country; and hope they will not be misled by two Men who are of no influence or consequence in this County or even in this Town where they are best known—this is not only my opinion but that of the principal Gentlemen of this place to who I have communicated my sentiments on the subject of an Artillery Company—

As a proof of Mr Joyners influence and conduct on the expedition he was sent to take the Powder from Maitland, you may form some Idea, when I tell you that some days after my return from Charles Town I accidentall fell in here, where I heard that a Canoe had come up from the camp at Bloody point, bringing an Account that Joyner, had but fifteen men, six of which were the Provincial Recruits left at the

Camp by Captain Barnwell, and I judging it expedient did send Captain John Bull with upwards of twenty Volunteers, who staid with Joyner and assisted in taking the Powder, and had he applied as he should have done to me, I could with the same ease have sent him Two Hundred men or more if necessary—

I do not mean to claim any merit on my part, or depreciate M:̲ *Joyner* in your esteem but to show you that he is a man of no influnce, and that a command of the sail he expects, will be taking him entirely out of his Eliment—In his own sphere I would give him the preference of a Command to any man in this County—

You may perhaps be a little surprised to find 400 lb of Powder being again left here, which was mention'd to me, tho' 1 approved of the Scheme, knowing the necessities of the People, to avoid *Censure* I declined to have anything to do with it—1 have the honor to be   Sir

Henry Laurens Esq:̲ r   Your most Obedient servant
President of the Council of Safety—   Step:̲ n Bull

Endorsed: Stephen Bull Esq—19 Aug.
         Answ:̲ d 23 Sept:̲ r 1775

[68.]

[ANDREW POSTELL TO THE COUNCIL OF SAFETY.]

Addressed: To
     The Honourable Gentlemen of the
     Council of Safety—
         at
     Charles Town

         Prince Will:̲ ms Parish Granville
                               County
To the Honourable Gentlemen the Council of Safety for the Province of S:̲ o Carolina, at Ch:̲ s Town

Agreeable to the resolves of the Honourable Gentlemen of

the Provincial Congress—do now Petition your Honours for Commissions, for a Troop of Horse now raised in the Parish & County above writ'en—By a number of Gentlemen (say Thirty) they were pleased to Elect me as their Captain— M![r]{.sup} Henry DeSaussure Lieutenant & M![r]{.sup} Thom[s]{.sup}. DeSaussure Cornet—and as soon as we have Commissions your Honours may depend on our readyness at the shortest notice to defend the Liberties of our Country—Your attention & speedy Compliance to your Humble Petitioners desire, will Oblige Gentlemen

        Your Very Hble Serv[t]{.sup}
20th{.sup} Septembr. 1775   Andrew Postell

Endorsed: Andrew Postell 20th{.sup}
    Sept[r]{.sup} 1775—Rec[d]{.sup} 23[d]{.sup}
    Commissions signed
    & delivered to Mess[rs]{.sup}
    Gee & Gray
     26 Septem 1775.[54]

[69.]

[HENRY LAURENS TO COL. STEPHEN BULL.]

        Charles Town. 23. Septem 1775
Sir.—

From various causes an answer to your several favours of the 18. 19. 20 & 24th{.sup} Ult[to]{.sup} has been long delayed—but not from any designed neglect.

Your intimations of the difficulty which you were under & of the apparent necessity for compelling some men in your Regiment to perform that Duty which all owe to their Country induced us first to put forth a Declaration calculated for that purpose as well as for Regulating the Militia in general, which we flattered our selves would have had all the

---

[54] From the private collection of A. S. Salley, Jr. See *The Sunday News*, Charleston. S. C., March 1?, 1899.

salutary effects which you wished for, so far were we from apprehending that offence would be given by such a measure to any of the Inhabitants of Country or Town except to such as we had in view whose murmurs are never to be regarded. but our order had not been made public 48 Hours before we were alarmed by accounts of a general dissatisfaction among the very people in Charles Town whom we had meant to relieve from an unequal & excessive share of the Duty of Nightly Guards the 12. alert active Volunteer Companies, these by certain Delegates after a public meeting presented an Address & Remonstrance to this Board & a petition to the General Committee. Copies of both, together with Copies of Reports on each by the Respective Committees appointed by us & by the General Commee. you will receive herewith to which we beg leave to refer you—We cannot tell yet what effect these Reports will have on the minds of the Remonstrants & Petitioners, but should they continue refractory, we fear advantages will be taken of the ill example by the disaffected throughout the Colony, of which Class we believe there are more within this Metropolis than without it in proportion to numbers—We make no doubt of your exerting your Influence on this alarming occasion in order to convince every reasonable man under your Command of the rectitude of our conduct & the necessity which we are all under of submitting to the regulations established by the Congress if we mean to defend the Rights of our Country—if there are any just cause for complaint redress will undoubtedly be granted at the next meeting of the Congress which must be on the 1st December & may be earlier—

This seeming disunion we hope will upon the whole produce very good ends—from apparent evil good will be brought forth we shall learn who are real Associates in their Country's Cause & who only subscribed the paper for temporary or sinister purposes.

We desire to avoid particularly adding to the disagreeable subject of any supposed censure on your conduct for detaining a part of the Public Gun powder being persuaded that your Motives were laudable & we hope you will forget that subject—

We are sorry however to inform you that the whole 1000! weight detained for your district is an over proportion of the public stock compared with the necessary demands from other parts of the Colony—in these circumstances we have judged it an indispensable duty, that we should further expostulate with our friends in Georgia before we part with the twenty Barrels detained for them at Beaufort—

The Governor continues on board the Tamar we are told that Moses Kirkland is gone to St Augustine by sea & last night the Officers of the Tamar seized a schooner belonging to Messrs Stone & Duval under pretence that she had Warlike stores on board because part of her Balast was Iron shot which the Owners had made use of for that purpose in the present & a former Vessel for many years past—Our difficulties seem to be increasing at this unlucky juncture when our friends & those whom we supposed to be with us are spliting into factions & withdrawing their hands from the public service—nevertheless we must struggle on & as our Cause is good still strive to surmount every obstacle & we shall get safely through—

By order of the Council of Safety

Ste—Bull Esqr Coll^o of the Granville County Regiment at
Sheldon

Endorsed: Copy 23^d Septem
1775.
To Coll^o Bull

PAPERS OF THE FIRST COUNCIL OF SAFETY OF THE REVOLUTIONARY PARTY IN SOUTH CAROLINA, JUNE-NOVEMBER, 1775.

[70.]

[COL. JOSEPH GLOVER TO HENRY LAURENS.]

Addressed : To
The Hoñble Henry Laurens Esqr
President of the Council of Safety—
Chas. Town.

Septr 22^d 1775

Sir./

I herewith send my return of the Officers and the Whole of the men, liable to bear Arms in the Colleton County Regiment of Foot under my Command, to the Council of Safety Agreeable to their directions to me. The two Saltcatcher Companys, you will Please Observe are the Largest, and all the male slaves from the age of sixteen to sixty years old, within the Bounds of those districts don't Exceed one hundred and twenty five, a small Proportion of slaves to the number of whites, Compared with the other Districts, I understand There are some Volunteer Companys formed & others a forming, and that some Commissions have been Obtained from the Council of Safety, without any Application Through me, as directed by your letter of the 26th July to me, although I gave as general a notification as possible thereof. I therefore Cannot Transmitt to you The Officers names of those. And am sorry to inform you the Regiment are Throw'n into the utmost Confusion, by the selecting of those Volunteer Companys. Especially in the patrole service For after the Committee of Intiligence gave information of the Battle at lexington, The Officers of this regiment mett Together and very Cheerfully came to a resolution to do their duty in every respect, The patrol duty was strictly attended to & our domesticks never behaved with more quiet & submission and the Officers never more Elert in Training their men, Imploying drillmasters, devideing their men into squads, and striveing who should Excell most in Bringing them on in their Exorcisis. But now the Patrol Service (which is one of the Materialest in the lower districts) Stagnated. In those districts where men are inlisted from are too little or no duty done & in other districts where the rendezvous are kept are over done several Officers have and are giveing up their Commissions they Complain of their men going away from them after being at the Expence & pains of Training them, Just, as they are persuaded or their humour takes them, The majority Consists Chiefly of men whose residence are of no long duration in any district, and will Elect & Palm Officers on the district, many of whom do not know how to Perform their duty, anything Equal to the Officers whom are displaced. It do not lay in my Power to Pirsuade them to keep their Commissions, They observe that they must be Subservant to their mens humours That if Proceeded against for neglect of duty They will go into some Volunteer Companys by which means all subordination and authority must be at an end, the Volunteer Companys, unless Limited to some Bounds or Restricted for a Certain time, will Plague their Officers. I am Credibly Informed of one mans haveing inlisted in the Fusaleers Company in Chas. Town, who is an Overseer at Godfreys savana and have since inlisted in two other Volunteer Companys, his former Officer of the district Ordered him into the ranks (his not having a Certificate) made him stand his Draught, his lott was to hold himself in readiness for the first march. this Shews the necessity of Confineing men to their duty and not to be left in a time of Exegincy to their Voluntary will and Pleasure, I have caused the malitia Troughout this regiment to be draughted agreeable to the Council of Safety's directions, but find The draughts will be all splitt to pieces by the Volunteer Companys now formed and Forming so that I find there will be many remnants of Companys who do not Enter with the Volunteers. Through the regiment Extent about one hundred and Twenty miles. I am at a loss how to Compose those men into a body and fear in any Emergency to be at a greater loss The Volunteer Companys having such a latitude. I have Caused the Council of Safety's Declaration of an alarm, To be Published to Every Company Through the Regiment— I think it my duty to give to the Council of Safety the above Information & state of the Colleton County Regiment as it stands at Present—I am with the utmost Obedience and regard for the Council of Safety—

Sir your Most Obediant Humble Servt

Joseph Glover

P. S I have Jus received an order for four Barrils of Powder from you. The Regiment are much in want of Ball and no Bayonets to be had

Endorsed: Jos-Glover. 22 Septr. 1775—Rec^d. 24th [55]

---

[55] From the private collection of A. S. Salley, Jr. See *The Sunday News*, Charleston, S. C., March 5, 1899.

South Carolina August ye 5th 1775 } An Accurate return of the Muster role, in the Colleton County Regiment of Foot Com^d by Coll^n. Jos^h. Glover—

Joseph Glover Colonel—Samuel Elliott Leutenant Colonel—James Laroch Major—Joseph Glover Junr Adjutant.

Districts	Captains	Lieutenants	Ensigns	Serjeants	Privates
Edisto Island	Joseph Fickling	John Seabrook & James Clark			
Wadmalaw Island	John Wilson	John Laroch	Wm Snely	2	95
John's Island	Thomas Ladson	Benjamin Mathews	Isaac Weight	2	53
Stono	John Sommers	John 56	Allen Miles	2	47
Willtown	William Skirving	Thomas Osborn	Morton Wilkinson	2	63
Beach Hill	W^m McClaughlin	Edward Perry & Richard Perry		2	66
Ponpon	Isaac Hayne	Thomas Roberts	Thomas Smith	2	41
Chehaw	Henry Hyrne	Peter B. Guerardeau	Thomas Hutchinson Junr	2	78
Round O	William Sanders	William Baker	Joseph Glover Junr	2	76
Horse Shoe	William Clay Snipes			2	55
Godfreys Savanah	Thomas Ladson	John Sanders	John Gough	2	68
Lower Saltcatchers	David Ferguson	Samuel Dunlap	Josiah Miles	2	84
Upper Saltcatchers	George Ford	Thomas 57	Jacob Carter	2	100
		Thomas Ford	George Ford Junr	2	131
				26	957

Returned by Joseph Glover.

56 Last name torn out.
57 Last name torn out.

Endorsed by Glover: The Colleton County, Regiment
—Return—

Endorsed by Henry Laurens: Return of the Colleton County Regiment 5 August 1775.[58]

[71.]

[ROLL OF CAPT. WILLIAM GASTON'S COMPANY.]

To the Council of Safety in Charles Town

South Carolina District Between Broad and Catawba Rivers adjoining the new aquisition and Broad River September 25th 1775 we the subscribers hereto have in Compliance With the Resolutions Entered into also Instructions given by the Provincial Congress held in Charles Town on Saturday June 17th 1775 and for the purposes therein mentioned associated and formed ourselves into a Voluntcer Company of horsemen And whereas by an Election held at the house of M? Francis Kirkpatrick this day by us the subscribers we have duely Elected and Chosen William Gaston to be our Captain Thomas Robins our first and James Kirkpatrick our Second Lieutenants we therefore humbly pray you to grant and give out Commissions or appointments for those our officers as Chosen

---

[58] From the private collection of A. S. Salley, Jr. See *The Sunday News*, Charleston, S. C., March 5, 1899.

SOUTH CAROLINA PROVINCIAL TROOPS 113

David Reed	Clayton Rogers	Jn⁰ Sadler
James Reed	Francis Bab	
James Dougherty	Charles Gillmore	
Jo^s Mc Cook	[59]	
James Robins	Robert Love	
William Bell	Moses Chery	
William Love	James Mc Creon	
Andrew Woods	William Rogers	
James Bell	James Elliot	
Frs Kirk patrick	John Gillespie	
John Love	John Grant	
John gallher	James Grant	
Robert Elliott		
Joseph Robison		
Robert Kirk Patrick		
Harrison Bell		
Patrick Duffy		
John Mc Cool		

Endorsed : Capt Fr: Kirkpatricks
Volunteer Company [60]

---

[59] Name obliterated.
[60] From the private collection of A. S. Salley, Jr. See *The Sunday News*, Charleston, S. C., March 19, 1899.

[CAPT. JOHN CALDWELL'S PAY BILLS.]

Pay Bill of Captain Caldwell's Company in the Regiment of Rangers Commanded By William Thomson Esquire.

Names of Officers, Non Commission, Officers and Privates	Date of Commissions and Attestations	Pay when Due	Amount
John Caldwell Captain	18 June 1775. to the	26th July	£133
Samuel Taylor 2d Lieutenant	17 July	26 July	20.....5
Oliver Towles } Serjants	26 June	26 July	25.....
William Coffell } Serjants	15 July	26 July	9.....6..3
David Murry	26 June	26 July	20.....
Laughlin Leonard	26 Ditto	26 Ditto	20.....
Andrew Huggins	26 Ditto	26 Ditto	20.....
John Huggins	26 Do	26 Do	20.....
James Huggins	26 Do	26 Do	20.....
William Huggins	26 Do	26 Do	20.....
Robert Owens	26 Do	26 Do	20.....
Andrew Caldwell	26 Do	26 Do	20.....
Benjamin Hodges	26 Do	26 Do	20.....
James Murry	26. Do	26 Do	20.....
John Mc Mahon	26. Do	26 Do	20.....
Robert Johnston	26. Do	26 Do	20.....
Charles Heard	26. Do	26 Do	20.....
William Forbes	26. Do	26 Do	20.....
Samuel Smith	26. Do	26 Do	20.....
William Cuningham 61	26. Do	26 Do	20.....

61 This is undoubtedly "Bloody Bill" Cuningham. It is commonly accepted that "Bloody Bill" was first a Whig and then a Tory. Sabine says so in his *American Loyalists*, and Judge O'Neall also says so in his *Annals of Newberry District*. There are several stories as to why he changed sides. Judge O'Neall says (*Annals of Newberry District*, sketch of Maj John Caldwell) that he had a nice horse that Captain Caldwell impressed; that Cuningham in the controversy with Capt. Caldwell gave offense, and Capt. Caldwell had him whipped, and that thereupon Cuningham deserted. Judge O'Neall probably mixed up the Cuningham story with that of Daniel McGirth, as it is the counterpart of the McGirth story. (See McCrady's *South Carolina in the Revolution, 1775-1780*; Johnson's *Traditions of the Revolution*; Harris' *Stories of Georgia*).

SOUTH CAROLINA PROVINCIAL TROOPS

Name	Date		Amount
Roger Mc Kinnie	26	Do	20
Timothy Mc Kinnie	26	Do	20
John Mc Mahan Junr	26	Do	20
Reuben Golding	26	Do	20
John Eakins	26	Do	20
Samuel Harper	26	Do	20
Anthony Harper	26	Do	20
Henry Willson	26	Do	20
Daniel Clarke	26	Do	10
Hezekiah Yancey	11	July	8
James Brown	14	July	3
			£705..11..3

John Caldwell being duly sworn upon the Holy Evangelist of Almighty God, maketh Oath that the above is a just and true Pay Bill of the men under his Command——

Sworn to Before me ..
this 26th September 1775

Jno Caldwell [62]

Geo᷎ Whitefield

Another tradition, given by the writer in his *History of Orangeburg County, 1704-1782*, ascribed the cause of his desertion to the hanging, by Capt. Jacob Rumph, of a Tory brother of William Cuningham. While this bears some semblance to the correct story it is much exaggerated and was only given by the writer as a tradition, and all traditions grow in the handing down process. A living member of the Cuningham family is authority for the last story, which is probably approximately true, which is that a party of lawless Whigs took William's crippled brother out of his house at night and whipped him, and that when his mother interfered she was roughly treated. This caused William to desert and declare the vendetta. He joined the British and rose to the rank of Major of Royal Militia. When the British army left Charles Town "Bloody Bill" left with it and settled at Nassau, New Providence, where he became a pensioner on the British. His death at Nassau was announced in the *Charleston Morning Post & Daily Advertiser* of January 30, 1787. On the 16th of December, 1779, Gov. Rutledge issued a proclamation, which was published in *The Charlestown Gazette*, January 17th and 18th, 1780, calling upon a number of deserters to surrender. Among these was William Cuningham.

[62] See Salley's *History of Orangeburg County, 1704-1782*, p. 414; vol. I. of this magazine, p. 120, *note*. John Caldwell was the maternal uncle of John C. Calhoun. (O'Neall's *Annals of Newberry District*.)

Pay Bill of Captain Caldwell's Company in the Regiment of Rangers commanded by William Thomson Esquire from 26th day of July to 26th August 1775.

Names of Officers, Non Commission Officers and Privates—	When Pay Commenced	Pay when Due	Amount
John Caldwell Captain	26 July	26 August	£108..
Samuel Taylor 2d Lieut	26. July	26 August	..69..
Oliver Towles } Serjants	26. July	26 August	..25
William Coffell }	26 July	26 August	..25
David Murry	Ditto	Ditto	..20
Laughlin Leonard	Ditto	Ditto	..20
Andrew Huggins	Ditto	Ditto	..20
John Huggins	Ditto	Ditto	..20
James Huggins	Ditto	Ditto	..20
William Huggins	Ditto	Ditto	..20
Robert Owens	Do	Do	..20
Andrew Caldwell	Do	Do	..20
Benjamin Hodges	Do	Do	..20
James Murry	Do	Do	..20
John Mc Mahan	Do	Do	..20
Robert Johnston	Do	Do	..20
Charles Heard	Do	Do	..20
William Forbes	Do	Do	..20
Samuel Smith	Do	Do	..20
William Cuningham	Do	Do	..20
Roger Mc Kinnie	Do	Do	..20
Timothy Mc Kinnie	Do	Do	..20
John Mc Mahan Junr	Do	Do	..20
Reuben Golding	Do	Do	..20
John Eakins	Do	Do	..20
Samuel Harper	Do	Do	..20
Anthony Harper	Do	Do	..20

10
15

	When Pay Commenced	Pay When Due	Amount		
Henry Williams		Do	..20		
Daniel Clarke		Do	..20		
Hezekiah Yancey		Do	..20		
James Brown		Do	..20		
Carried Over			£768	5..	..
Amount Brought Over			£768.	5..	—
Patrick Forbes	2 August	26 August	..16	0..	8
James Banks	18. Ditto	26 Ditto	..5.	0..	8
George Patterson	18. Ditto	26 Ditto	..5.		
			£794.	6..	4..

John Caldwell being duly Sworn upon the Holy Evangelists of Almighty God, maketh Oath that the above is a just and true Pay Bill of the Men under his Command

Jn.º Caldwell

Sworn to Before me this 26th September 1775. }
    Geo.ᵉ Whitefield

Pay Bill of Captain Caldwell's Company in the Regiment of Rangers Commanded by William Thomson Esquire from 26th day of Aug.t to 26th Septem.r 1775—

Names of Officers, Non-Commission Officers and Privates	when Pay Commenc'd	Pay when Due	Amount
John Caldwell Captain	26 August	26 Sept.r	£108.
Samuel Taylor 2.d Lieut	26 Aug.t	26 Sept.r	10
Oliver Towles ⎱ Serjants	26 Aug.t	26 Sept.r	15
William Coffell ⎰	26 Aug.t	26 Sept.r	
Daivd Murry	Ditto	Ditto	.69.
Laughlin Leonard	Ditto	Ditto	.25.
Andrew Huggins	Ditto	Ditto	.25.
John Huggins	Ditto	Ditto	20
James Huggins	Do	Do	20
William Huggins	Do	Do	20
Robert Owens	Do	Do	20
Andrew Caldwell	Do	Do	20
Benjamin Hodges	Do	Do	20
James Murry	Do	Do	20
John Mc Mahon	Do	Do	20
Robert Johnston	Do	Do	20
Charles Heard	Do	Do	20
William Forbes	Do	Do	20
Samuel Smith	Do	Do	20
William Cuningham	Do	Do	20
Roger Mc Kinnie	Do	Do	20
Timothy Mc Kinnie	Do	Do	20
John Mc Mahan Jun.r	Do	Do	20
Reuben Golding	Do	Do	20
John Eakins	Do	Do	20
Samuel Harper	Do	Do	20
Anthony Harper	Do	Do	20
Henry Williams	Do	Do	20

SOUTH CAROLINA PROVINCIAL TROOPS 119

	when Pay Commenc'd	Pay when Due	Amount		
Daniel Clarke	Do	Do	20		
Hezekiah Yancey	Do	Do	20		
James Brown	Do	Do	20		
		Carried over	£768.	5	
Amount Brought Over					
Patrick Forbes	26 August.	26 Septemr	£768.	5	
James Bankes	26 Augt	26 Septr	.20		
George Patterson	26 Augt	26 Septr	.20		
			.20		
			£828	5	

John Caldwell being duly Sworn upon the Holy Evangelists of Almighty God, maketh Oath that the above is a just and true Pay Bill of the Men under his Command

Jn°. Caldwell

Sworn to before me
this 26th September 1775
    Geoe. Whitefield

Endorsed: Capt Caldwells
    Paybills—
    Capt: Caldwell Pay Bills—

[73.]

[MELCHER GARNER TO THE REPRESENTATIVES OF ST. PAUL'S PARISH.]

Addressed: To
The Representatives of
S! Paul's Parish [63]

Gentlemen—

Wee received a letter from the General Committee, desireing us to have Stockade Forts built in Our Parish, wee will be much Obliged to you to Inform us in what manner the Expences are to be Defray'd, as wee are Entirely at a loss, how to Proceed,—wee allso Purpose meeting the Inhabitants to Fix on such Place or Places as will be Thought most Convenient for the same, Wee Likewise will be obliged to you to send us a Plan of a Fort & the Necessary Buildings for Accommodating the Inhabitants & c^{co}—Their will be three Forts Erected in the Parish,—by Order of the Committee

Melcher Garner
Chair,,man

Tuesday ye 26th Septr 1775

S! Pauls Parish

Endorsed: Rec^d. 29

Endorsed also: Melcher Garner 26 Septr 1775. Read in Council 1st Septr 1775
Parochial Forts

[74.]

[PLAN AND ESTIMATE OF REPAIRS NECESSARY FOR FORT LYTTLETON. [64]

An Estimate of the Repairs wanted at Fort Lyttelton
For the Plat form 415 feet Long & 18 feet Wide. Viz$_t$

---

[63] The representatives for St. Paul's Parish, elected Aug. 7th and 8th, 1775, were: Thomas Ferguson, Capt. Benjamin Elliott, Charles Elliott, Capt. Robert Ladson, George Haig and Capt. William Skirving —*The South-Carolina Gazette,* Thursday, Sept. 7, 1775.

[64] See *South Carolina Historical and Genealogical Magazine* for October, 1900, p. 303.

8 M feet of 2½ Inch Plank............
4500 feet Joyce. 6x8
2000 feet Cills .. 6x8   [Platform
2 Tapis Walls for the Cills under the £1600..—..—
100 lb Spikes
300 Bushels of Lime
Bricklayer, Carpenters & Labourers......
a Tapis break water wall 268 yds
6 M Bushels of Shells & Labourers....   ...446..—..—
5 M. Bricks for the Well & to Repair..
the Oven & Chimneys.
5 M feet of Inch Boards to repair
the Barracks, doors & Windows
4 M Bushels of Lime for the Well, Offi-   ...635..—..—
cers Barracks &c
Carpenters, Plaisterers, Bricklayers
and Labourers Wages................
Flooring and other Nailes, Locks, Hing-
es & Glasse for Gates, Doors & Windows.   ... 91.. 5..—
Repairing Gun Carriages, Getting the
guns out of the sand & up the Bank
into the Fort & Mounting the same &
Making Tomkins & other Necessa-   ....400..—..—
rys for the same with Ropes & Iron
Work.............................

                                £3172.. 5..—

Endorsed: Estimate for repairs
            of Fort Lyttelton
            Read in Council
            26 Septem 1775

Plan Endorsed: Plan of Fort Lyttel-
                ton at Beaufort.
                Rec'd 26 Septem 1775.

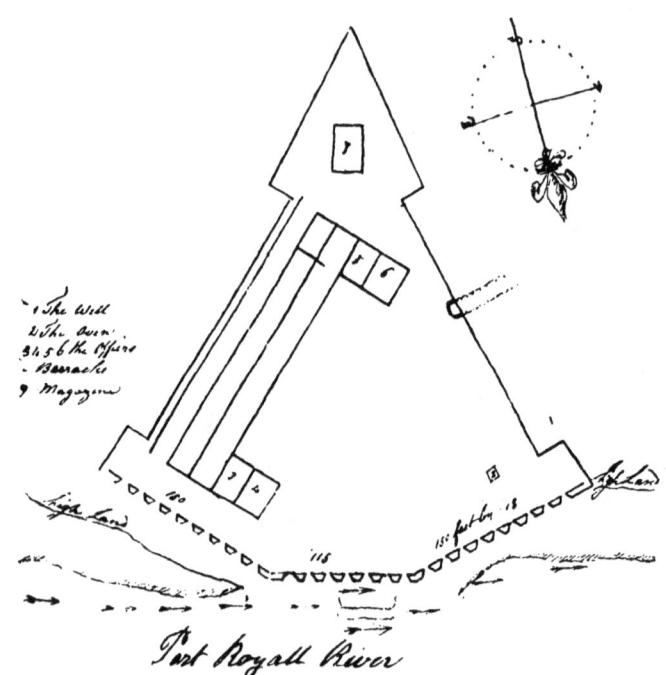

[75.]

[HENRY LAURENS TO WILLIAM HENRY DRAYTON.]

Charles Town 27th Septem 1775

Sir—

On Saturday last we received your Letter of the 17th together with the sundry papers which you refer to [65] & if Capt Wilson is detained one day more we will send by him the Declaration & Treaty to be printed in London but shall defer a publication here until we have an opportunity of considering the propriety of such a measure in your presence which we suppose will happen in the course of a few days. The Intelligence from the Cherokees received in Mr Wilkinson's Letter is very alarming, [66] we hope you have sent away the Good Warrior & his fellow travellers in good humour & that they will influence their Country Men to remain quiet & give us time to discover the perpetraters of the Murder intimated by Mr. Wilkinson—in the mean time we trust that you have taken proper measures for that purpose.

LeDespenser Packet arrived here from Falmouth with advices from London to the 3d. August—Accounts in brief are that Administration were sending more Troops and ships of war to America determined to persevere in the execution of their plan—General Gage in his Acct of the Bunker Hill affair of the 17th June transmitted to Lord Dartmouth owns about 1056 of the Kings Troops Killed & Wounded & his number of Officers rather exceeds our early advices.—We have heard nothing since the first of August from our Delegates.

By order of the Council
of Safety

The Honble. W. H. Drayton

Endorsed: Copy 27. Septem. 1775
Wm Henry Drayton

---

[65] See Gibbes's *Documents*, 1764-1776. [66] Ibid.

[76.]

[HENRY LAURENS TO COL. WILLIAM MOULTRIE.]

Charles Town. 28. Septem 1775

Sir—

Lieutenant John Allen Walter having signified to us in writing dated the 22º. Inst his desire to resign his Commission as Lieutenant in your Regiment We have after due consideration Resolved that he be permitted to resign. you will therefore accept his Resignation in form & notify the same to us in order that the Vacancy which will thereby happen may be properly supplied.

By order of the Council of Safety.

Collº Moultrie

Endorsed: Copy 28 Septem 1775
To Collº Moultrie

[77.]

[CAPT. JAMES JONES'S VOLUNTEER MILITIA COMPANY.]

We, whose names are here Underwritten, being deeply Impressed with the Calamitous Circumstances of the Inhabitants of America from the Oppressive Acts of the British Parlament, Tending to Enslave this Continent, do find it Necessary for the Security of our Lives and Fortunes, and above all, Our Liberty and Freedom, To Associate ourselves into a Volunteer Company under the Command of James Jones, And that we will hold ourselves in Readiness for Our mutual Security and Defence, to Obey all such orders as Shall be directed by our Provincial Congress.................. ....

SOUTH CAROLINA PROVINCIAL TROOPS

Henry Jourdon. Sen.r—	William Limmix...	John Maders—	Joshua Elkins—
Henry Jourdon. Jun.r	Alexander Brunston	George Brunston	Thomas Reavs. Sen.r
Joshua Stanley	John Ayers	William Jones	Thomas Reavs. Jun.r
William Stanley	William Ayers	Henry Taylor	Thomas Limmix Sen.r
Moses Bennett	Stephen Frank	Jeremiah Brown	Thomas Limmix Jun.r
Samuel Pickings	Martin Loadholt—	Benjamin Byrd	Amos Limmix
Josiah Brunston	Jacob Maders	Lewis Lee	Jacob Besinger
Gustavas Gulfus	Jacob Hier	Solomon Peters	Ephriam Jones
Thomas Jones Sen.r	Edmund Jones	John Tedders	Joseph Doelittle
Jacob Colson	William Wournell	Daniel Reavs	Daniel Buddiet
William Kierse	George Kierse—	John Morris	Charles Morris
William Brunston	James Morris	William Wood	Charles Cox
John Taylor	Henry Peeples	Mark Tapley	Benjamin Odom
Joseph Sykes	Timothy Caffle	Michael Odom	William Jones

126   SOUTH CAROLINA PROVINCIAL TROOPS

Endorsed: Capt. James Jones's Company of Volunteers at Salt Catchers— Commissioned 28 Septr 1775—[67]

[78.]

[DR. DAVID GOULD TO THE COUNCIL OF SAFETY.]

Addressed: To
The Worthy & Honourable Members of the Council of Safety for the Province of South Carolina

---

Illustrious Patriots./
     If the most Pressing necessity shall not be deemed a sufficient apology for the singularity of this address; I own myself unable to make any; and must submit to your censure.——

Perhaps it may be no easy task to determine why the unhappy are solicitous to conceal their infelicity; but certain it is, that this Propensity is so powerful: where any degree of delicacy presides in the mind: that every Person in the least acquainted with the human heart must be thoroughly convin'd of its distress when compel'd to proclaim it.——

It is of but little consequence: Gentlemen for you to be inform'd that in the early part of my life I quit the Land of my nativity, and pass'd a number of years in the West Indies; where the desire of independence enabled me to combat all the infirmities peculiar to that fatal Climate, till persevering diligence in the practice of medicine, had put me in possession of (what I tho't) a modest sufficiency for every future Care.——

---

[67] From the private collection of A. S. Salley, Jr. See *The Sunday News*, Charleston, S. C., March 12, 1899.

My unambitious views being thus satisfied, and the distresses which began to threaten my native Country (to which I feel every faculty of my soul indissolubly united determined me to return & share its destiny.——Accordingly all my property was shiped at different times, and on different Bottoms to North America, in one of which I took Passage myself; and after a most miserable & lengthy Voiage replete with inexpressible hazard and hardships I arriv'd at Boston a few days before General Gage; where I received the Melancholy news, that by ship-wreck & some other accidents to which Maritime affairs are liable, almost every shilling of my hard earn'd acquisitions was utterly lost.——

With a heavy, & almost disponding heart, I proceeded to New Jersey where I have two Children; and after spending some time with them, resolved to try my fortune one more among the Islands; in pursuance of this resolution on the 20th of March, I took shipping at New York & and Eleven days after was cast away at Cape Hatteras; from whence with much difficulty I got to Georgia; and being depriv'd by this accident of the very inconsiderable all, sav'd from my former misfortunes, have not had it in my Power to make a second attempt; and Consequently have ever since, been a distitute unhappy Wanderer, without a home.——

But the laudable preperations which are making for the preservation & defence of every sacred and valuable enjoyment, gives me leave to hope I may yet be rendered useful to society; and not intirely thrown by in the meridian of life, as a Worthless member in the Community.—I am not such a novice as to be ignorant of the obstacles which impede the success of a stranger, destitute of friends, interest, and acquaintance; and that employments are procured more easily by those who are more fortunate, but Gentlemen; let me beg you will oppose to those difficulties, the truely Pitiable situation to which I am reduc'd; and let this consideration excite you; generously to Imagine what it is impossible to discribe; the exquisite feelings of a Person of sensibility; accustomed to the Joys of society & the Conveniences of life; by fatal Mischances; at once secluded from both, Oblig'd to exist the

Child of dayly dependence, and compel'd by the indispensable calls of nature to accept the unpleasant Conditions.—(vile debasing necessity.) the universal benevolence of which your Characters bespeak you Possess'd; Join'd with these reflections; I flatter myself will supply the place of acquaintance, interest, & friends.——

Permit me Gentlemen; to inform you farther; that in the last War I spent several years in the service of my Country (chiefly in Character;) and during my residence in the Indies, served in a similar Capacity, for the verity of this I have sufficient vouchers; & should think myself happy in an opportunity of submitting them to the inspection of your Patriotick and honourable Board.——

Now Gentlemen: If, on perusing this Paper you shou'd think proper in any manner to honour me with your Commands, I shall endeavour to evince my gratitude by discharging any trust reposed in me, to the best of my abilities & with the utmost integrity.——

But on the Contrary: if my suit is fruitless, and I am given over a Prey to despair; I hope humanity & goodness of heart will induce you to Pardon this trouble & presumtion of a stranger; and forget the author; who cou'd never have been put on this expedient but as his last resources. ——

I have the honour to be with all Possible
        Respect: Worthy & Respectable
           Gentlemen your very obed.t
             & Most devoted

Cha.s Town   Humble servant
27 Sep.t 1775   David Gould [68]

P. S. any Commands directed to the care of Doct.r John Budd will be immediately obeyed.——

Endorsed: David Gould 27 Sept.r 1775
         Rec.d & Read in Council
         28th

---

[68] "Gould, David (Va). Hospital Surgeon, 8th September, 1777; Senior Hospital Surgeon in Virginia, 11th October, 1779; died 12th July, 1781."—*Officers of the Continental Army* (F. B. Heitman.)

[79.]

[HENRY LAURENS TO THE GEORGIA COUNCIL OF SAFETY.]

Charles Town So Carolina
29th Septem 1775.

Gentlemen

We wrote to you by the last Post to which we beg leave to refer—As the time approaches for the intended meeting of the Indian Commissioners at Salisbury in North Carolina & as the late accident of a Cherokee murdered & two more wounded by unknown White Men renders it essential for them to meet on the day appointed or sooner if possible, we embrace this favourable opportunity by the hands of Capt John Joiner for transmitting to you extracts from the Resolutions of the Continental Congress & from Letters from our Delegates together with a Copy of the Talk intended for the Indians & although you may have already received some of these, the repetition will be less prenicious than the want of any one part would be.—

We think the necessary alterations to be made & the signing of Mr. Hancocks name will be best done by the Commissioners when they are altogether therefore we have not attempted it.—We shall send duplicates of the papers now inclosed to you to Mr. Galphin & Mr. Wilkinson by expresses this day & you will furnish Mr. Rae with proper copies & such Instructions as you shall judge proper.—We are extremely glad to learn you have made a father acquisition of Gun Powder, the utmost frugality in the consumpt of what we have & Industry to add to our stores are equally necessary.——

By order of the Council of Safety

Council of Safety.
Savanna

Endorsed: Copy 29th Septem
1775
To The Council of Safety
at Savanna

[80.]

[HENRY LAURENS TO WILLIAM ERVEN.]

Charles Town So Carolina
29th Septem 1775.

Sir——

In answer to one part of your Letter of the 22d Inst I intreat you to believe that my remark upon a former Letter received from your Council of Safety without date was very innocently made & without meaning to give offence, tis my usual practice in corresponding, to Note the dates of Letters received as well as of such as I have written while these remain unacknowledged—omissions of dates are sometimes discovered even in the Letters of the most accurate & leisurely writers—Men who are full of business are more liable to such mistakes—& none more excusable for small undesigned errors that those who continually labour for the public—if this rule is not extended to me I shall be as full of blame as I am of faults every day—therefore I hope there will be reciprocal kindness & indulgence & you may rest assured of all proper respect & attention on the part of Sir

Your most Obedt Servt.
H L——

Endorsed: Copy to W. Erven
Esquire——
29 Sept 1775

[81.]

[HENRY LAURENS TO LADY SARAH CAMPBELL.[69]]

Madam

I am ordered by th C of S to acquaint Your Ladyship that such a Message by the hands of two Gentlemen was sent

---

[69] September, 1775, Lord William Campbell, the Royal Governor of South Carolina, having become alarmed at the power of the Council of Safety, withdrew from his home in Charles Town (the large brick

this afternoon to Ld W C. intreating His Excellency to return to C T— as the Council have hopes will induce His Ldship to gratify the wishes of the People & that nothing but the expectation of seeing His Ldship in Charles Town to Morrow has prevented their giving such orders as would have secured Your Ldyship, a safe passage to the Tamar with! hindrance or trouble—

If his Excy the Gov declines the Invitation which is sent Your Ladshp may rest assured that I will immedy apply for the Order & send it to Y! Ladshp if granted

Ans by 29 Septr 1775.

Endorsed: Copy to Lady Willm Campbell 29 Septr 1775

---

house now known as 34 Meeting Street) and went on board the man-of-war Tamar, then lying in Rebellion Roads. He was invited by the Council of Safety to return, but declined to do so. Lady Campbell evidently wrote to the Council of Safety to secure permission to join her husband, and this is the Council's reply. It is written on the blank side of a leaf of paper that was probably torn from the sheet upon which Lady Campbell wrote, for it contains the following address in a pretty hand :

To—
The Hoñble Henry Laurens Esq!
President of the Council of Safety
Chas Town

PAPERS OF THE FIRST COUNCIL OF SAFETY OF THE REVOLUTIONARY PARTY IN SOUTH CAROLINA, JUNE-NOVEMBER, 1775.

[82.]

[CAPT. SAMUEL WISE TO THE COUNCIL OF SAFETY.]

Addressed: To
 The Hoñoble the Council of Safety—
  address

To the Hoñoble the Councill of Safety
Honoble Gentlemen

I am Extremely sorry any incident should have arisen that wuld oblige me to send the Commission you were pleased to honour me with unto Mr Drayton, for haveing entered into the servis, with a heart full of Zeal for the Legal freedom of myself & fellow subjects of this Province in Particular and the Constitutional Rights of America in Generall, so nothing less than being dishonoured by a suspicion of want of Integrity to the great Cause of Constitutional Liberty, wuld have induced me to have taken this step, & I hope your Honours will be pleased to consider the bitterness of my feelings when Mr Drayton Refused to tell me the name of the Man who had thus disgraced me, but as my friends here seem to think that I have been rather hasty, if your Honours too should be of that Opinion, I shall be Exceedingly Greived, for it was never my intention to give the least offence, and beg leave to Submitt myself and Cause to your honours Judgment

      I am with great Respect
       your Honors
Charlestown   moste Obedt Humble servant
30 Sepr 1775   Saml. Wise [70]

Endorsed: Capt Sam Wise
    30 Sepr 1775.
    Read in Council 1st Octob.
    Referred to Mr Drayton—

[83.]

[THE GENERAL COMMITTEE TO THE COUNCIL OF SAFETY.]

In General Committee.[71]

---

[70] Samuel Wise was senior captain in the Rangers (See vol. I, p. 189). His resignation, as above, was not accepted. In September, 1776, the Rangers were taken upon the Continental establishment as a full infantry regiment, and on November 23rd Lt. Col. Thomson was appointed Colonel; Major Mayson was appointed Lt. Col., and Capt. Wise Major (Gibbes' *Documentary History of the American Revolution,* 1776-82, pp. 45-46). Maj. Wise was killed at the siege of Savannah, October 9, 1779.

[71] On July 6, 1774, a convention of the people of South Carolina met in Charles Town and passed resolutions condemning the British Parliament for shutting up the port of Boston, and looking to protection against oppressive measures. Before adjourning this Convention selected a committee of ninety-nine "to act as a General Committee to correspond with the committees of the other Colonies, and to do all matters and things necessary to carry out the resolutions of the convention." It was stipulated that twenty-one of this committee should

134 SOUTH CAROLINA PROVINCIAL TROOPS

Charles-Town, 2d October, 1775.

Resolved, That it be recommended to the Council of Safety, to direct a proper Intrenchment to be made, with all possible Expedition, on the Neck, at a proper Distance from Charles-Town; as a secure Retreat for the Inhabitants, should they be driven from the said Town.

A true Copy.

Pet^r Timothy, Sect^{ry}

Endorsed : P. Timothy
2^d Octob^r 1775

[84.]

[COMMISSION TO GEORGE GALPHIN.]

To George Galphin—of Silver Bluff. Esqr
By the Council of Safety for South Carolina convened at Charles Town the 2^d October 1775— ———

By virtue of Authorities vested in us by the provincial Congress of this Colony met at Charles Town in June last & confirmed by the Representatives of the United Colonies in America Assembled at Philadelphia in July following :

We do nominate & appoint You the said George Galphin Esquire to be a Commissioner for Indian affairs in the Southern department. AND. you are hereby authorized & empowered to treat with the said Indians in the name & on the behalf of the united Colonies in order to preserve peace and friendship with the said Indians and to prevent their taking any part in the present Commotions & you are to follow and obey all such Orders &

---

constitute a quorum and that the power of the General Committee was to continue until the next general meeting. This committee was continued until the formation of the independent government in March, 1776. Up to the formation of the Council of Safety in June, 1775, it was practically the executive power in South Carolina. After the formation of the Council of Safety its offices were chiefly advisory 'though it still retained some executive powers.

directions in Indian affairs as you may now or shall from time to time hereafter receive from the Representatives of the United Colonies, from the provincial Congress or from the Council of Safety for this Colony for the time being— And for all & every Act which you shall do or cause to be done by virtue of this Commission—this shall be your Warrant & Indempnification. Given under our hands & Seals at Charles Town aforesaid on the said 2ᵈ Octob 1775—

Endorsed: Copy 2ᵈ October 1775—
To George Galphin [72]

[85.]

[HENRY LAURENS TO THE GEORGIA COUNCIL OF SAFETY.]

Gentlemen

Charles Town So Carolina 3ᵈ October 1775—

We beg leave to refer you to our Letter of the 29ᵗʰ Ultᵒ which went by the hands of Mʳ Tebout from hence to Beaufort where Capt. Joiner was to take & convey it to you immediately—[73] We have not heard from you by the last mail & have nothing particular to trouble you with by the return but a Copy of the Commission which we have judged proper to give to Mʳ Galphin & Mʳ Wilkinson respectively—which, 'though we do not presume to offer it as a plan, may serve to give you information.—

We find that the Cherokees mentioned in our last were killed & wounded in your Colony, we think it very necessary to Advertise & offer a reward for discovery of the perpetrators— If you are of this opinion we will readily second you in the measure—

Endorsed: Copy 3ᵈ Octobʳ 1775

---

[72] On the margin of the commission is written: "To Edward Wilkinson of Keowee, Esquire," and the inference is that an exact copy was sent to Wilkinson. See No. 85.

[73] See January, 1901, magazine, p. 24

[86.]

[HENRY LAURENS TO THE GEORGIA COUNCIL OF SAFETY.]

Gentlemen.

I am ordered by the General Committee to inclose a Resolution Entered into this day in Commee on the Case of James Brisbane Esquire[74] to which we beg leave to refer—the Commee. request you to lay the Resolution before the proper board or Commee. in your Town in order that our Enemies may not receive shelter & comfort among our friends——

     I am Gentlemen
      Your most Obed^t Servt
Charles Town   H L President
 3^d October 1775—
     Under Cover as usual to W. Erven
          Esquire
    & sent to Philip Will to go by Post
Council of Safety at Savanna—

Endorsed: Copy 3^d Octob^r 1775—
  To the Council of Safety
   at Savanna

[87.]

[COL. JOSEPH GLOVER TO HENRY LAURENS.]

Addressed: To
   The Hon!. Henry Laurens Esqr^r
    President of the Council of Safety
      Charlestown

Sir   Octo^r ye 2^d 1775

Several Men, Who's Names are Subscribed To the within Assosiation on Edisto Island, To form themselves into a Volunteer Comp^y agreeable to a Resolution of the Provincial

---

[74] James Brisbane was one of the congratulators of Lord Cornwallis on his victory at Camden, Aug. 16, 1780, and was among those whose property was confiscated and persons banished by the Jacksonborough Assembly of 1782.

SOUTH CAROLINA PROVINCIAL TROOPS 137

Congress, have made Applycation To me to Procure, Commissions for the following Gentlemen to Command them Viz. Joseph Jenkins To Be their Captain Archibald Whaley First Lieut^n, Joseph Fickling Junr Second Lieut^t and Jeremiah Eaton Third Lieut^t, or Ensign I have Apply'd To the Governor Sometime ago for Those very Commissions, with some others which he refused to grant, I, therefore, Now Pray the Council of Safety will Direct Commissions To be Made Out for the Above Gentlemen If Approved of By them—I believe, it will Be Necessary for me To return the Inclos'd Paper, to the Officers, when The Council of Safety have done with it.

       I am
N:B: Sir
 Please Procure also an with Regard your
Ensigns Commission for the very Hum^l. Servt
Edisto Island, Old Militia, Company[75] Joseph Glover[76]

They have Choose Mr John Adams
to be Ensign of that Company

We the Subscribers do agree to Form ourselves into a Volunteer Company Under the Command of the Following Officers Mr Joseph Jenkins Captain Mr Archibald Whaley First-Lieutenant Mr Joseph Fickling Junr Second Liutenant The Uniform to be a Blue Coat with White Cuffs and Lappels with Jacketts & Breches of White, with a Fann Tail Hatt, To meett at least once a Week to goe through the Exercise We Farther Agree to the Orders of the Above Officers till such time Commission is Granted

---

[75] See January, 1901, magazine, p. 6.
[76] From the private collection of A. S. Salley, Jr. See *The Sunday News*, Charleston, S. C., March 5, 1899. The roll accompanying the letter was published in the same paper. The roll belonged to the collection left by the late Wm. Gilmore Simms, but is now owned by Maj. John Jenkins, of Charleston.

138 SOUTH CAROLINA PROVINCIAL TROOPS

Nath!. Adams	John Adams	John McMahan
Charles Elliott	Wm Stanyarne	Ric^d Cox
Samuel Eaton	Samuel Evans	William Mikell
Nath!. Morgan Jn^r.	William Wilson	David Adams Jn^r
James Crawford	Jeremiah Fickling	Whitem^h Seabrook
W^m. Furguson	John Fickling	
Ja^s. Murray	Wm Evans	
Benjamin Jenkins	Joshua Eaton	Ezekiel Wise
George McNorny	John Gregory	John Hanahan
John Theüs	Micah Jenkins	Thomas
John Wilson	Thomas Whaley	Elliott
John McLeod	Thomas Wescoat	Joseph Maxey
Richd Jenkins	Benjⁿ Edings	Robert Maxey
William Bonsall	William Reynolds	
Florence Flinn	George Cheney	
Isom Lowrey	Stephen Dulzer	
Wm Hanahan	John Docherty	
Jeremiah Eaton	Jno White	
Charles Flinn	John Desberry	
	Thos Skinner	

On reverse of page : Mr Jeremiah Eaton is allso appointed as Third Lieutenant

Endorsed : Coll^o Jos Glover
2^d. Octob 1775 presented to Council the 3^d.
Commissions signed the

[88.]

[PAPERS TRANSMITTED TO THE COUNCIL OF SAFETY BY CAPT. EZEKIEL POLK.]

So. Carolina New acquisition } Thaddeus Reed & Robert Davies } Came before me and Voluntarily made Oath that he will not Lift arms against the

Americans in their present Contest with Great Britain, nor do any thing by word nor Action, that he shall Know to be against the American Cause.

Sworn before me this 30th Sepr 1775
Ezek^l Polk ss

Endorsed by Polk: Reed &
Davies'
Oaths

South Carolina }
New acquisition } William West appeared before me and made Oath that he will not Lift arms against the americans in their present Contest with Great Britain, nor do any thing by word or action which He shall Know to be against the american Cause

Sworn to before me this } William West
2^d October 1775 }
Ezek^l. Polk ss

Endorsed by Polk: West
Deposition

South Carolina }
New acquisition } At a meeting of the Committee of this District on the 4th October 1775

Ordered, that in pursuance of the Recommendation of the Council of Safety of the 20th Sepr 1775 One large and commodious stockade fort be Built, in this District, as Near to the Centre of the Regiment, as Conveniency will permit.

A true Copy by order of Comittee
Ezek¹ Polk president[77]

---

[77] In June, 1775, the Provincial Congress elected Ezekiel Polk, then lieutenant colonel of the New Acquisition regiment, second captain in the regiment of Rangers (Ramsay's *Revolution of South Carolina*, Vol. I, pp. 34 and 36. *Collections South Carolina Historical Society*, Vol. 2, p. 24.) He organized his company and joined Major Mayson's camp at Ninety Six, Sunday, July 23, 1775. (vol I. of this magazine, p. 68),

[89.]

[HENRY LAURENS TO GEORGE GALPHIN]

Ch. Town 4 Octob 1775—

Sir.

Since closing our packet which you will receive with this we have Resolved to send to Keowee in order to be properly distributed among the Cherokees One Thousand pounds weight of Gun powder & 2000[1] Lead of which you will be pleased to inform Mr Wilkinson immediately & that he may expect it on the 20 Ins^t or a day or two sooner—We apprehend he will have sufficient time to make the distribution & for meeting you somewhere in the way to Salisbury & that you may both arrive at that town before the Day appointed—but in order to save time we repeat our desire that you will send a Messenger to him without delay & draw upon us for the expence.

By order of the Council
of Safety
H L
Presdt—

G G Esquire—

Endorsed: Copy to Geo Galphin
4 Octob. 1775
by a Man from Ph.
Wills—

---

after having had his progress to that point interrupted by Capt. Robert Cuningham's party of Tories. After remaining in Major Mayson's camp just a week he marched his men out of it on Saturday, July 29th, and sent them to their homes, and sent Maj. Mayson a letter announcing that he had quit the service. (Vol. 1, p. 70, Salley's *History of Orangeburg County, 1704-1782*, p. 414.) He afterwards adjusted his troubles with the Council of Safety and raised a company of volunteer militia and did good service in the "Snow Campaign" of November and December, 1775. Subsequent to the fall of Charles Town he was colonel of one of the regiments of "State Troops" under Gen. Sumter's command. He was a brother of Col. Thomas Polk, one of the Revolutionary leaders in Mecklenburg County, North Carolina, and of the same family as President Polk.

[90.]

[RETURN OF CAPT. THOMAS WOODWARD'S COMPANY FROM AUG, 1ST TO SEPT 20TH 1775[78].]

A Return to the pay Master of the officers non commissioners and privates of the Eight Company of Rangers commanded by Colo William Thomson from the 1st Day of August to the 20th of Sept 1775.—

			£	s	d
Thomas Woodward Capt	51 Days at 70/..........£		186	10	
1^t Lieu^t Richard Winn	51 Ditto .. 45/.................		114	—	
2^n Lieut John Woodward	Ditto..........45/...............		114	—	
Serj^{ts} John Smith...............Ditto...........................			41	13	4
William Boyd.............Ditto.............................			41	13	4
Drum^r William Wilson........Ditto	a 20 p^r Month....		33	6	8
John Owens...............Ditto......Ditto....................			33	6	8
James Picket............Ditto......Ditto.....................			33	6	8
James Owens..........Ditto......Ditto.....................			33	6	8
John Carr...............Ditto......Ditto.....................			33	6	8
John Carson............Ditto......Ditto....................			33	6	8
John Henderson......Ditto......Ditto....................			33	6	8
Daniel Oaks ....Ditto......Ditto.....................			33	6	8
Benj.. Mitchell.........Ditto......Ditto....................			33	6	8
Francis Henderson...Ditto......Ditto.....................			33	6	8
William Henderson..Ditto. ....Ditto.....................			33	6	8
Benj. May................Ditto......Ditto.....................			33	6	8
Jacob Frazier.........Ditto......Ditto.....................			33	6	8
Henry Wimpey ....Ditto......Ditto....................			33	6	8
Charnel Durham......Ditto......Ditto....................			33	6	8
James Anderson.......Ditto......Ditto....................			33	6	8
William Rayford......Ditto......Ditto....................			33	6	8
Mathew Rayford......Ditto......Ditto....................			33	6	8
		£	1089	16	8
Brought Over D^m ....£			1089	16	8
Benjamin McGraw...51 days..Ditto....................			33	6	8
Augustin Hancock...Ditto......Ditto....................			33	6	8
William Owens........Ditto......Ditto....................			33	6	8
John Mc Daniel ....Ditto......Ditto....................			33	6	8
Francis Mc Daniel ....Ditto......Ditto....................			33	6	8
Thomas Gather.........Ditto......Ditto....................			33	6	8
Prichard Stone........ Ditto......Ditto....................			33	6	8
John Jacobs.............Ditto......Ditto....................			33	6	8
John Bell................Ditto......Ditto....................			33	6	8
Joseph Owens.........Ditto......Ditto....................			33	6	8
Thomas Winingham.Ditto......Ditto....................			33	6	8
Edward Mc Graw.....Ditto .... Ditto....................			33	6	8
William Duggins......Ditto......Ditto....................			33	6	8
	Total——£		1523	3	4

[78] For the first return of this company, to August 1st, 1775, see Vol. I. of this magazine, pp. 122-123.

Thomas Woodward maketh Oath, That the above Pay Bill is just & true to the 20th Septemr 1775—
Sworn to before me this }
4th day of Octr 1775   }
   Tho: Charlton

PAPERS OF THE FIRST COUNCIL OF SAFETY OF THE REVOLUTIONARY PARTY IN SOUTH CAROLINA, JUNE-NOVEMBER, 1775.

[91.]

[PAY BILL OF CAPT. SAMUEL WISE'S COMPANY FROM SEPT. 1ST TO OCT. 1ST 1775.[79]]

Pay Bill of Captain Sam. Wise's Company, in the Regiments of Rangers, Commanded by Col?. William Thomson, from 1st Sept? till 1st Day October 1775——

Names of Officers & Privates				
Samuel Wise Captain, till the 20th (then resigned)	20 Days.	at 70/. ⅌ Day	£ 70,,	— —
John Donaldson. 1st Lieutenant	30 Days.	@ 45/. ⅌ do	67,,	10,, —
Joseph Pledger...2. Lieutenant	30. ditto	—45/. ⅌ do	67,,	10 —
Trustum Thomas. 1. Sergeant	30,, do	—£25., ⅌ Month	25,,	— —
Benjamin Hicks. 2 Sergeant	30,, do	—£25. ⅌ do	25,,	— —
1. Burgess Williams	30,, do	—£20. ⅌ do	20,,	— —
2. Thomas Dean	30,, do	—£20. ⅌ do	20,,	— —
3. Thomas Cochran	30,, do	—£20 ⅌ do	20,,	— —
4. Isham Gardner	30,, do	—£20. ⅌ do	20,,	— —
5 Edmund Hodge	30,, do	—£20. ⅌ do	20,,	— —
6. John Hodge	30,, do	—£20. ⅌ do	20,,	— —
7. Alexander Jernigan	30,, do	—£20. ⅌ do	20,,	— —
8. Bentley Fearson	30,, do	—£20. ⅌ do	20,,	— —

[79] See magazine for July 1900, pp. 189-90, for first return of this company.

144 SOUTH CAROLINA PROVINCIAL TROOPS

9. John Heard	30,,	do ...	—£20,, ⅌	do	20,,	—	—
10. Benjamin Fathern	30,,	do ...	—£20,, ⅌	do	20,,	—	—
11. John Booth	30.,	do ...	—£20. ⅌	do	20,,	—	—
12. Daniel Welch	30,,	do ...	—£20. ⅌	do	20,,	—	—
13. Dixon Pearce	30.,	do ...	—£20,, ⅌	do	20,,	—	—
14. Peter Hubbard	30,,	do ...	—£20,, ⅌	do	20,,	—.	—
15. Isham Hodge	30,,	do ...	—£20. ⅌	do	20,,	—	—
16. John Stubbs	30,,	do ...	—£20. ⅌	do	20,,	—	—
17. Thomas Conner	30,,	do ...	—£20. ⅌	do	20,,	—	—
18. Lewis Conner	30 ,	do ...	—£20. ⅌	do	20,,	—	—
19. Silvanus Cooper	30,,	do ...	—£20,, ⅌	do	20,,	—	—
20. John Wilson (Inlisted, 2d Inst. by Cap. PeyerimHoff. Exchanged for W. Morris)	˙8,,	do ...	—£20,, ⅌	do	18,,	13,,	4
Amount Carried Over					£653,,	13.,	4
Amount Brought Over					£653.,	13,,	4
21. Samuel Desurrencey	30. Days-	at£20. ⅌ Month			20,,	—	—
22. Daniel M c Daniel	30.	do ..	—£20. ⅌	do ..	20,,	—	—
23. Moses Mace	30.	do ...	—£20. ⅌	do	20,,	—	—
24. Isaac Lockhart	30.	do ...	—£20. ⅌	do	20,,	—	—
25. John Jones	30.	do ...	—£20. ⅌	do	20,,	—	—
26. Henry Wyly	30,,	do ..	—£20. ⅌	do	20,,	—	—
27. William Covington	30,,	do ..	—£20. ⅌	do	20,,	—	—
28. Jesse Smith	30,,	do ...	—£20. ⅌	do	20,,	—	—
29. Thomas Pearce	30,,	do ...	—£20. ⅌	do	20,,	—	—
30. Daniel Young	30,,	do ...	—£20. ⅌	do	20,,	—	—
					£853,,	13,,	4
Negroe Bob (.Drummer)	20,,	do ...	—£20. ⅌	do	13.,	6,,	8
					£867,,	0,,	—

John Donaldson Maketh Oath, That the above is a just & true Pay Bill of the first Company of Rangers to the first day of October 1775———

Sworn before me }
this 4th day Oct.r 1775 }
Tho: Charlton

Endorsed: Captain Samuel Wise
      Pay Bill from 1st Sept.r to 1st Oct.or 1775.

Endorsed also: Cap.t Wises
      Paybill—

[92.]

[JAMES BRISBANE TO HENRY LAURENS.[80]]

Addressed: To
             Coll Henry Laurens
             These

Sir

As I am about to put myself on my Travels deo Volunte on Sunday next I could do no less in Justice to myself than address a Line to you who attentively hear'd the Charge brought against me for acting the Honest Freeman and my defence. to enquire whether you as a private Gentleman or as Chairman of the Committe have seen a Letter addressed to Lord N—th by a Rice Planter dated Frontier of Carolina Augst 2^d 1775 And if so what your private Judgement of that Piece is—on the whole whether the Contents thereof indicate any Principles dangerous or that the author thereof can with Propriety be termed one of most dangerous of the Enemies to the Freedom of these Collonies.—If you have heard nothing of it there may be some mistery—It was delivered at the House of Peter Timothy in August for Publication if approved of by the Committe—

If you have any Letter to Wrights Neck you may depend on their being taken care off I mean to go & stay there for some Time if can be quiet there   Fare you well I am
                    Sir
                    Your most humble servant
Oct. 6th 1775—   James Brisbane
Henry Laurens Esqr

---

[80] See April 1901 magazine, p. 101.

[HENRY LAURENS TO JAMES BRISBANE.]

Sir.

In answer to your Letter of this Morning I do assure you that I never saw nor heard of the Rice Planter's Letter which you allude to, therefore I can form no opinion concerning its merit—I may venture to say it was never laid before the General Committee nor Council of Safety—because I have never been once absent from their meetings since April or beginning of May last.

you say you are to stay some time on Wrights Neck, do not attempt it without permission, rather remain where you are without going abroad till Wednesday next & then apply to the General Committee, perhaps, nay 1 think probably, upon a proper Representation of your Case they may indulge you to remain there (I mean at your Plantation) if not altogether, yet for some reasonable time beyond their late prescription, in hopes that you will not be instantly driven away I will not bid you farewell, but assure that that in all proper consideration I am Sir

Ansonburgh 6 Octo^{br} 1775.   your humble serv^t

Endorsed: James Brisbane
     6 October 1775 & an-
     swer same day—[81]

[93.]

[COL. WILLIAM THOMSON TO THE COUNCIL OF SAFETY.]

Addressed: To
     The Honourable the Council of Safety.
      Charles-Town. .

Amelia 29th Septr 1775./
The Honourable the Council of Safety.
Gent^n —

I yesterday return'd from Ninety six, & think it unnecessary to write of particulars, as I make no manner of doubt

---

[81] The copy of Laurens's reply to Brisbane was written on the back of the outside sheet of Brisbane's letter.

Mr Drayton has already given you the same. I have left seven Companies behind at Ninety six, in order to take a Tour farther into the Country.

An alarm has been given that an Indian of the Cherokees had been killed & two wounded in Georgia, which has disturb'd the minds of the back Inhabitants much. And Mr Drayton's opinion in this Case, concurs with my own, it is, that as the Rangers were raised in defence of the Country, the back settlers would think hard if they were not with them in case of danger. We have therefore order'd them to march for some time up amongst them but not to proceed within fifteen Miles of the Indian Line, for fear of alarming the Indians, & in order to appease the minds of the Inhabitants in those parts.

After which we have given leave of absence for a few days in order to recruit themselves & Horses, which is really requisite, when they are to meet at the Camp in Amelia which will be on the 24th October

After Mr Drayton had finish'd with Col: Fletchall, I took a ride to Fort Charlotte, & examin'd the whole; I think it is in very good order for defence & that there is a very good Company in it. While I was there I had the pleasure of seeing Fort-James on the Georgia side, taken possession of by some of the Georgians and Carolinians—at my return to Ninety six, I met with Mr Wilkinson from the Cherokee Nation who informed me that one of the Indians was killed & two wounded by some of the Georgia People I immediately gave orders to Lieutt Taylor of Fort Charlotte to take a party of Men with him & go in search of the Persons whom the Indians mistrusted had committed the fact & whose names this Mr Wilkinson mentioned to me. Inclosed you have a General return of my regiment of Rangers from the time of enlisting to the 20th Instant[82] which is as correct

---

[82] In his *History of Orangeburg County, 1704-1782*, the Editor of this magazine was unable to give, in his sketch of the 3d Regiment (Thomson's), any rolls of this regiment because he did not know of the existence of such rolls in the Historical Society's collection.

I could possibly make it from the returns given in by the different Captains.[83] Capt: Wise on that same Day resigned his Commission to M!̣ Drayton[84] & as he will inform you more particularly on that & every other Head I think it unnecessary to add any more—

    I remain
     Gentlemen
      Your most obed! hum serv!
         Wm Thomson

Endorsed: Coll^o W. Thomson
    29 Septem 1775
    Read in Council
    of Safety 7 Ooctober—

[94.]

[FIRST GENERAL RETURN OF THOMSON'S REGIMENT.]

A General Return to the Honorable the Council of Safety. of Colonel William Thomson's Regiment of Rangers from the time of inlisting to this 20th day of September 1775, inclusive—Viz!

---

[83] Several of "the returns given in by the different Captains" have been printed in former issues of this magazine and one in the present issue.

[84] He withdrew his resignation subsequently. See April 1901 magazine, pp. 97-98.

No of Privates	Names of Officers Non-Commissioned Officers and Privates.	Dates of Commissions and Attestations.	Age of Officers, Non-Commissioned Officers & Privates	Country where Born	Size of men.	Pay to this day
	Colonel William Thomson	18th June 1775				£ 570,, —,, —
	Major James Mayson	18. June "				427,, 10,, —
	Adjutant, John Easom .. from	1. Augst "				
	Serjt Major, Alexander Smith	1. Augst "				
	Captain Samuel Wise	18th June "	37,,	England	5 x 8	332,, 10,, —
	Lieuts { John Donaldson	18. June "	30,,	Do	5 x 10	213,, 15,, —
	{ Joseph Pledger	1. July "	25,,	Virginia	5 x 6	184,, 10,, —
	Serjts { Tristram Thomas	1. Do "	23,,	Maryland	5 x 6	66,, 13,, 4
	{ Benjamin Hicks	1. Do "	18,,	South Carolina	5 x 10	66,, 13,, 4
	Privates—Vizt.					
1	Burgess Williams	1. Do "	28,,	Virginia	6 x x	53,, 6,, 8
2	Thomas Dean	1. Do "	34,,	Do	5 x 10	53,, 6,, 8
3	Thomas Cockran	1. Do "	28,,	New England	5 x 10	53,, 6,, 8
4	Isham Gardner	1. Do "	22,,	South Carolina	5 x 10	53,, 6,, 8
5	Edmund Hodge	1. Do "	23,,	North Carolina	5 x 8	53,, 6,, 8
6	John Hodge	1. Do "	28,,	Do	6 x x	53,, 6,, 8
7	Alexander Jernigan	1. Do "	24,,	Do	5 x 10	53,, 6,, 8
8	Bentley Fearson	1. Do "	25,,	Maryland	6 x 2	53,, 6,, 8
9	John Heard	1. Do "	30,,	Pennsylvania	5 x 8	53,, 6,, 8

150 SOUTH CAROLINA PROVINCIAL TROOPS

No.	Name	Day	Month	Age	Origin	Size	£	s	d
10	Benjamin Fathern	3.	Do "	31,,	Virginia	5 x 10	51,,	6,,	8
11	John Booth	3.	Do "	22,,	Maryland	5 x 8	51,,	6,,	8
12	Daniel Welch	8.	Do "	37,,	Virginia	5 x 10	48,,	-	
13	Dixon Pearce	8.	Do "	38,,	Do	5 x 7	48,,		
14	Peter Hubbard	8.	Do "	19,,	South Carolina	5 x 8	48,,		
15	Isham Hodge	8.	Do "	25,,	Virginia	5 x 11	48,,		
16	John Stubbs	8.	Do "	21,,	South Carolina	5 x 9	48,,		
17	Thomas Conner	8.	Do "	24,,	Do	5 x 8	48,,		
18	Lewis Conner	8.	Do "	18,,	Do	5 x 10	48,,		
19	Silvanus Cooper	8.	Do "	31,,	Jerseys	5 x 6	48,,		
20	William Morris	8.	Do "	19,,	England	5 x x	45,,	6,,	8
21	Samuel Desurrencey	12.	Do "	22,,	South Carolina	5 x 4	45,,	6,,	3
22	Daniel McDaniel	12.	Do "	32,,	Do	5 x 8	45,,	6,,	8
23	Moses Mace	12.	Do "	27,,	Maryland	5 x 8	45,,	6,,	8
24	Isaac Lockhart	12.	Do "	23,,	New York	5 x 5	45,,	6,,	8
25	John Jones	12.	Do "	23,,	North Carolina	5 x 7	43,,	6,,	8
26	Henry Wyley	15.	Do "	23,,	Virginia	5 x 11	43,,	6,,	8
27	William Covington	15.	Do "	22,,	Maryland	6 x 1	43,,	6,,	8
28	Jesse Smith	22.	Do "	24,,	North Carolina	5 x 6	39,,	6,,	8
29	Thomas Pearce	22.	Do "	40,,	Virginia	5 x 8	39,,	6,,	8
30	Daniel Young	10	August "	22,,	Do	6 x 1	26,,	13,,	4
							£2297,,	8,,	4

A General Return of Col.º Thomson's Regiment of Rangers, Cont.ᵈ

Names of Officers, Non-Commission'd Officers and Privates.	N.º of Privates	Dates of Commissions and Attestations	Age of Officers Non-Commiss'd Officers & Privates.	Country where Born	Size of Men Feet-Inches.	Pay to this day
Captain John Caldwell		18th June 1775	35 Years	Virginia	......	332, 10, —
Lieuts { Samuel Taylor⁸⁵		17th July "	35 "	Pennsylvania	......	148, —, —
{ David Anderson		13th Septem "		Virginia	......	18, —, —
Sergts { Oliver Towles		26 June "	41 "	Virginia	5 x 6	70, 16, 8
{ William Coffell		15 July "	46 "	Maryland	5 x 8	54, 3, 4

85 "Died, on Friday the 20th of April last, in Pendleton county. Major *Samuel Taylor*. Throughout the revolution he proved himself a staunch whig, and an active brave soldier."—*City-Gazette and Daily Advertiser*, Tuesday, May 15, 1798. He began as second lieutenant of his company. (See January 1901 magazine, p. 9.)

152 SOUTH CAROLINA PROVINCIAL TROOPS

Privates, vizt.

#	Name	Date		Origin	Height			
1	David Murry	26 June	"	Virginia	6 x	23,,	56,,	13,, 4
2	Laughlin Leonard	26 Do	"	Do	6 x	27,,	56,,	13,, 4
3	Andrew Huggins	26 Do	"	Do	5 x 8	25,,	56,,	13,, 4
4	John Huggins	26 Do	"	Pennsylvania	5 x 7	28,,	56,,	13,, 4
5	James Huggins	26 Do	"	Virginia	5 x 10	26,,	56,,	13,, 4
6	William Huggins	26 Do	"	Do	5 x 7	21,,	56,,	13,, 4
7	Robert Owens	26 Do	"	Do	6 x	28,,	56,,	13,, 4
8	Andrew Caldwell	26 Do	"	Do	6 x	33,,	56,,	13,, 4
9	Benjamin Hodges	26 Do	"	Do	5 x 10	25,,	56,,	13,, 4
10	James Murry	26 Do	"	Do	5 x 8	20,,	56,,	13,, 4
11	John Mc Mahen	26 Do	"	Pennsylvania	5 x 8	21,,	56,,	13,, 4
12	Robert Johnston	26 Do	"	Do	5 x 7	27,,	56,,	13,, 4
13	Charles Heard	26 Do	"	Do	5 x 6	20,,	56,,	13,, 4
14	William Forbes	26 Do	"	Virginia	5 x 8	19,,	56,,	13,, 4
15	Samuel Smith	26 Do	"	Pennsylvania	5 x 10	19,,	56,,	13,, 4
16	William Cunningham	26 Do	"	Virginia	5 x 6	19,,	56,,	13,, 4
17	Roger Mc Kinney	26 Do	"	Pennsylvania	5 x 7	24,,	56,,	13,, 4
18	Timothy Mc Kinney	26 Do	"	Do	5 x 6	19,,	56,,	13,, 4
19	John Mc Mahen Jun	26 Do	"	Maryland	5 x 11	20,,	56,,	13,, 4
20	Reuben Golding	26 Do	"	Virginia	5 x	27,,	56,,	13,, 4
21	John Eakins	26 Do	"	Pennsylvania	5 x 5	20,,	56,,	13,, 4
22	Samuel Harper	26 Do	"	Virginia	5 x 10	23,,	56,,	13,, 4
23	Anthony Harper	26 Do	"	Do	5 x 10	24,,	56,,	13,, 4
24	Henry Willson	26 Do	"	Scotland	5 x 5	36,,	56,,	13,, 4
25	Daniel Clark	26 Do	"	Virginia	5 x 8	34,,	56,,	13,, 4
26	Hezekiah Yancey	11 July	"	Do	5 x 6	23,,	46,,	—,, —
27	James Brown	14 July	"	Ireland	5 x 6	20,,	44,,	—,, —
28	Patrick Forbes	2d August	"	Pennsylvania	5 x 6	16,,	32,,	3,, 4
29								
30							£2162,,	

SOUTH CAROLINA PROVINCIAL TROOPS 153

A General Return of Col? Thomson's Regiment of Rangers. Cont^d.

No. of Privates.	Names of Officers, Non-Commissioned Officers and Privates.	Dates of Commissions and Attestations.	Age of Officers, Non-Commissioned Officers & Privates	Country where Born	Size of Men Feet–Inch^s	Pay to this day
	Captain Ely Kershaw	18th June 1775	30 Years	England	6 x x	332,, 10,, —
	Lieuts { Francis Boykin	18. June "	21 "	North Carolina	5 x 10	213,, 15,, —
	{ Thomas Charlton	29. June "	29 "	Maryland	5 x 10	189,, —,, 7
	Serjts { Augustine Preestwood	1. July "	26 "	Virginia	6 x 1	66,, 13,, 4
	{ Thomas Pemble	1. Do "	28 "	Do	5 x 11	66,, 13,, 4
	Drummer Thomas Wood	1. Do "	26 "	Ireland	5 x 8	53,, 6,, 8
1	Privates—Robt Martin	1. Do "	28 "	Do	6 x 2	53,, 6,, 8
2	Newel Bearfoot	1. Do "	24 "	Virginia	5 x 4	53,, 6,, 8
3	James Saxon	1. Do "	20 "	Do	5 x 10	53,, 6,, 8
4	Uriah Goodwin	1. Do "	25 "	Do	6 x x	53,, 6,, 8
5	Jacob Cherry	1. Do "	23 "	Do	5 x 11	53,, 6,, 8
6	James Cook	1. Do "	23 "	England	5 x 3	53,, 6,, 8
7	Peregrine Magness	1. Do "	21 "	Virginia	5 x 9	53,, 6,, 8
8	John Gray	1. Do "	22 "	Do	5 x 11	53,, 6,, 8
9	Joseph Ferguson	1. Do "	23 "	Do	5 x 10	53,, 6,, 8
10	Benjamin Ferguson	1. Do "	23 "	Do	5 x 10	53,, 6,, 8
11	Mordicai Mc Kinney	1. Do "	24 "	Maryland	5 x 7	53,, 6,, 8
12	William French	1. Do "	30 "	Virginia	5 x 9	52,, 6,, 8
13	Richard Nicholls	1. Do "	21 "	North Carolina	5 x 10	53,, 6,, 8
14	Jeremiah Simmons	1. Do "	22 "	Ireland	5 x 8	53,, 6,, 8
15	Thomas Howell	1. Do "	24 "	Maryland	5 x 9	53,, 6,, 8
16	Thomas Coursey	1. Do "	28 "	North Carolina	5 x 10	53,, 6,, 8
17	John Payne	1. Do "	22 "	South Carolina	5 x 8	53,, 6,, 8
18	John Wright	1. Do "	22 "	Maryland	5 x 9	53,, 6,, 8

	Name			Age		Birthplace	Size	£ s d
19	Hugh Gaston	1.	Do "	23	"	Ireland	5 x 10	53,, 6,, 8
20	Robert Gaston	1.	Do "	25	"	..Do	6 x 2	53,, 6,, 8
21	Alexander Gaston	1.	Do "	21	"	..Do	6 x x	53,, 6,, 8
22	George Gray	1.	Do "	24	"	Virginia	5 x 10	53,, 6,, 8
23	John Steel	1.	Do "	22	"	Ireland	5 x 9	53,, 6,, 8
24	John Swilla	1.	Do "	26	"	Virginia	5 x x	53,, 6,, 8
25	Aaron Alexander	1.	Do "	29	"	..Do	6 x 5	53,, 6,, 8
26	Robert White	1.	Do "	35	"	Ireland	6 x ?	53,, 6,, 8
27	Henry Harmon	1.	Do "	30	"	Virginia	5 x 10	37,, 3,, 8
28	William Weatherford	25.	Do "	29	"	..D'	6 x x	33,, 6,, 8
29	Samuel Sessions	1. August		28	"	..Do	6 x x	30,, 6,, 8
30	John Montgomery	4.	Do "	24	"	Ireland	5 x x	
							£2463,, 5,, —

SOUTH CAROLINA PROVINCIAL TROOPS 155

A General Return of Col.º Thomson's Regiment of Rangers. Cont.d

No. of Privates	Names of Officers, Non-Commissioned Officers and Privates.	Dates of Commissions, and Attestations.	Age of Officers, Nm-missioned Officers & Privates.	Country where b[orn]	Size of Men Feet-Inch.s	Pay to this day
	Captain Robert Goodwyn	18th June 1775	34 Years	Virginia	6 x 2	332,, 10,, —
	Lieut.s { David Hopkins	25. June "	38 "	Do	5 x 6	198,, 7,, —
	{ William Mitchell	2. July "	28 "	Do	5 x 10	182,, 5,, —
	Serj.ts { Merry M.c Guire	25 June "	23 "	Do	5 x 5	71,, 13,, 4
	{ John Johns	25. Do "	22 "	Do	5 x 10	71,, 13,, 4
	Drummer, Henry Frits	25. Do "	18 "	South Carolina	5 x 5	57,, 6,, 8
	Privates—Viz.t					
1	Thomas Miller	25 Do "	19 "	Ireland	5 x 9	57,, 6,, 8
2	James Randolph	25. Do "	25 "	Virginia	5 x 9	57,, 6,, 8
3	James Anderson	25. Do "	20 "	South Carolina	5 x 5	57,, 6,, 8
4	Benjamin Hodge	25. Do "	19 "	Do	5 x 9	57,, 6,, 8
5	William Partridge	25. Do "	18 "	Do	5 x 7	57,, 6,, 8
6	Henry Wyley	25. Do "	30 "	Ireland	5 x 4	57,, 6,, 8
7	John Snelling	25. Do "	19 "	South Carolina	5 x 9	57,, 6,, 8
8	Elijah Peters	25. Do "	21 "	North Carolina	5 x 11	57,, 6,, 8
9	Lewis Broadway	25. Do "	18 "	Do	5 x 6	57,, 6,, 8
10	Lewis Coon	25. Do "	19 "	South Carolina	5 x 6	57,, 6,, 8
11	Jesse Killingsworth	25. Do "	20 "	Do	5 x 7	57,, 6,, 8
12	Hext Chappell	25. Do "	19 "	Virginia	5 x 10	57,, 6,, 8
13	Charles Devor	25. Do "	26 "	Pennsylvania	6 x 1	57,, 6,, 8
14	Joseph Wells	25. Do "	34 "	North Carolina	6 x 1	57,, 6,, 8
15	Conrad Coon	25. Do "	21 "	South Carolina	5 x 10	57,, 6,, 8
16	Gardner Williams	25. Do "	26 "	Virginia	5 x 6	57,, 6,, 8
17	William Lee	25. Do "	21 "	North Carolina	6 x 1	57,, 6,, 8

13	John Jackson	25.	Do	"	38	South Carolina	5 x 9	6,,	8
19	Solomon Peters	25.	Do	"	23	North Carolina	5 x 9	6,,	8
20	William Hubbard	25.	Do	"	24	Virginia	5 x 7	6,,	8
21	Gilbert Gibson	25.	Do	"	26	South Carolina	5 x 6	6,,	8
22	Gilbert Gibson (Congarees)	16.	July	"	21	Do	5 x 11	13,,	8
23	William Foust	1.	July	"	25	Do	5 x 6	6,,	8
24	John Tapley	1.	Do	"	21	Virginia	5 x 6	6,,	8
25	Burrell Foust [86]	1.	Do	"	20	South Carolina	5 x 7	6,,	8
26	William Lacerty	6.	Do	"	24	North Carolina	6 x 8	6,,	8
27	Bryant Adams	6.	Do	"	46	Do	5 x 10	6,,	8
28	William Winningham	6.	Do	"	35	South Carolina	5 x 11	6,,	8
29	John Gibson	16.	Do	"	26	Do	5 x 9	13,,	4
30	Benjamin Gibson	16.	Do	"	20	Do	5 x 7	13,,	4
							£2553,,	8,,	4

[86] "Burril, Son of Caspar & Naomy Foust; born January 11th 1756. Suscep:,, John Parks, Henry & Anne Hertel.."—Rev. John Giessendanner's church register of the townships of Amelia and Orangebnrgh, 1739-1761, in Salley's *History of Orangeburg County, 1704-1782*, p. 159.

SOUTH CAROLINA PROVINCIAL TROOPS 157

A General Return of Col. Thomson's Regiment of Rangers. Cont.

No of Privates	Names of Officers, Non-Commissioned Officers and Privates.	Dates of Commissions, and Attestations.	Age of Officers, Non-Commissioned Officers & Privates	Country where Born.	Size of Men. Feet-Inch.	Pay to this day
	Captain Edwd. Richardson	18th June 1775	28 Years	South Carolina	5 x 10	332,, 10,, —
	Lieuts. { Lewis Dutarque	18. June "	29 "	Do	5 x 10	213,, 15,, —
	{ Moses Vance	1 July "	32 "	Virginia	5 x 8	184,, 0,, —
	Serjts. { Reuben Bromfield	25 June "	21 "	Do	6 x x	71,, 13,, 4
	{ Joseph Fox	25 Do "	30 "	South Carolina	6 x x	71,, 13,, 4
	Drummer James Buchanan	1st July "	34 "	Ireland	5 x 8	53,, 6,, 8
	Privates—Vizt					
1	Andrew Hannah	25th June "	25 "	Ireland	5 x 9	57,, 6,, 8
2	Charles McKinney	25. Do "	21 "	South Carolina	5 x 9	57,, 6,, 8
3	Robert Spurlock	25. Do "	27 "	Virginia	5 x 10	57,, 6,, 8
4	Benjamin Franklin	25 Do "	21 "	Do	5 x 9	57,, 6,, 8
5	David Brunson	25. Do "	31 "	South Carolina	5 x 10	57,, 6,, 8
6	Ezekiel White	25. Do "	21 "	Do	5 x 10	57,, 6,, 8
7	Zeth Poole	25. Do "	20 "	North Carolina	5 x 9	57,, 6,, 8
8	Dennis Hinson	25. Do "	23 "	Virginia	5 x 8	5,, 6,, 8
9	Joseph Smith	25. Do "	27 "	Pennsylvania	5 x 7	57,, 6,, 8
10	William Poole	1. July "	17 "	North Carolina	5 x 8	53,, 6,, 8
11	William Rogers	1. Do "	23 "	Maryland	5 x 10	53,, 6,, 8
12	Johnston Parish	1. Do "	24 "	Virginia	5 x 8	53,, 6,, 8
13	Edwin Ferrel	1. Do "	21 "	Do	5 x 8	53,, 6,, 8
14	John Mattison	1. Do "	19 "	Do	5 x 8	53,, 6,, 8
15	Richard Singleton	1. Do "	17 "	South Carolina	5 x 5	53,, 6,, 8
16	Micajah Wallis	1. Do "	20 "	Virginia	5 x 8	53,, 6,, 8
17	Isaac Hilton	1. Do "	31 "	Do	5 x 8	53,, 6,, 8

#	Name	Day	Month		Days		Origin	Dim		£	s	d
18	John Hilton	1.	Do	"	16	"	South Carolina	5 x 8			53,,	6,, 8
19	William Hilton	1.	Do	"	23	"	Virginia	5 x 6			53,,	6,, 8
20	Isaac Brunson	1.	Do	"	26	"	South Carolina	5 x 8			53,,	6,, 8
21	Josiah Brunson	1.	Do	"	25	"	Do	5 x 8			53,,	6,, 8
22	William Hood	1.	Do	"	45	"	Do	5 x 8.6			53,,	6,, 8
23	William Sloan	1.	Do	"	29	"	Do	6 x 8			53,,	6,, 8
24	Michael Morgan	11.	Do	"	23	"	Lancaster	5 x 8			46,,	6,, —
25	John Belcher	15.	Do	"	31	"	Virginia	5 x 9			43,,	6,, 8
26	John Brunneau	28.	Do	"	24	"	Do	5 x 8			35,,	6,, 8
27	Abraham Poole	1.	July	"	23	"	Do	5 x 10			53,,	6,, 8
28	Benjamin McKinney	25.	June	"	39	"	North Carolina	5 x 9			57,,	6,, 8
29	John Bromfield	7.	Septr	"	20	"	Virginia	5 x 9			9,,	6,, 8
30	Charles Fortenor	10	Do	"	20	"	North Carolina	5 x 8			7,,	6,, 8
										£2442,,	1,,	8

SOUTH CAROLINA PROVINCIAL TROOPS 159

A General Return of Colo Thomson's Regiment of Rangers. Contd.

No of Privates	Names of Officers, Non-Commissioned Officers and Privates.	Dates of Commissions, and Attestuations.	Age of Officers, Non-Commissioned Officers & Privates	Country where Born	Size of Men Feet. Inchs.	Pay to this day
	Captain Thomas Woodward........	18th June 1775	46 Years	Virginia........	....	332,, 10,, —
	Lieuts. { Richard Winn;...........	18 June "	25 "	...Do...........	....	213,, 15,, —
	{ John Woodward........	1 July "	28 "	...Do...........	....	184,, 10,, —
	Serjts. { John Smith...............	18 June "	28 "	...Do...........	5 x 10	76,, 13,, 4
	{ William Boyd............	29 Do "	27 "	Ireland........	5 x 8	68,, 6,, 8
	Drummer William Wilson........	15 July "	24 "	...Do...........	5 x 9	43,, 6,, 8
	Privates—Vizt					
1	James Picket...................	24 June	22 "	Virginia........	5 x 11	58,, —,, —
2	John Owens....................	24 Do	31 "	...Do...........	5 x 11	58,, —,, —
3	Benjamin Mc Graw.............	23 Do	21 "	South Carolina.	5 x 5	58,, 13,, 4
4	Benjamin May..................	18 Do	20 "	Virginia........	5 x 6	61,, 6,, 8
5	James Owens...................	27 Do	33 "	...Do...........	5 x 10	56,, —,, —
6	John Carr......................	27 Do	36 "	...Do...........	6 x x	56,, —,, —
7	John Carson....................	27 Do	26 "	Maryland.......	5 x 9	56,, —,, —
8	Benjamin Mitchell..............	27 Do	21 "	Ireland.........	6 x 1	56,, —,, —
9	John Henderson................	27 Do	26 "	Pennsylvania...	5 x 9	56,, —,, —
10	Daniel Oaks....................	27 Do	30 "	...Do...........	5 x 11	56,, 6,, 8
11	William Rayford................	28 Do	25 "	South Carolina.	5 x 10	55,, 6,, 8
12	William Owens.................	28 Do	36 "	Pennsylvania...	5 x 6	55,, 6,, 8
13	Edward Mc Graw...............	29 Do	30 "	South Carolina.	5 x 10	54,, 13,, 4
14	John Jacobs....................	29 Do	25 "	Virginia........	5 x 11	54,, 13,, 4
15	James Anderson................	29 Do	22 "	South Carolina.	5 x 11	54,, 13,, 4
16	Jacob Frazier...................	29 Do	27 "	......Do........	5 x 9	54,, 13,, 4
17	Henry Wimpey..................	29 Do	25 "	Virginia........	5 x 8	54,, 13,, 4

160 SOUTH CAROLINA PROVINCIAL TROOPS

18	William Henderson	29	Do	23	"	South Carolina	5 x 7	54,,	13,,	4
19	Francis Henderson	29	Do	21	"	Virginia	5 x 5	54,,	13,,	4
20	Mathew Rayford	30	Do	20	"	South Carolina	5 x 6	54,,	—,,	
21	John Mc Daniel	30	Do	28	"	Virginia	5 x 10	54,,	—,,	
22	Francis Mc Daniel	30	Do	26	"	....Do	5 x 10	54,,	—,,	
23	Charnel Durham	1st	July	21	"	....Do	6 x 1	53,,	6,,	8
24	Augustine Hencock	1.	Do	20	"	....Do	5 x 8	53,,	6,,	8
25	Thomas Gather	8.	Do	32	"	Maryland	6 x x	48,,	—,,	
26	Pritchard Stone	8.	Do	44	"	Virginia	6 x 10	48,,	—,,	
27	John Bell	14.	Do	24	"	Ireland	5 x 10	44,,	—,,	
28	Joseph Owens	14.	Do	35	"	Virginia	5 x 10	44,,	—,,	
29	Thomas Winningham	14.	Do	40	"	South Carolina	6 x x	44,,	—,,	
30	William Duggins	15.	Do	19	"	Virginia	5 x 6	43,,	6,,	
								£2524,,	8,,	4

SOUTH CAROLINA PROVINCIAL TROOPS 161

A General Return of Colo. Thomson's Regiment of Rangers. Contd.

No of Privates	Names of Officers, Non-Commission'd Officers and Privates.	Dates of Commissions and Attestations.	Age of Officers, Non-Commissioned Officers & Privates	Country where Born.	Size of Men Feet-Inch.	Pay to this day	
	Captain John Purves...	18th June 1775	29 Years	Scotland	5 x 10	332,,	10,,
	Lieuts { William Martin	21. June "	28 "	Virginia	6 x x	207,,	—
	{ John Carraway Smith	1. Septem: "	24 "	North Carolina	6 x x	45,,	—
	Serjts { George Liddle...	19th August "	21 "	Maryland	5 x 10	25,,	16,, 8
	{ David Burks...	8. July "	30 "	Virginia	5 x 9	60,,	—,,
	Drummer, William Colter.	9. Septem "				9,,	
	Privates—Vizt						
1	William Skinner...	8th July	21 "	North Carolina	5 x 8	48,,	13,, 4
2	Samuel Norwood...	10. Do	22 "	Virginia	5 x 9	46,,	6,, 8
3	James Sexton...	12. Do	21 "	Pennsylvania	5 x 7	45,,	6,, 8
4	Flud Mitchell...	12. Do	18 "	Virginia	5 x 5	45,,	6,, 8
5	William Moseley...	12. Do	22 "	Do	5 x 9	45,,	6,, 8
6	Theophilus Norwood...	19. Do	20 "	Do	5 x 10	40,,	13,, 4
7	John Jackson...	19. Do	18 "	Do	6 x x	40,,	13,, 4
8	Peter Mc Mahen...	19. Do	18 "	Ireland	5 x 6	40,,	13,, 4
9	John Rassel...	19. Do	18 "	Maryland	5 x 9	40,,	13,, 4
10	Thomas Hallum...	19. Do	29 "	Virginia	5 x 9	40,,	13,, 4
11	James Robinson...	20. Do	17 "	Ireland	5 x 2	40,,	—
12	John Warnock...	21. Do	20 "	Do	5 x 7	39,,	6,, 8
13	Michael Warnock...	21. Do	18 "	Pennsylvania	5 x 10	39,,	6,, 8
14	Samuel Nelson...	22. Do	28 "	Scotland	6 x x	38,,	13,, 4
15	Patrick Smellie...	22. Do	19 "	North Carolina	5 x 9	38,,	13,, 4
16	John Pretter...	22. Do	40 "	Ireland	5 x 11	38,,	13,, 4
17	James Mc Elwee...	22. Do			5 x 5	38,,	13,, 4

162 SOUTH CAROLINA PROVINCIAL TROOPS

	Name	Date	Age		Birthplace	Size	£	s	d
18	James Russel	22. Do	19	"	...Do	5 x 7	38,,	13,,	4
19	John Jordan	22. Do	28	"	North Carolina	5 x 7	38,,	13,,	4
20	Arthur Sharborow	19. August	23	"	......Do	5 x 10	20,,	13,,	4
21	Thomas Moore	25. Do	35	"	Virginia	6 x 1	17,,	6,,	8
22	Thomas Jackson	26. Do	21	"	Ireland	5 x 8	16,,	13,,	4
23	Robert Johnston	26. Do	20	"	Pennsylvania	5 x 9	16,,	13,,	4
24	Patrick Morris	30. Do	30	"	Virginia	5 x 11	14,,	13,,	4
25	James Daviun	1. Septem	26	"	Ireland	5 x 8	13,,	6,,	8
26	John Anderson	1. Do	19	"	South Carolina	5 x 4	13,,	6,,	8
27	James Martin	1. Do	17	"	Virginia	5 x 5	13,,	6,,	8
28	Edward McKay	5. Do	21	"	Pennsylvania	5 x 11	10,,	13,,	4
29	William Harbison	6. Do	18	"	Ireland	5 x 7	10,,	—,,	—
30	John Hunter	9. Do	27	"	...Do	5 x 10	8,,		
							£1617,,	13,,	4

SOUTH CAROLINA PROVINCIAL TROOPS 163

A General Return of Colº Thomson's Regiment of Rangers. Contd.

No of Privates	Names of Officers, Non-Commissioned Officers and Privates.	Dates of Commissions and Attestations.	Age of Officers, Non-Commissioned Officers and Privates.	Country where Born	Size of Men Feet-Inch	Pay to this day
	Captain John Lewis Peyer im Hoff	11th August	37 Years	South Carolina	....	143,, 10,, —
	Lieuts { Felix Warley	21. June "	26 "		....	207,, —,, —
	{ David Monaghan	26. Augst "	21 "		5 x 9	58,, 10,, 8
	Serjts { George Standley	27. Do "	38 "		5 x 8	20,, 16,, —
	{ Isaac Jordan	28. Do "	27 "			20,, —,, —
	Privates—Vizt					
1	Josiah Jordan	28. Do "	17 "		5 x 6	16,, —,, 8
2	Jethro Moore	28. Do "	30 "		5 x 8	16,, —,, —
3	Lewis Mc Glaham	28. Do "	19 "		5 x 6	16,, 6,, —
4	William Curtis	26. Do "	28 "		6 x 2	17,, —,, —
5	John Lynch	12. Sept "	26 "		6 x x	6,, —,, —
6	John Uhrhy	9. Do "	19 "		5 x 6	8,, —,, —
7	James Mann	18. Do "	18 "		5 x 3	2,, —,, —
8	James Scott	18. Do "	21 "		5 x10	2,, —,, —
9	David Dillard	1. Do "	19 "	Virginia	5 x 7	2,, 6,, 8
10	Simon Martin	19. Augst "	25 "	England	5 x 7	13,, 13,, 4
11	Thomas Moore	30. Do "	18 "	North Carolina	5 x10	20,, 13,, 4
12	Joseph Leigh	30. Do "	50 "	Virginia	6 x x	14,, 13,, 4
13	William Leigh	30. Do "	35 "	England	5 x11	14,, 13,, 4
14	Thomas Hanshaw	2d Septem	30 "	Pennsylvania	5 x 9	12,, 13,, 4
15	John Price	9. Do "	34 "		5 x 7	8,, —,, —
16	Thomas Hagen	9. Do "	31 "		5 x10	8,, —,, —
17	James Letterling	11. Do "	22 "		5 x 8	6,, 13,, 4
18	Harrod Sutherton	15. Do "	22 "		5 x 8	4,, —,, —
19	John Edwards	12. Do "	26 "		5 x 6	6,, —,, —
20	Philip Murphey	12. Do "	22 "		5 x 6	6,, —,, —
21	James Murphey	9. Do "	21 "		5 x x	8,, —,, —
22	John Gill Jun	8. July	19 "		5 x x	48,, —,, —
23	William Morris					£720,,	10	—

164 SOUTH CAROLINA PROVINCIAL TROOPS

A General Return of Col. Thomson's Regiment of Rangers. Cont'd.

Nº of Privates	Names of Officers, Non-Commissioned Officers and Privates.	Dates of Commissions and Attestations	Age of Officers, Non-Commissioned Officers & Privates	Country where Born	Size of Men (Feet-Inchs.)	Pay to this day
	Captain Charles Heatly	12th Augst 1775	26 Years	South Carolina	6 x x	140,, —,, —
	Lieuts { Richard Brown	20 June "	32 "	Ireland	5 x 4	209,, 10,, —
	{ Francis Taylor	13 Septr "	25 "	Virginia	5 x 8	18,, —,, 4
	Serjts { Edward Leger	15th August "	27 "	South Carolina	5 x 5	29,, 3,, 4
	{ Alexr Mc Kenzie	15 Do "	39 "	Scotland	5 x 7	29,, 3,, 4
	Privates—Vizt.					
1	John Surginor	15 Augst "	19 "	Ireland	5 x 9	23,, 6,, 8
2	John Cyders	15. Do "	23 "	South Carolina	5 x 5	23,, 6,, 8
3	Daniel Wootan	18. Do "	40 "	Virginia	5 x 6	21,, 6,, 8
4	John Rotten	20. Do "	40 "	Do	5 x 6	20,, —,, 8
5	Thomas Burdell sr.	15. Do "	19 "	South Carolina	5 x 10	23,, 6,, 8
6	John Wootan	20. Do "	16 "	Virginia	5 x 7	20,, —,, —
7	William Lucas	20. Do "	24 "	South Carolina	5 x 8	20,, —,, —
8	George Coband	20. Do "	21 "	England	6 x x	20,, —,, —
9	Peter Burns	20. Do "	42 "	Ireland	5 x 8	20,, —,, —
10	William Porter	20. Do "	23 "	Virginia	5 x 9	20,, 6,, 8
11	Isaac Vaughan	22 Do "	23 "	Georgia	5 x 8	19,, 6,, —
12	Joseph Williams	25 Do "	21 "	Virginia	5 x 8	18,, —,, —
13	John Killingsworth	25. Do "	35 "	North Carolina	5 x 10	18,, —,, 8
14	Solomon Floyd	26. Do "	27 "	Virginia	5 x 6	17,, 6,, 8
15	Dennis Mc Carty	26. Do "	22 "	Ireland	5 x 8	17,, 6,, 8
16	Charles Boyle	26. Do "	45 "	North Carolina	5 x 6	17,, 6,, 8
17	William Mc Graw	28. Do "	30 "	Ireland	5 x 8	16,, —,, —
18	William Runnolds	28. Do "	37 "	Virginia	5 x 10	16,, —,, —

SOUTH CAROLINA PROVINCIAL TROOPS

19	Andrew Mc Elvene	29.	Do	"	22	"	Ireland	5 x 7	15,,	6,,	8
20	Richard Pearson	29.	Do	"	27	"	Virginia	5 x 6	15,,	6,,	8
21	Ormand Morgan	31.	Do	"	26	"	...Do	5 x 7	14,,	-,,	
22	Benjamin Wade	31.	Do	"	24	"	...Do	5 x 10	14,,	6,,	8
23	William Thomas	1.	Septr.	"	30	"	...Do	5 x 7	13,,	6,,	8
24	John Mc Lain	1.	Do	"	28	"	Ireland	5 x 7	13,,	6,,	8
25	Robert Crockat	2.	Do	"	23	"	Virginia	5 x 7	12,,	13,,	4
26	James Hawkins	4.	Do	"	18	"	...Do	5 x 5	11,,	6,,	8
27	Joseph Trotter	4.	Do	"	20	"	North Carolina	5 x 10	11,,	6,,	8
28	John Glass	4.	Do	"	22	"	Virginia	5 x 10	11,,	6,,	8
29	Joshua Glass	4.	Do	"	25	"	...Do	5 x 11	11,,	6,,	8
30	John Miller	1.	July	"	38	"	...Do	5 x 6	53,,	6,,	8
									£1026,,	10,,	—

87 "On Sunday July 25.. In Orangeburgh Church.—Thomas, Son of John & Elizabeth Burdell; born March 3d 1756. Suret. Adam Snell, Conrad & Magdalen Yutzy.".—Rev. John Giessendanner's church register of the townships of Amelia and Orangeburgh, 1739-1761, in Salley's *History of Orangeburg County, 1704-1782.*

166 SOUTH CAROLINA PROVINCIAL TROOPS

A General Return of Col? Thomson's Regiment of Rangers. Cont.ᵈ

Colonel Thomson	570,,	—,,	—
Major Mayson	427,,	10,,	—
Captain Wise's Company	2297,,	8,,	4
Captain Caldwell.....Do	2162,,	3,,	4
Captain Kershaw ...Do	2463,,	5,,	—
Captain Goodwyn...Do	2553,,	8,,	4
Captain Richardson Do	2442,,	1,,	8
Captain Woodward..Do	2524 ,	8,,	4
Cantain Purves......Do	1617,,	13,,	4
Captain Peyer im Hoff...Do	720,,	10,,	--
Captain Heatly ....Do	1026,,	10,,	—
	£18804,,	18,,	4
Adjutant, Easom		,,	,,
Serjt Major, Smith		,,	,,
Doctr Rogers from 1st July to the 20th September Inst: 82 Days @ 45/ ℔ day.................£ 184.10.—	£		
Pay master, John Chesnut ⎫ Commission dated 18th ⎬ 285.—.— June to 20th Septr 95 ⎪ days a 60/ ℔ day— ⎭			
Allowed for Cloathing 297 men a £15 ℔ man......... 4455.—.—	4924,,	10,,	—
		,,	,,

The above General Return is an exact Copy taken from the respective Returns delivered in to me—[88]

Amelia 29tʰ September 1775.

Wᵐ Thomson.

Endorsed: Coll? Thomson's Return of the Regiment of Rangers—
see endorsement on
Mr Kershaw's ge-
-neral Account—
Returned in behalf of
Mr Chesnut Pay Master
13tʰ October 1775—

---

[88] It will be observed that very few of the men of this regiment were born in South Carolina. This is owing to the fact that the regiment was raised in the up-country of South Carolina which had not been settled twenty years before. It will also be observed that more of them were born in Virginia than elsewhere, which goes to show that Virginia furnished the greatest number of the up-country's settlers, and this is one reason why the people of the up-country are such good people.

SOUTH CAROLINA PROVINCIAL TROOPS

[95.]

[FIRST GENERAL PAY-BILL OF THOMSON'S REGIMENT.]

A General Return of the pay due to the Regiment of Rangers, Commanded by Colonel William Thompson Esq͟r

		£ s. d.	£ s. d.
Colonel Thompson from 18 June to 20th Oct͟r is 125 days £6			750 — —
Major James Mayson.... ditto........................is 125 days 90†			562. 10. —
Alexander Rogers Surgeon—ditto.................is 125 days 45†			281. 5. —
John Chesnut. paymaster,. ditto...... ......is 125 days 60†			375,, — —
Captain Wise pay Bill to 1 Septem͟r	1766. 16. 8		
ditto.. to 1 October	867..........		2633,, 16. 8
Captain Caldwell's ditto to 26 July...............	705. 11. 3		
ditto to 26 August	794. 6. 4		
ditto to 26 Septem͟r	828. 5 —		2328,, 2. 7
Captain Kershaw's ditto to 1 August.............	969. 11. 8		
ditto to 1 Septem͟r	938,, ...		
ditto to 20 October	1516. 13. 4		3424. 5,, —
Captain Goodwyn's ditto to 1 August.............	1112,, ...		
ditto to 20 Sept͟r	1523. 3. 4		
ditto to 20 October	910........		3545. 3,, 4
Captain Richardson's dͦ to 1 August..................	971,, —		
ditto to 1 Sept͟r	918. —		
ditto to 20 October...............	1516. 13. 4		3405. 13,, 4
Capt. Woodward's ditto to 1 August..............	997. 14. 8		
ditto to 20 Sept͟r	1523. 3. 4		
ditto to 20 October	910		3430. 18.. —
Captain Purves.. ditto to 22 August.................	1002. 11. 8		
ditto to 22d Sept͟r	948. 8. 4		1951. — —
Capt͟n Peyre Im Hoff ditto to 1 October	797. 12. 4		908. 1. 3
Captain Heatly.. ditto to 20 Septem͟r	910.........		1707. 12. 4
ditto to 20 October..............			
Advanced for 297 Suits Cloaths £15 ⅌ Suit			4455 — —
			£29758. 7. 6

Cr
By Cash sent ⅌ Colonel Thompson[89] 1000
By ditto sent ⅌ Captain Woodward............ 5000
By ditto reced by Mr Loocock............ 4000
By ditto reced by ditto 5514. 14. 8
                                    15514. 14. 8
                                    £14243,, 12. 10

Errors Excepted

for John Chesnut Paymaster

Joseph Kershaw

[89] See *Collections* of the South Carolina Historical Society, vol. 2, p. 40.

Endorsed: Mr Kershaw's
General Return
of the Regiment of
Rangers—afterwards
extended to the 20 Octob^r
1775—the whole Amount
for Officers & Men
to that day—————
£16884 13. 8
Ordered in Council of
Safety to be paid &
Paid accordingly——

PAPERS OF THE FIRST COUNCIL OF SAFETY OF THE REVOLUTIONARY PARTY IN SOUTH CAROLINA, JUNE–NOVEMBER, 1775.

[96.]

[CAPT. WILLIAM FULLWOOD'S COMPANY OF VOLUNTEER MILITIA.]

We whose names are hereunto subscribed do certifie that we have chosen the Undermentioned Gentlemen for officers of a Company of Volunteers, to be immediately under the Command and Direction of the Committee of safety in the Province of South Carolina. we hope our choice may be approved of.

    Capt William Fullwood—Captain
    Lieu^t John Gambell 1st Lieu^t
    Lieu^t James Davis 2^d Lieu^t

Given under our hands the 30th September 1775.——

SOUTH CAROLINA PROVINCIAL TROOPS 171

1 William Martin	19 John Laferty	38 John Frierson Jr
2 James Conyers Jr	20 John Pursor	39 James Mc Calla
3 Saml Davison	21 Patk Fagan	40 William Gamble
4 Edwd Dickey	22 Evan Benbow	41 Robt Reily
5 James Dickey	23 William Carson	42 John Rafield
6 Edwd Drake	24 Corns Dysert	43 Robt Thomson
7 John Woods	25 Hugh Davis	44 Arthr White
8 John Wimpee	26 Ebenr Bagnal	45 John Bagnal
9 William Mc Coy	27 John Vertu	46 William Milwee
10 William Floyd	28 Benja Davis	47 John Milwee
11 David Anderson	29 John Liveston	48 Robt Gamble
12 James Thomson	30 James Woods	49 Randal Platt
13 William Brunson Sr	31 John Platt	50 Corns Donavan.
14 Danl Conyers	32 John Nelson	
15 William Mc Elveen	33 Thos Levans	A True Coppy.
16 John Webb	34 Ethelridge Pitman	
17 Isaac Roland	35 Henry Montgomery	
18 William Taylor	36 William Montgomery	
	37 Malcum Kerr	

Endorsed: Capt Wm Fullwoods
Volunteer Company
Commissions granted
October 1775.[90]

[97.]

[COMMISSIONERS FOR FORT LYTTLETON TO THE COUNCIL OF SAFETY.]

Addressed: To
Council of safety
Charles Town

Beaufort 3d October 1775.

Gentlemen
We have Received a Resolve of the Council of Safety, Impowering us to put Fort Lyttleton into proper Repair[91] and for which purpose you have granted Three Thousand two Hundred Pounds.—we have this day drawn on you in fav. of Thos Heyward Junr Esqr for a Thousand

---

[90] From the private collection of A. S. Salley, Jr. See *The Sunday News*, Charleston, S. C., March 19, 1899.

[91] See issues of this magazine for October, 1900, p. 303, and January, 1901, p. 15 et seq.

pounds of said sum, as we shall have Occasion for so much soon to pay workmen which are to be Employ'd, in mean time you may be assured we shall use our best endeavours to Expedite the work.

                We are Gentlemen
                      Your Hble servants
                      John Joyner
                      Tunes Tebout.
                      Andrew Aggnew
                      Jas Cuthbert
                      D∴ DeSaussure

Endorsed: Commissioners for Fort Lyttleton 3ᵈ Octob 1775 Reported in Council the 8ᵗʰ

[98.]

[CAPT. EZEKIEL POLK TO HENRY LAURENS.]

Addressed: To
        Colⁱ Henry Laurens Esqʳ
            President of the Council
                of Safety
℘ʳ Mʳ Burns   Charles Town——

                        2ᵈ October 1775
Sir.

    I Flattered myself that I would Recive an answer to my Letter of the 12ᵗʰ Sepʳ last by Mʳ Henry; I am partly in a State of inactivity, I Took my Company & five Companies of the Militia & Volunteers, in Order to Join Colⁱ Thompson, but had not Marched far till we Received Certain Intelligence that Colⁱ Fletchall had Decamped; I have made a Tour among the Tories on Kings Creek, some of whom seem Determined not to subscribe the association; I have Thought that forcing them to subscribe would not sufficiently secure them, therefore have taken a middle course with them, as you will find by the Inclosed Deposition; I thought it prudent at this Dangerous Crisis to proceed in this manner as some have already Declared, that although the Want of Necesaries has Obliged them to Subscribe yet they would Join the other party if they must fight; I have sworn several of them in this manner;[92] and Expect a number at my house to morrow for that purpose; this is their Voluntary act, and perhaps time may make them active on our side.

I Receved the Order of the Council of Safety of 20th Sepr which I will lay before the Committee To morrow for their Consideration ;——

     Sir I am with Zeal & Esteem
      your most Obedt
Excuse Incorrectness Humble
I write in haste   Servant
      Ezek! Polk

o Col! Henry Laurens Esqr—

Endorsed: Capt Ezek. Polk
   2d October 1775 Recd
   & Read in Council the
   12th Answd 13

[99.]

[COL. RICHARD RICHARDSON TO THE COUNCIL OF SAFETY.]

Addressed: To
   The Honable Council of Safety
      Chas Town—
℔r favr Mr. Moore

Gentlemen

 Mr Isham Moore first Lieutt of Capt Mattw Singletons Company, or Troop, of Light horse; wait on You, by whom I transmit the Return made to Me by Capt Singleton. They

---

[92] See the April issue of this magazine, p. 103 et seq.

were Embodied sometime before I was call'd out by the Hon^eble Mr Drayton; and was on Service at their Own Expence the time Specified in the Inclos'd Return : You will no Doubt make such provission for the Return as are agreeable to the Resolutions &^c and if the Officers and Company meet with Your Approbation will Comission them Accordingly—I shall take the Liberty of Transmitting Such Other Returns of Some other Troop of Light horse and militia as Make Returns to me; the Expence Upon the Whole will be Very Triffleing—I have the Honour

to be. Gentlemen Your Most
Obedient Hble Servt
Richd Richardson

Council of Safety } St Marks 7th Octr 1775—

Endorsed: Coll^o Richardson
7th October 1775
Recd 12th & offered
Read the 13th & Answ^d [93]

[The accompanying return.]

A true Roll of the Company or Troop of Light-Horse Embodied under the Command of Captain Matthew Singleton, of Saint Mark's Parish, on the High Hills of Santee, which was Out on the Provincial Service of South Carolina : under the Command of Colonel Richard Richardson : Commencing the 13th day of September 1775; and Discharged the 22^d Day of the said Instant.[94]

---

[93] From the private collection of A. S. Salley, Jr. See *The Sunday News*, Charleston, S. C., March 12, 1899.

[94] From the private collection of A. S. Salley, Jr. See *The Sunday News*, Charleston, S. C., March 12, 1899. The original roll of this company, handed in at its organization Aug. 26, 1775, was published in this magazine for July, 1900, pp. 184-186.

Isham Moore } Lieuts.	Wm Brunson	James Mc Cormack
John Singleton }	Peter Matthews	Zach Harrel
Joseph Hill } Serjts.	Jesse Temples	Josiah Wheet
Caleb Gayle }	Alex^r Holliday	Isaac Jackson
Richd Wells..Drum^r	Ephraim Pcole	Thos Jackson
Thos Morfet	Jacob Brigman	Drewry Fletcher
Josiah Gayle	Charles Goodwin	Ed^d Hill
Willis Ramsey	Henry Wheeler	Samuel Devise
Richd Harvin	Hope Ridgway	Sabe Stone
Saml Tines	James Allen	Thomas Neil
Robt Tines	Joseph Rogers	David Neil

The above return of Two Lieutenants Two Sergeants one Drum and Twenty Eight Privates— Capt Mat Singleton made Oath to be just & True 27th Sept 1775 before Wm Richardson J P

Endorsed: Capt M. Singleton's
Company of Horse

[100.]

[CAPT. ROBERT LIDE'S COMPANY OF VOLUNTEER MILITIA.]

To the Honourable the Council of Safety of South Carolina

The humble Petition of Sixty of the Inhabitants on the North East Side of Pee Dee River, from Browns Creek to the Three Creeks, in St Davids Parish

Sheweth

That your Petitioners, concious of the Injustice of Several Acts of the British Parliament, past in the Reign of his present Majesty, and being desirous to serve their Country by aiding and assisting their Brethren, the good people of this Colony, in their opposition of every foe, as becomes every good Citizen to do, have formed a Company of Volunteers and have chosen Robert Lide Esqr to be their

176 SOUTH CAROLINA PROVINCIAL TROOPS

Captain, Mr Thomas Powe to be their first Lieutenant, and Mr William Watkins to be their second Lieutenant

Your Petitioners therefore pray that your Honours will be pleased to Issue the requisite Commissions for the above Named Gentlemen as soon as may be, and your Petitioners as in duty bound shall ever pray

Philip Perry	Richard Whittington	Theodorick Webb
Willis Studdivent	Ephraim Whittington	Samuell Moore
Owent Whittington	Jessee Brown	Jessee Mixon
Jerrimiah Rowell	William Warrington	Thos Davis
Joseph Allison	Thomas Sweat	John Cone
James Coleman	Solomon Studdivent	Jordon Purkins
Josiah Cox	John Kenneday	Joseph Harper
Manuell Cox	James Findlay	Isaac Purkins
John Cox	Matthew Murphey	Cornelius Mixon
Francis Whittington Junr	Thos Baker	John Rabon
Joshua Stroud	Francis Kenneday	Dale Baker
Michael Mixon	Alexander Craig	Charles Rabon
Griffen Nunnery	William Sweat	Nathan Sweat
Jacob Blackwell	William Cherry	Joseph Owens
Samuel Brown	Joseph Dobbs	William Bodirford
Abel Lewis	Isaac Turbeveal	John Townsen
Maurice Murphey Junr	Richd Kerby	Light Townsen
James Harris	Reuben Jenkins	Benja Baker
		George Cherry
		Isaac Wolf
		David Lee
		Jno Heath
		Jno Mixon
		Drury Lee

Endorsed: Volunteer Company
Robt Lide Captain
9th October 1775—[95]

---

[95] From the private collection of A. S. Salley, Jr. See *The Sunday News*, Charleston, S. C., March 19, 1899.

SOUTH CAROLINA PROVINCIAL TROOPS 177

[101.]

[HENRY LAURENS TO BENJAMIN JENKINS.]

Sir—

I am ordered by the Council of Safety to acknowledge the Rec.t of your Letter of the 10th Ins.t & to acquaint you that they have Issued the proper quantity of Gun Powder for the Colleton County Regiment & put it under the direction of Coll.o Glover to whom the Captains of the Militia & Volunteer Companies on Edisto Island must apply for their proportion. Whenever you send a Boat, provided it shall be before the meeting of the Congress, the Council of Safety will order four four-pound Cannon together with a proper quantity of Corn Powder to be delivered for the service you point out, but they are informed that there are not any 4.t Shot in Charles Town—perhaps you may think it best to postpone this business to the meeting of Congress when other pieces of Cannon for which suitable shot may be found, may then be ordered.—

I am Sir

Charles Town 13 Octobr 1775.   Your most obedient servant

Benjamin Jenkins Esquire.—

Endorsed: Copy 13th Octobr 1775
    To Capt Polk[96]
    & B. Jenkins

[102.]

[OATH OF NEUTRALITY TRANSMITTED BY CAPT. POLK.[97]]

South Carolina }
New acquisition }   Robert Black, Joseph Black, William Wilson, Daniel Ponder, Nathaniel Harison John Black, Jacob Garner, James Black

---

[96] The name of Capt Polk is scratched out by lead pencil, and beneath Henry Laurens's endorsement is written, by lead pencil, the word "Gunpowder" in the handwriting of Prof. William J. Rivers.

[97] See No. 98, p. 261.

Came before me and Voluntarily made Oath that they will not, (unless Compelled in Self Defence) lift arms against the americans in their present Contest with Great britain nor Do any thing by word or action which they shall know to be against the american Cause,

Sworn before me this
3ᵈ of October 1775—
Ezek! Polk ss

Robert Black
Jacob Gerdner
Joseph Black
John Black
Daniel Ponder
James Black
Nathaniel Harris[n]
William Wilson

Endorsed: 5 Neutral affida-
-vits from Coll?
Polk. Recᵈ 14 Octob 1775

PAPERS OF THE FIRST COUNCIL OF SAFETY OF THE REVOLUTIONARY PARTY IN SOUTH CAROLINA, JUNE-NOVEMBER, 1775.

[103.]

[RETURN OF CAPT. EZEKIEL POLK'S CO. OF RANGERS.]

A return of the Officers noncommissioned officers and Privates of the   Company of Rangers Commanded by Col? William Thompson Esq! from 18th day of June to the 7th day of October 1775 [98]

---

[98] It will be remembered that when the Provincial Congress of South Carolina elected officers for the regiment of Rangers in June 1775 Ezekiel Polk was elected one of the captains and Samuel Watson one of the lieutenants. They were both commissioned by the Council of Safety on June 18th. Captain Polk recruited a company and joined Major Mayson's camp at Ninety Six on Sunday, July 23, 1775 (Vol. I. of this mag., p. 68). He remained in camp just a week, and on Saturday, July 29th, marched out of it, sent his men to their homes and wrote Major Mayson a letter announcing that he had quit the sirvice (Vol. I., p. 70). For this he was dismissed from the service, but he explained his conduct satisfactorily to Wm. Henry Drayton, special representative of the Council of Safety, and was reinstated by the Council to the command of his company independently of the 3d Regiment (Rangers), but under the command of Col. Thomson (Vol I., p. 192). This is the first return of the company.

180 SOUTH CAROLINA PROVINCIAL TROOPS

				£	s	d
7th July 1775		Ezekiel Polk. Capt — 111 Days @ 70/		3.88		
11 July.	,,75.	Samuel Watson Ft. Lieutt 111 Days @ 45/		244		
7th July	,,75.	William Polk Sd Do 92 Days @ 45/		207		
		Thomas Alexander Serjt 92 Day -- @ £25 ⅌ mn		75		4
		Jonathan Fitchet Do 88 Days -- @ £25 ⅌ M		71		
		Alexr Stuart Drummer 92 Days @ £20 ⅌ N		60		

Privates

				£	s	d
7th July	,,75	Jonathan Potts 92 Days @ £20 ⅌ M		60		
7th July	,,75	Samuel Wilson 92 Days @ £20 ⅌ M		60		
Do		Robert Adams 92 Days @ £20 ⅌ M		60		
Do		William Alexr 92 Days @ £20 ⅌ M		60		
8th July	,,75	James Brown 91 Days @ £20 ⅌ Mh		59		8
10 July	,,75	James Hawthorn 90 Days @ £20 ⅌ Mh		58		4
10 July	,,75	John Cancillor 90 Days @ £20 ⅌ M		58		4
10th July	,,75	Benjamin Rowan 90 Days @ £20 ⅌ M		58		4
11th July	,,75	John Janes 89 Days @ £20 ⅌ M		58		
Do		James Nickels 89 Days @ £20 ⅌ Mt		58		
Do		Josiah Porter 89 Days @ £20 ⅌ Mt		58		
Do		John Caruth 89 Days @ £20 ⅌ Mt		58		
Do		James Barron 89 Days @ £20 ⅌ Mt		58		
Do		Daniel Shaw 89 Days @ £20 ⅌ M		58		
Do		John Knox 89 Days @ £20 ⅌ M		58		
Do		John Miller 89 Days @ £20 ⅌ M		58		
Do		Thomas Clemens 89 Days @ £20 ⅌ M		58		
12th July	,,75	Samuel Callwell 88 Days @ £20		57	6	8
Do		Alexr Adams 88 Days @ £20 ⅌ M		57	6	8
Do		David Calhoon 88 Days @ £20 ⅌ M		57	6	8
Do		Benja Brown 88 Days @ £20 ⅌ M		57	6	8
Do		William Ridley 88 Days @ £20 ⅌ M		.57	6	8

Date		Name		Rate			
12th July	,75	George Adams	88 Days	@ £20 ⅌r M.	57	6	8
15th July	,75	John Gordan	85 Day	@ £20 ⅌r M.	55	6	8
17 July	,75	Charles Patrick	83 Days.	@ £20 ⅌r M.	54		
18 July	,75	James Crawford	82 Days	@ £20 ⅌r M.	53	6	8
Do	—	Alexr Campbell	82 Days	@ £20 ⅌r M.	53	6	8
		those men have Received £50 Each, & if the officer, with whom they were Chooses to keep them, upon letting me know, I can list 2 in their Room—99					
Do		Robert McCleary	82 Days	@ £20 ⅌r M.	53	6	8
21st Augt	75	Isaac Horner	47 Days	@ £20 ⅌r M.	31	6	8
21st Augt	75	Alexr Nickels	47 Days	@ £20 ⅌r M.	31	6	8

South Carolina

Capt. Ezekiel Polk came before me & declard upon oath that the above return of the officers & privates is Just & true ——

Sworn before me this
9th of October 1775.

    Tho : Charlton

                Ezekiel Polk

Endorsed: Return of Captⁿ Polk's Company brought in to Council of Safety by Mr Kershaw 14 Octob 1775.

---

99 James Crawford had been reënlisted or transferred to Capt. Charles Heatly's Company. 3d. Regt., or Rangers. (See Vol. I, p. 295.)

[104.]

[HENRY LAURENS TO CAPT. ARNOLDUS VANDER HORST.]

Sir.

I am ordered to inclose & return you the Account which was laid before the Council of Safety this Morning upon which is a Bill, on the Colony Treasurers payable to your order for £86.3.9 for provisions &c made use of by your Company in the late service at Haddrel's point—the Council observe that your Company have relinquished a further claim which they had upon the public for £203.0.3—& have ordered me to return you thanks & to request you to return their thanks to your Officers & Men.   I am &c

16 Octob 1775
Capt Arnolds Vanderhorst
   Christ Church

Endorsed: Copy 16th Octobr 1775
   Capt Vanderhorst

[105.]

[HENRY LAURENS TO COL. WM. MOULTRIE.]

Sir—

I am ordered by the Council of Safety to desire you will immediately order an equiry to be made howmany Seamen are inlisted in the Regiments of Foot, & to make a return of the names & numbers of the whole to Morrow. & to enquire of such Seamen if they are willing to change the service by acting on board the Colony Schooners where their pay will be considerably advanced—   I am
      Sir
Charles Town   Your most obedient
19th October 1775. & most hum Servt

Colonel Moultrie.

Endorsed: Copy 19th Octobr 1775
   To Collo Moultrie

[106.]

[GEORGE GALPHIN TO THE COUNCIL OF SAFETY.]

Addressed: To
              The Honabl Concil of Safty
                   Ch : Town

Gentm

I belive I mentind by the Express the other Day that mr Rae my nevey & son was gon up to the Creeks with the amnison & a talk from the gentm of the Committe in Savannah & a talke from my self the ancer to them is In Closed mr tatte give out a talke from Sir James Wright & Capt Stuart the same Day thire ancer is Likeway In Closed about half the uper Towns is in the Interest of west floarada & has youse all thire Interest to bringe the rest of the nattion to thire way of thinking but they Could not preswade them to it nor it will not be in there power to Do it in Case they are sepleyd from hear as usall they are all at home & very unEasey for want of amnison to go out a hunting as this is the month they go out for there winter's hunt they Disiere that this talk may be sent to the beloved men of Ch : Town & Georgia & for me to send up there ancer Emedeatly Let it be good or bad if the gentm of the Committe in Savvanna wood but Let part of the goods & amnison know on Savvanna beloning to the merchts hear Come up that Everey trader might have 2 horse Load of amnison to Carey up know it wood satisfy them tho it is not more than half what they uselly Carey wee have Lost half the uper Towns allredy & if they had been suppleyd as usall wee should not Lost one Town of them but they have sent there trade to pensacollo & they have brought up plenty of amnison for them holms [100] had anuff a Do to stope severele of the trader that Deale Down hear from going to pencacollo for goods and amnison

---

[100] David Holmes. (See Vol. I., p. 124.)

& in Case there is no amnison goe to them till the Commissinor.^s meet.^s at Salsberry[101] & has finssh.^t there bissness there the seson for hunting will be over & there will be no passeyfying them & they will say all the talk we have sent them is nothing but Ly.^s for they ware tol^d there wood be nothing but Lying talk^s sent them from these two provences one of the heed men tol^d holms that m.^r tatte[102] give out a talke some time ago to the Indian.^s & tol^d them they ware not to belive any talke but what Came from Capt Stuart or the governo.^r if any man brought any other talk^s there he wood sen^d them in Irions near the great watter holms Chaleng^d tatte with it in the square before all the Indian^s he Deny.^d it, the fellow got up that tol^d holms & he tol^d tatte he was a Lyer he Did say say so & florish.^t his hatchet a bout that holms had a nuff a Do to passefy him as Long as m.^r Rae & holms was in the nattion m.^r tatte gave out no ba^d talk^s I no if the gent.^m of the Committee ha^d a fue Line^s from you they wood sen^d the amnison up Emedeatly I have wrote them as pressing as I Can but for fear they shoul^d not sen^d it if you wood be kinde a nuff to InClose me a Letter for them I wood sen^d it from hear to them I will forfet my Livef to Keep the Lower Creek.^s peasable if they are Suply.^d & the will keep the uper Creek^s peasable there is some of the heed men of the Lower Town.^s to be at my hous by the Last of the month it will be verey unLuckey if I shoul^d be gon before they Come Down they sent me word by holms that I migh^t Depen^d upon there being Down it wase tol^d in the Creek.^s that the govern.^r of penesacollo & Capt Stuart was going to sen^d amnison throw the Creek.^s to the Cherek.^s I have wrote the Creek.^s & tol^d some of the hee^d men that was hear, as sone as the good^s & ammison Came in it wood be sent to them they have been tol^d the good^s is Come in there will be no puting them of any Longer if they finde we tell them Ly.^s they will not belive a talke that is sent them what

---

[101] See letter of Henry Laurens, dated Sept. 29, 1775, to the Georgia Council of Safety, Vol. II., p. 24.

[102] Tate.

is the youse of Commissinor^s if it is not in there power to have the Indian^s Seply^d all the talk^s they Can give them will be of no youse D holms write^s you by this Expres^s plase pay the Express 20£ Carriing

      I am Gent^m your most Obe^d
       humbele Servent George Galphin
          O^{br} 15 1775

P: S it was say^d in the Creek^s that m^r Ch: Stuart with 50 men was sone to be there the Reson the Indian^s menttion^t the Diferent Contery people in there talk^s they ware tol^d the Irish & the amercan^s had Joine^d againest the Englus^s & Scoth

Endorsed: Geo Galphin, 15 Octo.
    1775—Received & Read
    in Council the 21.st
    Answered as within
    the 22^d ——

[107.]

[HENRY LAURENS TO GEORGE GALPHIN [103].]

       Charles Town 22^d Octobr. 1775—
Sir—

We thank you for your favour of the 15th Ins^t which together with the Sundry Talks & Letters said to have accompanied it, came safe to hand yesterday & we immediately took the subject matter under our consideration.—

It appears from your opinion, from Mr Holmes's intelligence & from the politick Indian Talks, that we have no other means for keeping our Indian Allies in peace & friendship with us but that of supplying them with Ammunition Clothing &cc as usual, we therefore cannot withhold our assent that such Goods should be sent among them, & we shall

---

[103] This copy of Henry Laurens's answer to Galphin was written on the inside of the wrapping sheet of Galphin's letter to the Council of Safety. (See the endorsement to that letter.)

impart our sentiments on this head by Tuesday's Post to the Council of Safety at Savanna, we apprehend, our Letter by Post will sooner reach their hands than if it went through yours—you will nevertheless write to them if you see it necessary.—

We think it of great moment that you should have a personal interview with those Indians expected the latter end of this month at your House & therefore recommend, to delay your intended journey to Salisbury even to the 5th or 6th November if they do not arrive sooner; it will be very proper that those Indians should be well informed of the appointment of Commissioners for the sole purpose of conducting the Trade with them, & of the several departments of Commissioners, as well as by what authority appointed—the novelty & dignity of this grand plan will excite their curiosity, strike them with awe & tend to confirm their resolutions to remain neuter at least till they shall learn & see the effects of the new arrangement; if you find it necessary to remain at home so long as the 5th or 6th November you may apprize Mr Wilkinson of the case he may go on before you & if we compute the distance truly you will have time enough to join your Colleagues on the 12th or a day sooner, & perhaps be as early for business as any of them—the first day is, generally in all new Assemblies, spent in establishing preliminary rules & modes for proceeding—but we wish that at least one of the Commissioners nominated for his Colony should be at Salisbury on the very day appointed for meeting.

We have paid the Messenger who brought your Letter Twenty Pounds.

By order of the Council of Safety

George Galphin Esquire—

[108.]

[CAPT. ROBERT GOODWYN'S PAY BILLS.]

A Return to the paymaster of the Officers Non Commissioned officers & privates of the Second Company of Rangers Com-

SOUTH CAROLINA PROVINCIAL TROOPS 187

manded by Col.º William Thomson from 1 day of August to the 20th of Sep.r 1775——

Cap.tn—Robert Goodwyn	—	51 days at 70.s /		£178-10-0
1 Leu.t —David Hopkins	51	. D.to	... 45 /	.. 114- 0--
2 Leu.t —William Mitchell		D.to	....45 /	.. 114——--
Scarj.ts Merry M.c Gwyer		......D.to	....	41-13-4
John Johnes		.... D.to	....	41-13-4
Drumer. Henry frits		..........D.to@20/p.r Month		33- 6 8
1 Will.m fust[104]		..........D.to	....	33- 6.8
2 Thomas Millar		........D.to	....	33- 6-8
3 James Randolph		.......D.to	....	33- 6-8
4 John Gibson..		......D.to	....	33. 6-8
5 James Anderson		.......D.to	....	33- 6-8
6 Benjamin Hodge		......D.to	....	33- 6-8
7 William partridge		.....D.to	....	33- 6-8
8 Henry Wyley		........D.to	....	33- 6-8
9 William Lassater		......D.to	....	33- 6-8
10 Briant Addams		........D.to	....	33- 6-8
11 John Sneling		.. D.to	....	33- 6-8
12 Elijah peters		..........D.to	....	33- 6-8
13 Lewis Broadway		.......D.to	....	33- 6 8
14 Lewis Coon..		......D.to	....	33- 6-8
15 Jesse killingsworth		.....D.to	....	33- 6-8
16 Hix Chappell.		.......D.to	....	33- 6-8
17 Gilberd Gibson		........D.to	....	33- 6-8
18 John Tapley		.........D.to	....	33- 6-8
19 Charles Dever		.... D.to	....	33- 6-8
20 Gilberd Gibson Con.s [105]		. D.t	....	33- 6-8
21 Joseph Wells		.........D.to	....	33- 6-8
22 Gunrod[106] Coon ...		...D.to	....	33- 6-8
23 Gardner Williams		......D.to	....	33- 6-8
24 William Lee		..........D.to	....	33- 6-8
25 Burwell Fust[104] ...		...D.to	.. ..	33- 6-8

[104] Foust. (See Vol. II., p. 180.)
[105] Gilbert Gibson, of the Congarees. The other Gilbert Gibson was probably from Orangeburgh.
[106] Conrad Kuhn.

188 SOUTH CAROLINA PROVINCIAL TROOPS

26 Benjamin Gibson	D^{to}	33-	6-8
27 John Jackson	D^{to}	33-	6-8
28 William Winingham	D^{to}	33-	6-8
29 Solomon peters	D^{to}	33-	6-8
30 William Hubbar[107]	D^{to}	33-	6-8

£1523.3.4

Capt Robert Goodwinn Maketh Oath that this is a just & True Return to the pay Master of the Officers Noncommission Officers & privates in his Company

Robert Goodwyn

Certif^d & sworn to Before me the 20th Oc^t 1775

R Winn J. P.

A Return to the paymaster, of the Officers Non-commissioned officers And privates of the Second Company of Rangers Commanded by Col^o William Thomson from the twentieth of September to the Twentieth of October 1775

Cap^{tn}... Robert Goodwyn 30 days. @70^s / p^r day		£105-	0-0
1 Leut.. David Hopkins 30 days @. 45/ p^r day		067-10-0	
2 Leut.. William Mitchell	D^{to}	067-10-0	
Searj^{ts} .. Merry Mc Gwyer	D^{to}	025-	0-0
John Johnes	D^{to}	25-	0-0
Drumer. Henry Frits	D^{to}	20-	0-0
1 William Fust	D^{to}	20-	0-0
2 Thomas Millar	D^{to}	20-	0-0
3 James Randolph	D^{to}	20-	0-0
4 John Gibson	D^{to}	20-	0-0
5 James Anderson	D^{to}	20-	0 0
6 Benjamin Hodge	D^{to}	20-	0-0
7 William partridge	D^{to}	20-	0-0
8 Henry Wyley	D^{to}	20-	0-0
9 William Lassater	D^{to}	20-	0-0
10 Briant Addams	D^{to}	20-	0-0
11 John Sneling	D^{to}	20-	0-0
12 Elijah peters	D^{to}	20-	0-0

[107] Hubbard. (See Vol. II., p. 180.)

SOUTH CAROLINA PROVINCIAL TROOPS

13	Lewis Broadway.....D.to...........	20-	0-0
14	Lewis Coon.........D.to...........	20-	0-0
15	Jesse killingsworth...D.to...........	20-	0-0
16	Hix Chappell.......D.to...........	20-	0-0
17	Gilberd Gibson.....D.to...........	20-	0-0
18	John Tapley.......D.to...........	20-	0-0
19	Charles Dever.....D.to...........	20-	0-0
20	Gilberd Gibson Con.s..D.to...........	20-	0-0
21	Joseph wells.......D.to...........	20-	0-0
22	Gunrod Coon......D.to...........	20-	0-0
23	Gardner williams.....D.to...........	20-	0-0
24	William Lee.......D.to...........	20-	0-0
25	Burwell Fust.......D.to...........	20-	0-0
26	Benjamin Gibson....D.to...........	20-	0-0
27	John Jackson..... D.to...........	20-	0-0
28	William Winingham..D.to...........	20-	0-0
29	Solomon peters......D.to...........	20-	0-0
30	William Hubbard....D.to...........	20-	0-0

£910 ,, ,,

Cap.t Robert Goodwin Maketh Oath that the above is a just & True Return of the Officers non Commission Officers & privates

Sworn to Before me the 20.th October 1775   Robert Goodwyn
                     Rich.d Winn J P

Endorsed: Cap.t Goodwyns
          Paybill—
Endorsed also: Pay Bill
          For the
          20.th day of Oc.tr

[109.]

[CAPT. ELY KERSHAW'S PAY BILL.]

A Return of the Officers Non Commissioned Officers & Privates of the third Company of Rangers Commanded by Col.o William Thomson from the first day of September to the Twentieth day of October 1775—

190 SOUTH CAROLINA PROVINCIAL TROOPS

Ely Kershaw Cap.t —	50 days..a 70/..	£175.	,,.	,,
Francis Boykin 1st Lieut	50 days..a 45/..	112,,	10.	,,
Thomas Charlton 2d Lieut	50 days..a 45/	112,.	10.	,,
Thomas Pemble Serg.t ..				
1 Month & Twenty days.a £25.℔ Month		41,,	13,,	4
Augustine Prestwood Serg.t d.o ..a d.o		41,,	13,,	4

Privates

1	Thomas Courson..			
	1 Month & 20 days.a £20 ℔ Month	33,,	6,,	8
2	Henry Harmon...ditto..a d.o	33,.	6,,	8
3.	Robert Martin....ditto..a d.o	33,,	6,,	8
4.	Alexander Gaston.ditto..a d.o	33,.	6,,	8
5.	Joseph Furguson..ditto..a d.o	33,.	6,,	8
6.	BenjaminFurgusonditto..a d.o	33,.	6,,	8
7	Richard Nickells..ditto..a d.o	33,,	6,,	8
8.	George Gray.....ditto..a d.o	33,.	6,,	8
9	John Gray.......ditto..a d.o	33,,	6,,	8
10.	Jacob Cherry ....ditto..a d.o	33,,	6,,	8
11	Mordicai M.cKinnieditto..a d.o	33,,	6,,	8
12	Thomas Howell...ditto..a d.o	33,,	6,,	8
13	Peregrine Magness ditto..a d.o	33,,	6,,	8
14.	John Payne......ditto..a d.o	33,,	6,,	8
15	James Saxon.....ditto..a d.o	33,,	6,,	8
16.	John Steel...... ditto..a d.o	33,,	6,,	8
17.	Jeremiah Simmonsditto..a d.o	33.,	6,,	8
18.	William French...ditto..a d.o	33,,	6,,	8
19.	John Swilla......ditto..a d.o	33,,	6,,	8
20	James Cook......ditto..a d.o	33,.	6,,	8
21.	Newill Barefoot ..ditto..a d.o	33,,	6,.	8
22.	John Montgomery.ditto..a d.o	33,,	6,,	8
23	Samuel Sessions...ditto..a d.o	33,,	6,,	8
24.	Aaron Alexander .ditto..a d.o	33,,	6,,	8
25	Robert Gaston....ditto..a d.o	33,,	6,,	8
26.	Uriah Goodwyn ..ditto..a d.o	33,.	6,,	8
27.	Robert White ... ditto..a d.o	33,,	6,,	8
28.	Hugh Gaston.....ditto..a d.o	33.,	6,,	8
	Carried Over.....	£1416,,	13,,	4,,

SOUTH CAROLINA PROVINCIAL TROOPS

   Bro! Over....................£1416,, 13,, 4,.
29. William Weatherford..
   1 Month & 20 days a £20 ℔ month . 33,, 6,, 8
30. John Wright.........ditto..a d?... 33,, 6,, 8
  Thomas Wood Drummer ditto..a d? 33,, 6,, 8

            £1516,, 13,, 4

 Ely Kershaw maketh Oath, That the above is a just & true Pay Bill of his Company to the 20th day of October 1775—

Sworn before me   }   Ely Kershaw.
this 4. day October 1775
 Tho : Charlton

Endorsed: Cap! Kershaws
     Paybill—

PAPERS OF THE FIRST COUNCIL OF SAFETY OF THE REVOLUTIONARY PARTY IN SOUTH CAROLINA, JUNE-NOVEMBER, 1775.

[110.]

[CAPT. EDWARD RICHARDSON'S PAY BILL.]

A Return of the Officers Non Commissioned Officers & Privates of the fifth Company of Rangers Commanded by Col. Wm Thomson Esqr from the first day of September to the 20th day of Octr 1775.———

Edward Richardson Capt..	50 days	a 70/...	£ 175.	,,	,,
Lewis Dutarque 1 Lieut	50 days	a 45/...	112,,	10.	,,
Moses Vance 2d Lieut	50 days	a 45/...	112,,	10.	,,
Rubin Broomfield Sergt.	1 Month & 20 days	a £5	41,,	13	4
Joseph Fox........do....	...do	a do	41,,	13.	4
Privates					
1 Andrew Hannah............	do	a £20 ₱ mth	33,,	6,,	8
2 Charles Mc Ginney...	do.....	a do	33.	6.	8
3 Robt Spurlock......	do.....	a do	33,,	6.	8
4 Benjamin Franklin.......	do.....	a do.	33.	6.	8
5 David Brunson.............	do.....	a do	33.	6.	8
6 Ezekiel White...	do.....	a do	33.	6.	8
7 Seth Pool	do.....	a do	33.	6.	8
8 Wm Pool..	do.....	a do	33.	6.	8
9 Denny Hinson	do.....	a do	33.	6.	8

10	Wm Rogers	do	a do	33	6.	8
11	Johnston Parish	do	a do	33.	6.	8
12	Edwin Ferrill	do	a do	33.	6.	8
13	John Mattison	do	a do	33	6.	8
14	Richd Singleton	do	a do	33.	6.	8
15	Micajah Wallace	do	a do	33.	6.	8
16	Isaac Hilton	do	a do	33.	6.	8
17	John Hilton	do	a do	33.	6.	8
18	Wm Hilton	do	a do	33.	6.	8
19	Isaac Brunson	do	a do	33.	6.	8
20	Wm Griffin	do	a do	33.	6.	8
21	Josiah Brunson	do	a do	33.	6.	8
22	Michael Morgan	do	a do	33.	6.	8
23	Wm Hood	do	a do	33.	6.	8
24	Joseph Smith	do	a do	33.	6.	8
25	Abraham Pool	do	a do	33.	6.	8
26	James Buchannan Drummer	do	a do	33.	6.	8
27	Benjamin Mc Kinnie	do	a do	33.	6.	8
28	John Bronaugh	do	a do	33.	6.	8

```
                    Carried Over .............. £1416,, 13,, 4
                    Amount Brt. Over .......... £1416. 13,, 4
29 Wm Sloan  from 1 Sept to 20 Octr  £20 ⅌ Month.  33.  6. 8
30 John Belcher     do             a do           33,,  6,, 8
31 John Broomfield  do             a do           33.   6. 8
                                              £ 1516,, 13,, 4
```

Edward Richardson Maketh Oath, That the above is a just & true Pay Bill of his Company to the 20th day of Octr 1775——
Errors Exetd

Sworn to before me this }
9th day Octr 1775.   }
Richd Richardson

Endorsed : Capt Richardsons
            Pay bill——

[111.]

[CAPT. THOMAS WOODWARD'S PAY BILL.]

A Return to the pay Master of the Eight Company of Rangers Commanded by Colonel William Thomson from the 20th Sept to the 20th October 1775.

				£	s	D
	Thomas Woodward Capt.	30 Days	a 70/—	105		
1	Lieut. Richard Winn	Do	45/	67	10	
2	Lieut. John Woodward	Do	Do	67	10	
Serjts	John Smith	Do	£ 25. Month	25		
	William Boyd	Do	Do	20		
	John Owens	Do	Do	20		
	James Picket	Do	Do	20		
	James Owens	Do	Do	20		
	John Carr	Do	Do	20		
	John Carson	Do	Do	20		
	John Henderson	Do	Do	20		
	Daniel Oaks	Do	Do	20		
	Benj. Mitchell	Do	Do	20		
	Francis Henderson	Do	Do	20		
	William Henderson	Do	Do	20		
	Benj. May	Do	Do	20		
	Jacob Frazier	Do	Do	20		
	Henry Wimpey	Do	Do	20		
	Charnel Durham	Do	Do	20		
	James Anderson	Do	Do	20		
	William Rayford	Do	Do	20		
	Mathew Rayford	Do	Do	20		
	Benj. Mc Graw	Do	Do	20		
	Augustin Hencock	Do	Do	20		
	William Owens	Do	Do	20		

SOUTH CAROLINA PROVINCIAL TROOPS

John McDaniel		Do	20	0 0
Thomas Gather		Do	20	0 0
Prichard Stone		Do	20	0 0
			£ 770	—

Brought Over Dr £770

	Days		£	pr. Month
John Jacobs	30		20	
John Bell		Do		Do
Joseph Owens		Do		Do
Thomas Winningham		Do		Do
Edward McGraw		Do		Do
William Duggins		Do		Do
Omt. William Wilson Drumr.		Do		Do
			£ 910	— ,,

South Carolina

I Thomas Woodward do Certify that. the the Sums as they Stand Stated against the Several persons Named that is in my Company is a just Act and Return Sworn to & Certif.d before me the 20th Oct.r 1775

        Rich.d Winn J P

Endorsed : Capt. Tho.s Woodwards 20th
          Paybills

[112.]

[CAPT. CHARLES HEATLY'S PAY BILL.]

Pay Bill of Capt. Heatley's Conpy in the Regiment of Rangers Commanded by William Thomson Esqr. up to the 20th Octr. 1775 Inclusive——

Names of Officers non commission'd officers & Privates——	Dates of Comissons & attestations	Time in Service—		Amount		
Capt. Chs Heatley		30 Days	a £3.10. ⅌ day	£	105.	
Lieut. Rd Brown		30. Do	a. £2.5. ⅌. Do.		67.	10
Lieut. Fras Taylor		30. Do	a. Do ⅌. Do.		67.	10
Edwd Leger ⎫ Sergts		1 month	a. £25. ⅌ month		25.	
Alexr. Mc Kinsey ⎭		1. Do	a. Do. ⅌. Do.		25.	
John Surginor		1 Do	a. £20 ⅌.		20.	
John Siders		1 Do	a. Do.		20.	
Thos Burdell		1 Do	a. Do.		20.	
Danl Wootan		1 Do	a. Do.		20.	
John Rottin		1 Do	a. Do.		20.	
John Wootan		1 Do	a. Do.		20.	
William Lucas		1 Do	a. Do.		20.	
Geo. Coband		1 Do	a. Do.		20.	
Petr Burns		1 Do	a. Do.		20.	
Wm Parler		1 Do	a. Do.		20.	
Isaac Vaugin		1 Do	a. Do.		20.	
Joseph Williams		1 Do	a. Do.		20.	
Jno Killingsworth		1 Do	a. Do.		20.	
Solomon Floid		1 Do	a. Do.		20.	
Denise Mc Carty		1 Do	a. Do.		20.	
Chs Boiles		1 Do	a. Do.		20.	
Wm Mc Graw		1 Do	a. Do.		20.	

SOUTH CAROLINA PROVINCIAL TROOPS

Wm Runnalds	1	Do	a	Do	20	—	—
Andrew Mc Kelvey	1	Do	a	Do	20	—	—
Richd Persons	1	Do	a	Do	20	—	—
Osmand Morgan	1.	Do	a	Do	20	—	—
Benja Wade	1	Do	a	Do	20	—	—
Wm Thomas	1	Do	a—Do	Do	20	—	—
Jno Mc Clain	1	Do	a	Do	20	—	—
Robt Crockett	1.	Do	a	Do	20	—	—
Jas Hawkins	1	Do	a—Do	Do	20	—	—
Joseph Trotter	1	Do	a—Do	Do	20	—	—
John Glass	1	Do	a...Do	Do	20	—	—
Joshua Glass	1	Do	a—Do	Do	20	—	—
Jno Miller	1	Do	a—Do	Do	20	—	—
Jas Crawford	1	Do	a—Do	Do	20	—	—

₩ Chs Heatley————£ 910— 0— 0—

Brought ovr ... £ 910— 0— 0—

Charles Heatley maketh Oath that the above is a Just & True Bill of his Companey to the 20th of Octr 1775—

Sworn to befor me } John Purves
this 3rd of Octr 1775 }

Endorsed : Capt Charles Heatley's
Paybill £910

[113.]

[ALEXANDER INNES TO GOVERNOR TONYN. [108]]

Cherokee in Rebellion Road 15th Oct.r 1775

Sir,

I did myself the honor to write to your Excellency by Colo. Kirkland[109] some time ago; and at the same time sent all the packets that came by the two preceding Mails. I now convey to your Excellency those brought by Pond, & am at the same time to beg a thousand pardons for the liberty I took in opening your News papers, as by some neglect Lord Williams were not sent and in our present forelorn situation you may judge how anxious we must be to read any thing from England. It was Committee like freedom, but we dont stick at higher Crimes then felony or breach of trust in this Province— The Governor has left me very little interesting to say of affairs here, there are great divisions amongst the Leaders, & I firmly believe the majority of the people of Charles Town are against all their measures.

The state of the back Country Mr Kirkland could fully inform you of, & the event of Draytons expedition plainly shows what might have been done there, had there been any decent force here : by what infatuation or neglect these unhappy provinces to the southward have been so totally abandoned, for such a space, I cannot imagine, but the reflection of what I have seen drives me almost distracted.

The 2d of July Capt. Tollemache sailed from this harbour for Boston, perfectly well informed of the state of this & the neighbouring Provinces of N. Carolina & Georgia with the strongest remonstrances from the three Governors both to Gen. Gage & the Admiral; and so little regard has been paid

---

[108] Alexander Innes was Secretary to Lord William Campbell, Royal Governor of South Carolina. Patrick Tonyn was Royal Governor of East Florida. This letter was captured by representatives of the Council of Safety.

[109] Moses Kirkland, the traitor

to them, that not even a line has been received from either. But I have done with this cursed subject.

The Cherokee is a great acquisition to us, Cap. Ferguson with good sense, politeness, and skill in his profession has the warmest zeal for the good of the Service : he is none of those luke warm officers with which we have long been cursed, and we have only to regret his force is so unequal to his spirit. De Brahm who he brought out has been plaguing us with his being impeded in carrying on the service he was order'd, but the Governor (who has moved from the Tamer to this ship) has cut him very short. A fine time to talk of his surveys of a Country that we are in a doubt to whom it may belong— I shall be happy on every occasion to receive your commands, & am with the most
    perfect Esteem & respect
   Sir
     Your Excellency's most obedient
     & obliged hble servant
      Alex. Innes

N B I take the Liberty of
inclosing under your Excellency's
Cover a few lines to Mr Penman
to request his good offices to this
poor skipper. I shall be much
mortified if my old friend is the
Malcontent you alude to.

His Excellency Governor Tonyn

I will not trouble your Excellency with Mr Penmans letter I have given it to the Master.——

Endorsed : Alexander Innes
    to
   Govr Tonyn
   15 Octr 1775

[114.]

[ORDER TO DELIVER POWDER TO MOSES COTTER. [110]]

deliver ⅌ Order Wᵐ Hy. Drayton Esqʳ to Moses Cotter for the use of the Cherokees

$\left. \begin{array}{l} 38\text{-}^a/4^1 \\ 4\text{-}^a/8 \end{array} \right\}$ Contᵃ 1000ᴸᴮ Powder

[115.]

[HENRY LAURENS TO THE COMMITTEE FOR SAXE-GOTHA TOWNSHIP.]

Charles Town. 24. October 1775

Gentlemen—
The affairs of this Colony must be reduced to a very precarious situation when the information of Mʳ Lewis Dutarque & Ralph Humphreys is to supercede the orders of those who are authorized & required to do every thing which shall to them seem needful & expedient for the defence security & protection of this Colony— how do you think public business can be conducted if the orders of men properly authorized & who devote their whole time to public service without fee or reward, are to be thus interrupted & impeded--

Mʳ Lewis Dutarque was in the Council of Safety a very few days ago after he had come from the Congree— he gave us no such information as you speak of, he has therefore either too hastily informed you or he has been extremely deficient in his Duty as an Officer & an Associate, by failing to lay before us, intelligence of such vast importance—

---

[110] The Council of Safety had resolved to send two thousand pounds of powder to Keowee to be distributed among the Cherokee Indians and had written Indian Agent George Galphin to that effect on October 4, 1775 (See Vol. II. of this magazine, p. 105). This is the order to the custodian of some of the Council's powder to deliver one thousand pounds to Moses Cotter, the wagoner assigned to haul it.

We should have hoped that you would have forwarded the execution of the Council of Safety's Orders[111] & we hope you will do so upon receipt hereof— be assured we act upon good grounds & have nothing else in view but the public welfare——

By order of the Council of Safety

We desire you will do your endeavours to forward
the Waggon with Safety & order the Waggoner
to deliver the Letter directed to Mr Wilkinson
to Mr Pearis as we suppose Mr Wilkinson will be gone from
Keowee to attend his Duty at Salisbury—
We have ordered an escort of Rangers
to conduct the Waggon[112] & request
your assistance if needful—
Messrs William Arther
     William Goodwin
     Jacob Richman
     Ralph Humphreys—
          at Congree

Endorsed: Copy 24. Octob^r 1775
     To Mess^s Arther
          Goodwin
          Richman
          & Humphreys

---

[111] These orders seem to have been in reference to the forwarding of the powder to the Cherokees.

[112] The escort, consisting of two sergeants and eighteen privates under Lieut. Thomas Charlton and Uriah Goodwin, a cadet, of the Rangers (3d Regt.), was, on Tuesday, October 31st, overpowered by a party under Patrick Cuningham and the powder taken away. (See Cotter's affidavit, *Moultrie's Memoirs*, Vol. I, p. 97.)

[116.]

[HENRY LAURENS TO EDWARD WILKINSON.]

Charles Town. 24. Octobr. 1775.

Sir—

We are sorry to find that from misapprehensions the Ammunition intended for the Cherokee Indians to be distributed by you has been detained at Congrees— we have now ordered it to be sent forward immediately but as we have no expectation of your having time to take upon you the distribution we have authorized Mr Richard Pearis to transact that business & we desire you will deliver to him the Letter which we wrote to you by the Waggon in which the ammunition is put & direct it to him for his Government in acting in your stead—

We hope you will not fail to be at the meeting of the Indian Commissioners at Salisbury on the 10th Novem^r Mr Galphin, will probably be delayed; two or three days—from a necessity for attending certain Creek Indians who are to be at his House about the latter end of this month——

By order of the Council
of Safety—

Edward Wilkinson Esqr —

Endorsed: Copy 24th Octob^r 1775.
To E. Wilkinson

[117.]

[HENRY LAURENS TO RICHARD PEARIS.]

Charles Town 24. October 1775.

Sir—

We have received your Letter of the 15th Ins^t & shall give the contents full & proper consideration—in the mean time we are sorry to learn that the Ammunition vizt 1000^{tw} Gun Powder & 1000^{tw} Lead intended for the Cherokees has been stopped & detained at Congaree—it is necessary that it should be forwarded & properly distributed— but as we have no hopes of meeting M:̣ Wilkinson at Keowee, presuming that he will have been set out upon his journey to Salisbury before this can reach you, we desire that you will receive the ammunition, open M:̣ Wilkinson's Letter & follow the Instructions given to him as if they had been directed immediately to yourself, & also in M:̣ Wilkinsons absence take a Letter which we now direct to him—

You shall hear from the Provincial Congress in due time relative to recalling M:̣ Cameron, but we desire that you will not abate your vigilance to counteract his schemes & projects — We cannot forbear expressing our good opinion of M:̣ Wilkinson & our hopes that upon further investigation you will find that you had mistaken his principles & his conduct— We have no partiality for any man but him who is a fast & steady friend to American Liberty—if M:̣ Wilkinson shall here after be found to be or to have been faulty, he shall receive no countenance from us— but we cannot condemn any man unheard we hope you will either prove clearly that he has acted contrary to the Interest of America in order that he may be properly, distinguished—or, that you will endeavour to colesee with him for common benefit--

By order of the Council
Richard Pearis— of Safety.

Endorsed: Copy 24.th Octob:̣ 1775
To Rich.d Pearis
Endorsed also: Copies to be
Entered——

[118.]

[HENRY LAURENS TO LT. COL. WILLIAM THOMSON.]

Charles Town, 25. October 1775.

Sir—
We lately ordered a Waggon containing 1000.tw Gun powder & 1000.tw Lead to proceed to Keowee & to lodge that Amunition in the hands of Edward Wilkinson Esquire

in order to be distributed among the Cherokees, this was done after mature deliberation & after long consultation with our friends in Georgia as well as under the sanction & direction of the Representatives of the United Colonies at Philadelphia—notwithstanding all this, the Committee at Congaree have thought proper to stop the Waggon, under pretence that the people in the frontier will not allow the Ammunition to pass & ground their apprehensions upon a report made to them by Lieutenant Dutarque, who was in Town & in the Council of Safety a few days ago but intimated no such danger to us.—public business cannot be conducted with benefit to the Colony if orders are to be thus questioned & interrupted —or if we are to account for our motives & proceedings to every man in the Colony—the Indians can procure Ammunition without our help—& therefore for every good and obvious reasons, we think it expedient to supply them with a little— In order that the present intended supply may go forward without further impediment, we desire you will order an Officer's Guard immediately to escort & protect the Waggon & to see that the powder & Ball are safely delivered to Mr Richd Pearis as we conclude that Mr Wilkinson will have left Keowee & be on his way to Salisbury, in which case the Letter which the Waggoner has for him must also be delivered to Mr Pearis for his guide in making the distribution.—

By order of the Council
of Safety

Order the utmost dispatch to be made by the Waggoner.——
To Colonel Thomson or the Commanding Officer of the Regiment of Rangers at Camp—

Endorsed ; Copy 25th Octob^r 1775
          To Coll^o Thomson

SOUTH CAROLINA PROVINCIAL TROOPS

[119.]

[ROLL OF CAPT. DARIUS DALTON'S COMPANY OF VOLUNTEER MILITIA.]

Addressed: To the Honble Council of Safety/
Charles Town

Prince Williams Parish—20.th Octo.^r 1775

Gentlemen/

We whose Names are under written; having formed ourselves into a Company of Volunteers, either to Act as Horsemen or Footmen, in defence of our Liberties & Country, which so loudly calls upon us for so doing; do with due submission--Petition the Honble the Council of Safety, to grant unto us Commissions for Our Officers which we have chosen by a Majority of Votes, Viz.^t . . Darius Dalton Capt Charles Browne first Lieu.^t , Joseph Ainger second Lieu.^t & James Gowen third Lieu.^t under the Names of the Swift & Bold—for which we shall be thankfull—

We are with respect—

P.. S.. As we have sent a boy down with this, by whom the Commissions may be sent- - - - - - - - - - - - - - - - - - - } Gentlemen/

Y.^r Most humble servants

John Cockran	Darius Dalton - -
Saml Jones	Charles Browne
Thos Marshall	Joseph Ainger
George Farrar	James Gowen
Richd Keating	Isaac Hirde
Josiah Tilley	Francis Thos Greene
Stephen Swan	James Francis Dalton
James M.^c kewn	Joseph Dopson
Nathl Tilley	Jacob Auton
Francis Chosohne	John Barlow—
Joseph Alexander	And.^w Mc Carley

206 SOUTH CAROLINA PROVINCIAL TROOPS

William Harvey
Thos. Stone——
James Stone——
John Ferguson
Wm Smith . -.
Florence Dunnovant
Wm Murray . . . .
John Keating . . . .
Andw Fornea . . .
James Miscampbell
John Swinney
Cornelius Mc. Cartey
John Prescotte . . 54—

Richd. West—
John Bonneu - - -
John Gatch
John Russell
Benja. Dean
John Malkin
John Allen—
Daniel Ellis - -
Seth Prior——
John Stoney—
John Lesur—
Turner Myrick
Saml. Fletcher
John Roberts
Robert Anderson
Moses Grainger
Peter Boizell
John Adam Eirick
Phillip Ulmer   30

Endorsed: Capt Charles Brownes
Volunteer Company
of Dragoons—
Commissions granted the
28th October 1775—[113]

[120.]

[HENRY LAURENS TO THE COMMISSIONERS FOR THE COLONY TREASURY.]

Gentn

Pay to William Woodward Fifty Pounds for an express from Edwd W—— Esq from Keowee (Indian affairs) By order of the Council of Safety 30 October 1775

H L

---

[113] From the private collection of A. S. Salley, Jr. See *The Sunday News*, Charleston, S. C., March 12, 1899.

To J N
P B
W G Esq^rs
Commiss^rs for Colony Treasury—[114]

Endorsed: Copy 30.th Octob^r
1775
To the Commissioners of
the Treasury

[121.]

[CAPT. SAMUEL BOYKIN TO THE COUNCIL OF SAFETY.]

Granbey. 16.th October. 1775
To The Hono^ble Council of Safety.

Gentlemen

I am Sorry it was nott in my Power to comply. with your directions, it was Occasioned by the Indians being taken very sick one of them Died on his way home and two more at their Town, and Several more very. sick, A few days after I returned home I was taken Extreemly Ill with the feaver, or should have wrote you before this, I was at the Catabaw Town A few days Ago. and the Indians has gott much better, and are willing to come down at any time you may think proper, as the Sickley season of the year is now Over. I should. be glad you would lett we know when they may be Wanted Again— by the desire of M^r. Thomas Fargason I have paid twenty five Indians Under my Command two hundred & fifty pounds which is ten pounds Each

---

[114] John Neufville, Peter Bacot and William Gibbes. The latter was then the owner of the house (which he had built a few years before) now used as the Women's Building at the South Carolina Inter State and West Indian Exposition.

man which sum Should be glad you would pay M^r. Joseph Kershaw. I am Gentlemen

    Your Most Humb^{le} Servt.
     Samuel Boykin

Endorsed : Capt. Sam Boykin
   16th October 1775—
   Rec^d & presented to the
   Council of Safety 30th [115]

---

[115] From the private collection of A. S. Salley, Jr. See *The Sunday News*, March 19, 1899.

PAPERS OF THE FIRST COUNCIL OF SAFETY
OF THE REVOLUTIONARY PARTY IN SOUTH
CAROLINA, JUNE-NOVEMBER, 1775.

[122.]

[ROLL OF CAPT. JOHN JENKINS'S COMPANY OF VOLUNTEER MILITIA.]

John Jenkins Capt
Benj.^{a} Reynolds } first Lieut.
William Fripp Junr } second
Benjamin Toomer - - - - - 4
William Chaplin Ju.^{r} 5
William Adams Jur 6
Joseph Jenkins 7
William Maltby 8
John Fripp Ju.^{r} 9
Thos Ladson— 10
Benj^a Ladson 11
William Reynolds Senr 12
William Sims 13

George Stevens	14
William Chaplin Sen.r	15
Charles Floyd	16
Charles Sams	17
Tho.s Russle	18
James Reynolds Sen.r	19
James Reynolds Ju.r	20
Richard Reynolds	21
William Fripp Sen.r	22
Paul Fripp	23
Robert Rutherford	24
Joshua Snowden	25
Joshua Toomer	26
Allen Meckee—	27
William Barns	28
John Barnes—	29
Thomas Fripp	30
Tho.s Bell -	31
John Meckee	32
James Allen	33
John Fendin	34
Cornelias M.c Carty	35
David Scott	36
William Scott	37
William Meckee	38
Michael Shireman	39
Isaac Fendin	40
Stephen Rivers	41
John Coburn	42
James Shickels	43
John Miller	44
Benjamin Scott	45
Sam.l Green	46
Joseph Williams	47
John Chaplin Se.r	48
John Chaplin Ju	49

Joseph Oswald .. 50
Thomas Prichard . 51
Thomas Jennings .. 52
Richard Scott ... 53

Endorsed: Volunteer Company
Captain John Jenkins
St Helena
Commissions signed
20 October 1775 [116]

[123.]

[ANDREW CUMMING TO HENRY LAURENS.]

Addressed: To
Henry Lawrense Esqr
President of the
Council Safety
Charles Town

Gentlemen
In Consequence of ye Resolutions of the Provincial Congress have sent down a List of a Number of men who are willing to enter into a Volunteer Company under my Command I therefore Pray you may grant me a Commission And to ye rest of the Officers Agreable to their request as you' observe on the Back of the List sent, I am Gentlemen with respect – ——
Your most obed^t Hum^{ble} Servt
Octr ye 30th 1775
Andrew Cumming
To
Henry Lawrense Esqr

[116] From the private collection of Yates Snowden, Esq. See *The Sunday News*, Charleston, S. C., March 12, 1899.

Endorsed: Andrew Cumming's
application for Com-
-missions granted
30 October 1775—[117]

[124.]

[CAPT. ANDREW CUMMING'S COMPANY OF VOLUNTEER MILITIA.]

South Carolina ⎫ We whose names are underwritten being
Saltcatchers & ⎬ deeply impressed with the Calamitous Cir-
Edisto District ⎭ cumstances of the Inhabitants of America
from the oppressive Acts of the British Parliament tending
to enslave this Continent do find it nessisary for the security
of our Lives and Fortunes and above all our Liberty and
Freedom to Associate ourselves into a Volunteer Company
Agreeable to the Resolution of the Congress And that we will
hold ourselves in readiness for our mutual Security and
Defence to obey all such orders as shall be directed by The
field Officers of the Colleton County Regiment of Foot.
Given under our hands this 9th Day of October, One Thous-
and seven hundred and seventy five

---

[117] From the private collection of A. S. Salley, Jr. See *The Sunday News*, Charleston, S. C., March 5, 1899.

SOUTH CAROLINA PROVINCIAL TROOPS 213

And:w Cumming—	William Pellum	Edw:d Canaday—	Jesey Mc. Clendon
Samuel Padget	John Slater—	Frederick Touchstone	Thomas Byrd
Will:m Lott	Edw:d Pellum—	Hardy Howel	Abraham X (his mark) Odum
W:m Parker—	George Weir—	William Arnet	William Casten
W:m Mitchel	Willis Elzey—	John B (his mark) Brunston	James W (his mark) Ward
Joseph Howel	Tho:s Wethrington	Peter X (his mark) Graham	Thomas Z (his mark) Zachry
Henry Touchstone j	Jacob Hunter	John X (his mark) Graham	William X (his mark) Valantine
Abraham Blitchindon	William Blitchindon	Moses Gayter	James X (his mark) Welch
Peter presler	Robert Cannon	Benj:n X (his mark) Blackledge	John Cain
David moore	George Petis	James Hollen	Tho:s B (his mark) Broom
John Ford	Rich:d Wethrington	George Stuart	William X (his mark) Davis
Tho:s X (his mark) Studavant	Caleb Bright	Jeremiah J (his mark) Brown	Jacob Sojurner
John Touchstone	Henry Crum	Reuben X (his mark) Golightly	John X (his mark) Innan
Jonas Touchstone	John Patrick		Robert Gilbert
John Cannon			
Benj:n B (his mark) Stanley			

Thomas M (his mark) Manton	
Henry Smith	
Leven L (his mark) Roten	
John X (his mark) Lane	
John S (his mark) Slater Jun:r	
Christopher T (his mark) Tonchstone	
John Hickmon	
Robert R (his mark) Brown	
Samuel Glover	
James I (his mark) Speers	
Jacob X (his mark) Frank	
James Simpson	
Patrick Cain	
John Gilbert—	

We The within Subscribers have Proceeded to Elect Officers to Command The said Company within mentioned and Do Choose Andrew Cumming To Be Captn Patrick Cain first Lieutenant Samuel Paget second Lieut^t Henry Crum Ensign And Pray Commissions may be Obtained for them ——

Endorsed: Capt A. Cummings
Volunteer Company
Commissions granted
30 October 1775—[118]

[125.]

[JAMES SKIRVING, JR., TO HENRY LAURENS.]

Addressed: To
Henry Lawrens Esqr——
President of the Council of
Safety —·—

Sir

As I have been prevail'd on to Accept the Command of a Company of Gentlemen Volunteers in the Parish of St Bartholomews and having inlisted a Sufficient Number, presume from the Temper of the times, that I am to Apply to the Council of Safety for my Commission, Mr Charles Shepheard first, and doct^r Mathew Kennedy second Lieutenant, Mr James Postell Ensign, I do Apply, I have the Honor to be
Sir
Your most Obed^t Servt
James Skirving Junr

To
Henry Lawrens, Esqr President
of ye Council of Safety

---

[118] From the private collection of A. S. Salley, Jr. See *The Sunday News*, Charleston, S. C., March 5, 1899.

Endorsed: James Skirving Junr
No date
Read & Commiss.^s sign'd
in Council [119]

[126.]

[LIST OF PUBLIC RECORDS SENT TO DORCHESTER
FOR SAFE-KEEPING.]

List of Sundry Cases &c of Public Records sealed with the seals of Respective offices & the president of the Council of Safety 24th Octobr 1775—& sent on board the Schooner Sally Thomas Curling Master to Dorchester—(viz)
From the Commons Pleas Office—11. Boxes Records

    Crown——D^o—— 2. Ditto————
    Auditors—D^o—— 1. Ditto————
    Chancery--D^o—— 2. Ditto————
    Surveyor Generals— 3. Presses & one Chests
    Registers Office— 3. Ditto Boxes
    Secretarys Ditto— 10. Boxes. Box marked N.º 8.
    remans in the Office as it contains Records of Wills, & the Originals are sent to Dorchester——

S O Boxes N.º 1 a 7 and N.º 9 a 11
C P O. Boxes from N.º 1. to 11 Sessions 2 Boxes N.º 1 & 2.—
  3 Presses & 1 Chest—Chancery—Troup [120] 2 Boxes
R. M. C. Boxes from N.º 1. to. 3. { Auditors
             { Office Books 1 Box—
      Received 27th October 1775 by the
      hands of Joshua Ward at Dorchester
      the above Boxes, Presses & Chest——

---

[119] From the private collection of A. S. Salley, Jr. See *The Sunday News*, Charleston, S. C., March 12, 1899.
[120] John Troup, Register of the Court of Chancery.

a true Copy from
the orginal Examined
with Tho. Bee Esquire
by Henry Laurens.

(Signed)
Rich Waring
Jn? Glaze
Richard Walter——

In the Council of Safety
30th October, 1775.

Endorsed: Copies relative to Public Records the Originals deliver'd to Mr President Drayton in Congress this 2^d Novem 1775 [121]

[127.]

[CAPT. EDWARD LACEY'S COMPANY OF VOLUNTEER MILITIA.]

South Carolina   Camden District Turkey Creek
We the subscribers being desirous of raising & forming a Volunteer Company as well for the defence of this Neighbourhood in particular as for the province in General do request of the honoble the Council of Safety,—Commissions for the same and that Edwd Lacey be appointed Captain Charles Miles be appointed first Lieutenant and That patrick Mc Griff be appointed Second Lieutenant of the said Company

Edwd Lacey
Frances Graves
Wm Brown
Richard Mils
James M^cneall
James Hagans

ould Miles Jas
Aaron Hall

---

[121] The Second Provincial Congress of South Carolina, the deputies to which had been elected on Monday and Tuesday the 7th and 8th and Monday and Tuesday the 28th and 29th of August, 1775, met in Charles Town on Wednesday, November 1, 1775, and selected William Henry Drayton for its president, and Peter Timothy for its secretary.

Palmore Rindrick
Ja^ses Lacey
Josiah Hill
Charles Miles
Reuben Lacey
Turner Kendrick
James Morrow
Edward Bell
Daniel Travers
Hugh Simpson
John Miles
Alexander Brown
Valinetine Bell
John
   montgomery
Joseph Robison
Hamilton Brown
Robert montgomry
Thomas mones
William mones
Wm Williams
Patrick Mc Grieff

This is to Certify that We the subscribers do agree that m^r Ja^s Miles Sang^d Bring Our Commissons

          Edwd Lacey
          Charles Miles
          Patrick Mc Grieff
          Ja^es Lacey Clark

Endorsed: Capt. Edwd Lacey's
      Volunteer Company—[122]

---

[122] From the private collection of A. S. Salley, Jr. See *The Sunday News*, Charleston, S. C., March 19, 1899.

[128.]

[CAPT. ELIAS DUBOSE'S COMPANY OF VOLUNTEER MILITIA.]

South Carolina/.

Whereas the provincial Congress, have deemed it necessary that for the more immediate protection of the good people of this colony, whose liberties & rights are threaten'd by the arbitary hand of despotism that they should be trained to the use of arms have resolved that any fifty men meeting and associated together should have a power to elect their own officers; And Whereas We the Inhabitants of St David's Parish fully convinced of the propriety of the said resolve, do associate & form ourselves into a Voluntier Independant Company, & for the better regulation of said Company do chuse, nominate & appoint Elias Dubose to be Captain Daniel Dubose—first Lieut^{nt} Isaac Dubose second Lieu^t in the aforesaid Company of Voluntiers—to be under the direction & subject to the Command of the Provincial Congress & Council of Safety & likewise do enter into following agreements with each other ———

1. We will go forth & defend the rights of our Country whenever the provincial Congress & Council of Safety shall deem it necessary & that we will pay implicit obedience to our officers — —
2. That to attain a knowledge of the art military we will punctually attend at the time & place of training when & where our officers shall appoint—under the fine of   for non attendance.
3. That our Company shall consist but of fifty privates & Sarjeants

Elias Dubose
Isaac Dubose
Dan^{el} Dubose
Andrew Dubose
Jo^s Dubose — —

William jones
Abraham Brown
Levi Brown
Cornelus Atwood
Josiah Clements

SOUTH CAROLINA PROVINCIAL TROOPS 219

John Courtney Juner
Joseph Chandler
James Curtis
James Marler
James Courtney
Isaac Dubose
William Prescott
Richard Mims
John Esam
John Jones
Thomas Rows
William Prescott
Elish Dubose
James Perkins
Francis Benton
John Dubose, Sen.
John Pigott Junr
John Warren
John Norwood
Nathaniel Piget
Benj. Curtis
Aaron Benton
Thos. Harrisson
Robert Courtney, Sen.
Samuel Courtney
Robert Courtney Jur

James Curbey
John Hardee
John Warren Sen.
Will. Sims
John Pigott Senieer
Benj. Sowl
Mc. kinny Sowl
Abraham alquien

Endorsed: Capt. Dubose's
Volunteer Company[123]

---

[123] From the private collection of A. S. Salley, Jr. See *The Sunday News*, Charleston, S. C., March 19, 1899.

220 SOUTH CAROLINA PROVINCIAL TROOPS

[129.]

[RETURN OF COL. MOULTRIE'S REGIMENT NOV. 6, 1775.]

Monthly Return of the 10 Companies in the 2nd So: Carolina Regiment of Foot commanded by Col. William Moultrie

Companies	Field			Commissiond			Staff					Serjeants					Drums & Fifes			Effective Rank & File												Arms		
	Colonel	Lt Colonel	Major	Captains	1st Lieuts	2nd Lieuts	Adjutant	Qur Master	Pay Master	Surgeon	Surg. Mate	Fit for duty	Sick	on Duty	recruiting & on furlough	Total	fit for duty	Sick	Total	Fit for duty	on Duty	on Command	on Furlow	Sick Prest	In Hospital	Absent	Recruiting	Discharged	Deceased	Total	Fit for Service	Unfit Serve	Ramrods wanting
Field Officers	1	1	1																											3			
Capt. Elliott's				1	1	1						3				3	4		4	41					4	2		2	3	64	40	3	1
" Marion's				1	1	1						1	1		1	3	1		1	30	6	2	2	1	4	10		2	1	64	17	9	6
" P. Horry's				1	1	1						1		1		2	1		1	30	7	2	3	3	7	5		1	2	62	28	12	
" D. Horry's				1	1	1						3		1	1	3	1		1	26	8	3		5	1	1		4		56	30	30	6
" Eveleigh's					1									1		3	1		1	29	4		1	2	4	2		2		58	10	3	20
" Mc Donald's				1	1	1						2		1		2	1		1	16	5	1	1	3		8		3	2	32	8	4	
" Harleston's				1	1	1						2		1	1	2	2		2	26	4	1		5	4	1			1	55	10	1	3
" Huger's				1	1	1						2		1		3	1		1	33	4	3	1	1	2			2	1	38	12	2	6
" Mason's					1	1						3				3	2		2	30	4			1		1	2			54	18	2	4
" Motte's					1	1																3		1		1			1	48	16	5	10
Staff Officers							1	1	1	1	1																			5			
Totals	1	1	1	7	9	8	1	1	1	1	1	17	1	5	4	27	15		15	282	46	18	25	21	26	32	2	18	11	557	217	51	74

Captains, Eveleigh & Chas. Motte with } recruiting   At the head Quarters in the new Barraks the
Lieuts. Peronneau & John Harleston   6th November 1775—

Sixty five Stand of arms delivered   A Dellient adjutant
to Mr. John Huger to be repaired

Endorsed: Return of 2 Regim̅t̲
6 Nove̅m 1775.

[130.]

[COMMITTEE FOR LITTLE RIVER TO COUNCIL OF SAFETY.]

Gentlemen, Little River October 23ᵈ 1775——
Six of us being part of the Committee for this place duely elected by those Qualified to vote for Deputies in Provincial Congress; Calling an extra meeting on Business as we found occasion. Did write to the Committee of intelligence on the 13th Sepr last [124] (which letter was laid before your Committee) desiring that Daniel Robbins Coaster & Trader of this place should be publickly advertised for Violating the Resolves enter'd into by your Committee on the 14th August Last, by employing a Certain James Hamilton who refused signing the General Association when Offered to him by the Commander of this Company of Foot Militia, and also could not Shew a Certificate wherein he had signed one similar thereto in either of the United Colonies, and Also Trading with (persons who had not signed any Association) in presence of two of this Committee which two are Men of Veracity. Upon those Violations as we thought them, by unanimous consent three of this Committee waited on the said Danl Robbins desiring he would attend their meeting, which he refused to Comply with, After deliberating on the same we thought him Inimical to the Liberties of America. And as we had not any Publick money refered it to you to have him Stigmatized, but on his return were Surprized to hear him say that he was Cleared by the General Committee on the strength of which he used the Chairman with disrespect and contempt, and said he was informed their was no Committee this side of Geo. Town. The last assertion we thought beneath our inquiry, and as we had no answer from you in

---

[124] See Vol. I. of this magazine, pp. 204-205. That letter was addressed to the Committee of Intelligence, as this one also evidently was, but both that and this were turned over to the Council of Safety, for they bear endorsements in the handwriting of Henry Laurens, President of the Council of Safety.

regard to his being cleared from the Complaint we laid before you (which we can make good.) Should have thought Robbins reported a falsity had not Mr Josias Allston been in Chas town at the same time and was inform'd by two of the Members of your Committee that the said Danl Robbins was Cleared. From this affair we think we appear in so despicable a light as a Committee that one Mans assertion should reach farther than Six. We the Subscribers do resolve to Act no more as a Committee for this place. We ever had our Country' Cause at Heart and if we should be called upon with our Muskets or our purses none will be more ready to exert either or both in the Cause of Liberty. as far as they will extend.————

We do not presume to advise, not being Capable; We Only mention that in this Company of Foot Militia their is about Eighty Effective Men and not one half, nay we may say three fourths has more then three Charges of Ammunition, However you are the best Judges if proper to Supply them, or to have the Need full Lodged in the Hands of a Judicious Person, if such a one can be found at this Place. This is a Sea Port and liable to be pillaged by Sea Rovers, the safety of our Families and Interests are dear to us and would protect them if in our power————

The following is a Charge Contracted by this Committee.

To Robert Bell for Carrying a Negroe to be heard before the Geo. Town Committee on. Accusation of being Concerned in an Insurrection	£5–0–0
To Hugh Stanaland to goe express to Geo. Town with the Carsons Letters and other Papers	5–0–0
	£10–0–0

We are Gentlemen your most Obedient Serv.^ts

Michel Bellins	Saml Dwight
John Allston Junr	Josias Allston
Samuel Price	Dennis Hankins
Daniel Morrall	Alex.^r Dunn

SOUTH CAROLINA PROVINCIAL TROOPS 223

Endorsed: Commee. Little—
   River 23 Octob 1775
   Reported upon
   10th Nov. P M

Endorsed also: Committee.
   Wm Parker
   M— Edwards
   &
   the Delegates of the
   District

[131.]

[CAPT. WILLIAM MILLS'S COMPANY OF VOLUNTEER MILITIA. [125]]

] der Captin William Mills and Also to serve Him, in
] lomies Parish in the Volunteer Company and Allso
] at Any Tim when the said Captain Calls on me
] der My Hand this 11th day of August 1775

		unanimously chosen Wm Mills Captain
	] James Stuart	
	] Charles Smith	
	] William Moore 30	
	] Abraham Taylor	
	] Milles Reyly	
	] Arter Ashworth	
	] Richard Morpor	Hugh Wasson 1t Lieut
	] Petterson Gillett	Thos Loyd. 2d Lient
	] Ceder Kennedy	Peter Payn. 3 . do
	] Eron Tillmon	
Iseme Copland	William Harvy	
John Smyly	Thomas Conney	
John Wiggins	William Loyed 40	
Joab Benton	George Carter	

---

[125] This document is badly mutilated, only parts of the agreement and roll being left. The bracket show where the words are torn off. The original belongs to the private collection of A. S. Salley, Jr. See *The Sunday News*, Charleston, S. C., March 19, 1899.

William Pons	Jac.ᵇ Paget	
Petter Payne	W.ᵐ Paget	
Robert Harper	Hugh Wason	
John Celly	Mi[ ] Franke	
[ ] Cogby	Lamb [ ]	
[ ] Brown	Tho.ˢ Cog[ ]	

[The bottom part torn the entire width of the sheet.]

Endorsed: [Top torn off]
          Volunteers S͛ [[126]
          Parish

Endorsed also: Capt Mills's
                Volunteer
                Company

[So far as the Editor of this magazine is aware all of the originals of the first Council of Safety's papers that are in the collection of the South Carolina Historical Society have been published in this magazine since January 1, 1900. About twenty more, which were purchased by him several years ago from the estate of the late William Gilmore Simms and which he published in *The Sunday News* (Charleston, S. C.) in March, 1899, have been republished here in order to make them more accessible to students. One roll, that of Capt. Benjamin Screven's company of volunteer militia, which was published in *The Sunday News* March 12, 1899, has been omitted because the Editor possesses only an imperfect copy of the original.

In addition to the incomplete journal and other papers of the first Council of Safety that appeared in Vol. 2 of *Collections of the South Carolina Historical Society*, other papers of that Council have appeared in Drayton's *Memoirs of the American Revolution,* in Gibbes's *Documentary History of the American Revolution,* 1764-1776, and in other works on the American Revolution.]

---

[126] St. Bartholomew's Parish apparently.

INDEX

-A-

Adams, Alexr. 180
 David Jr. 138
 George 181
 John 137, 138
 Nathl. 138
 Robert 180
 William Jr. 209
Addams/Adams, (Briant,
 Bryant) 156, 187, 188
Adinger, ___ 22, 27
 (Mr) 21
Aggnew, Andrew 172
Agnew, John 66
Ainger, Joseph 205
Alexander, Aaron 37, 154, 190
 Joseph 205
 Thomas 180
Alexr., William 180
Allen, James 55, 175, 210
 John 206
Allison, Joseph 176
Allston, John Jr. 75, 222
 Josias 75, 222
Alquien, Abraham 219
Anderson, David 151, 171
 James 40, 141, 155, 159, 187, 188, 194
 John 99, 162
 Robert 206
Aney, Frederick 15, 20
Archer, Francis 19
Armstrong, Saml. 66
Arnet, William 213
Arther, William 201
Ashworth, Arter 223
Askew, John 66
Atwood, Cornelus 218
Auton, Jacob 205
Ayers, John 125
 William 125

-B-

Bab, Francis 113
Bachhannan, James 38
Bacot, Peter 207
Bagnal, Ebenr. 171
 John 171

Baker, Benja. 176
 Dale 176
 Moses 20
 Thos. 176
 William 111
Ball, Elias Jr. 76
 Isaac 77
Bankes/Banks, James 117, 119
Barefoot/Bearfoot, (Newill, Newel) 36, 153, 190
Barlow, James 12, 16
 John 205
Barnes, John 210
 Joseph 15, 20
Barns, William 210
Barnwell (Capt) 34, 104
 John 13, 15, 18, 21
Barrett, Edward 17
Barron, James 13, 17, 180
Bee, Tho. 216
 Thomas 1
Belcher, John 158, 193
Bell, Edward 217
 Harrison 113
 James 113
 John 141, 160, 195
 Robert 222
 Thos. 210
 Valinetine 217
 William 113
Bellins, Michel 222
Belsher, John 39
Benbow, Evan 171
Bennett, Moses 125
Benton, Aaron 219
 Francis 219
 Joab 223
Berriman, James 14, 19
Besinger, Jacob 125
Bird, John Geor. 77
Black, James 177, 178
 John 177, 178
 Joseph 177, 178
 Robert 177, 178
Blackledge, Benjm. 213
Blackwell, Jacob 176
Blake (Capt) 69
 John 35
Bland, Edward 66
Blitchindon, Abraham 213
 William 213
Bodirford, William 176
Boiles, Chs. 91, 196

Boizell, Peter 206
Bonds, Robert 20
Bonneu, John 206
Bonsall, William 138
Boote, ___ 48
Booth, John 60, 144, 150
Bossly, Josh 77
Boswood, James 20
Bowman, Samuel 16
Boyd, William 39, 141, 159, 194
Boyes, Alexander 66
Boykin, Francis 36, 153, 190
 Samuel 207, 208
Boyle, Charles 164
Brantley, Nathl. 77
Bremar, Peter 52, 57
Bremars, Francis 23
Brett, Christopher 17
Brewton, Miles 1
Brice, Robert 20
Brient, Daniel 20
Bright, Caleb 213
Brigman, Jacob 55, 175
Brindly, Luis David 77
Brisbane (Mr) 101
 James 136, 145, 146
Broadway, Lewis 155, 187, 189
Bromfield, John 158
 Reuben 38, 157
Bronaugh/Bronnaugh, John 38, 193
Broom, Thos. 213
Broomfield, John 193
 Rubin 192
Broughton, Alexr. 77
 Thos. 77
Brown, ___ 79, 224
 Abraham 218
 Alexander 217
 Benja. 180
 Hamilton 217
 James 115, 117, 119, 152, 180
 Jeremiah 125, 213
 Jessee 176
 John 18
 Levi 218
 Rd. 196
 Rich 92, 99
 (Richard, Richd.) 38, 91, 164
 Robert 213

Brown (cont)
  Samuel 176
  Wm. 216
Browne, Charles 205, 206
Brunneau, John 158
Brunson, Charles 55
  David 157, 192
  George 55
  Isaac 158, 193
  James 55
  Josiah 158, 193
  Mathew 55
  (William, Wm.) 55, 175
  William Sr. 171
Brunston, Alexander 125
  David 38
  George 125
  Isaac 38
  John 213
  Josiah 38, 125
  William 125
Buchanan/Buchannan, James 157, 193
Buck, Amos 12, 17
  (William, Wm.) 14, 20
Buckman, Michael 12, 16
Bucks, David 98
Budd, John (Dr) 128
Buddiet, Daniel 125
Budding, John 20
Bull (Col) 45, 100, 107
  John 40, 104
  Stephen 54, 74, 101, 104, 105, 107
Burdell, Elizabeth 165
  John 165
  (Thomas, Thos.) 91, 164, 165, 196
Burke, John 18
Burks, David 161
Burns (Mr) 172
  (Peter, Petr.) 91, 164, 196
Burt, Thomas 20
Butler, Thomas 77
Byrd, Benjamin 125
  Thomas 213
Byrne, Chrisr. 15, 20
  Gerald 20
Byrnes, Garrat 15
Byron,_____ 95

-C-

Caffle, Timothy 125
Cain, John 213
  Patrick 213, 214
Caldwell,_____ 37
  (Capt) 5, 6, 8, 9, 11, 114, 166, 167
  Andrew 114, 116, 118, 152
  John 114, 115, 116, 117, 118, 119, 151
Calhoon, David 180
Calhoun (Mr) 5
  John C. 115
Calhoun/Calhone/Colhone, John Ewing 52, 57
Callwell, Samuel 180
Cameron,_____ 69, 80
  (Mr) 7, 203
Campbell, Alexr. 181
  Andw. 77
  David 77

Campbell (cont)
  L. Wm. 82
  Peter 77
  Robert 13, 18
  Sarah (Lady) 130, 131
  William (Lord) 130, 198
  William Johnston 20
Canaday, Edwd. 213
Canady, Matthew 18
Cancillor, John 180
Cannon (Mr) 95
  John 213
  Robert 213
  Roger 14, 19
Capers, (Thomas, Thos.) 52, 57
Carigon, James 20
Carr, John 39, 141, 159, 194
  Thomas 90
Carson, John 39, 141, 159, 194
  William 171
Carter, George 223
  Jacob 111
Caruth, John 180
Casten, William 213
Cattell, (Benj., Benjn.) 15, 20, 21
  Wm. 12, 15, 16, 21
Cattles (Capt) 101
Caulfield, Daniel 13
Celly, John 224
Chaddock, (Thomas, Thos.) 14, 19
Chambers, Jacob 55
Chandler, Joseph 219
Chaney, Bailey 78
Chaplin, John Jr. 210
  John Sr. 210
  William Jr. 209
  William Sr. 210
Chappell, (Hix, Hext) 155, 187, 189
Charlton (Lt) 48
  Tho. 142, 144, 181, 191
  Thomas 36, 153, 190, 201
Cheney, George 138
Cherry, George 176
  Jacob 36, 153, 190
  William 176
Chery, Moses 113
Chesnut, John 166-168
Chesson, Tinson 16
Chosolme, Francis 205
Claera, John 14, 20
Clark,_____ 69
  Daniel 152
  James 111
  Jases. Lacey 217
Clark/Clarke, (Sampson, Samson) 52, 57
Clarke, Arthur 70-72
  Daniel 115, 117, 119
Clay, Joseph 28, 66, 67
Clemens, Thomas 180
Clements, Josiah 218
Coachman, James 32, 33
Coband, (George, Geo.) 91, 164, 196
Coburn, John 210
Cochran (Capt) 77
  (Mr) 29
  Thomas 60, 143
Cockran, John 205
  Thomas 149
Coffell, William 114, 116,

Coffell, William (cont)
  118, 151
Cog( ), Thos. 224
Cogby,_____ 224
Cogdell, G. 47
Cole, Wm. Hamilton 52, 57
Coleman, James 176
Colson, George 13, 18
  Jacob 125
Colter, William 99, 161
Commander, Thomas 77
Conaly/Conely, Thomas 13, 18
Cone, John 176
Conelly, Thomas 17
Conn, Thomas 52
Conner, Lewis 60, 144, 150
  Thomas 60, 144, 150
Conney, Thomas 223
Connor, Thomas 57
Conyers, Danl. 171
  James Jr. 171
Cook, James 37, 153, 190
  John 19
  William 14, 19
Coon, Lewis 155, 187, 189
Cooper, James 17
  Silvanus 60, 144, 150
Copithorn, John 25
Copland, Iseme 223
Cordal, Henry 16
Corker, John 19
Cornel, Jack 42
Cornwallis (Lord) 136
Cotter,_____ 201
Moses 200
Coursey, Thomas 153
Courson, Thomas 190
Courtney, James 219
  John 219
  Robert Jr. 219
  Robert Sr. 219
  Samuel 219
Covington/Covinton, (William, Wm.) 60, 144, 150
Coweson, Thomas 37
Cox, Charles 125
  John 176
  Josiah 176
  Manuell 176
  Ricd. 138
Craie, Isham 18
Craig, Alexander 176
Crawford, James 92, 138, 181
  Jas. 197
Crockat/Crocket/Crockett, (Robert, Robt.) 92, 165, 197
Crosbee, Peter 20
Crum, Henry 213, 214
Cullian, Francis 19
Cumming, Andrew 211-214
Cuningham,_____ 79
  Patrick 201
  Robert 140
Cuningham/Cunningham, William 114-116, 118, 152
Cunningham,_____ 31
  (Capt) 6, 11, 30
  Patrick 5
  Robt. 5
Curbey, James 219
Curtis, Benja. 219
  James 219
  William 163

Cuthbert, Jas. 172
Seth Jno. 90
Cyders, John 164

-D-

Dalton, Darius 205
  James Francis 205
Danniles, John 20
Dartmouth (Lord) 123
Davelin, James 99
Davies, Robert 138, 139
Davis, Benja. 171
  Hugh 171
  James 170
  John 16, 52, 57
  Thos. 176
  William 213
Davison, Saml. 171
Daviun, James 162
Day, Joseph 52, 57
  Wm. 51, 57
Deadman, Jeremiah 18
Dean, Benja. 206
  Thomas 60, 63, 67, 143, 149
Deans, _____ 69
DeBrahm, _____ 199
Delagaye (Mr) 34
Dellient, A. 220
Demer, _____ 50
DeSaussure, D. 22, 44, 172
  (Dan, Daniel) 28, 34, 54, 59, 63, 64, 81, 82, 93
  Henry 105
  Thoms. 105
Desberry, John 138
Desurrencey, (Samuel, Sam.) 60, 144, 150
Dever, Charles 187, 189
Devise, Samuel 175
Devor, Charles 155
Dickey, Edwd. 171
  James 171
Dillard, David 163
Dobbs, Joseph 176
Docherty, John 138
Dodds, John 14, 19
Dods, James 66
  Samuel 66
Doelittle, Joseph 125
Doggett, (Richard, Richd.) 14, 19
Doharty (Lt) 22
Donaldson, John 59, 143, 144, 149
Donavan, Corns. 171
Dopson, Joseph 205
Dougherty, James 113
  Patrick 52, 57
Downs (Mr) 68
Drake, Edwd. 171
Drayton, _____ 2, 47, 198, 224
  (Capt) 52
  (Mr) 44, 50, 61, 62, 83, 132, 133, 147, 148, 174, 216
  C. 81
  Charles 51, 56, 57, 58
  William Henry 1, 44, 50, 62, 63, 67, 69, 78, 81, 93, 94, 96,

Drayton, William Henry (cont)
  97, 123, 179, 200, 216
Dubose (Capt) 219
  Andrew 218
  Daniel 218
  Elias 218
  Elish 219
  Isaac 218, 219
  John Sr. 219
  Jos. 218
Duffy, Patrick 113
Duggins/Duggans, William 40, 141, 160, 195
Dulzer, Stephen 138
Dunlap, Samuel 111
Dunn (Mr) 48
  Alexr. 75, 222
Dunnovant, Florence 206
Durham (Charnel, Charnal) 40, 141, 160, 194
Dutarque (Lt) 204
  Lewis 38, 157, 192, 200
Duval (Mr) 107
Duvoux, John 17
Dwight, Saml. 75, 222
Dysert, Corns. 171

-E-

Eakins, John 115, 116, 118, 152
Easom, _____ 166
  John 149
Eaton, Jeremiah 137, 138
  Joshua 138
  Samuel 138
Eden, Joshua 52, 57
Edings, Benjn. 138
Edwards, _____ 223
  (Mr) 23
  John 163
  William 19
Egan, Edmund 95, 96
Eirick, John Adam 206
Elkins, Joshua 125
Elliot, James 113
Elliott (Capt) 33, 220
  B. 67
  Benjamin 1, 120
  Charles 120, 138
  Robert 113
  Samuel 111
  Thomas 138
Ellis, Daniel 206
Ellison, John 66
  Robert 65, 66
Elzey, William 16
  Willis 213
Erven, W. 136
  William 66, 67, 130
Esam, John 219
Evans, Henry 12, 16
  Samuel 138
  William 13, 18
  Wm. 138
Eveleigh (Capt) 220

-F-

Fagan, Patk. 171
Fardo, Geo. Jno. 51

Fargason, Thomas 207
Farill, Lewis 77
Farmer, James 55
Farnell, James 17
Farrar, George 205
Fathern, (Benjamin, Benjn.) 60, 144, 150
Fearson, (Bentley, Bently) 60, 143, 149
Fendin, Isaac 210
  John 210
Fenwicke/Fenwick, (Thomas, Thos.) 51, 56, 57
Ferguson (Capt) 199
  David 111
  George 18
  John 206
  Thomas 1, 120
Ferguson/Furguson, Benjamin 37, 190
  Joseph 37, 153, 190
Ferrel/Ferril/Ferrill, Edwin 38, 157, 193
Fickling, Jeremiah 138
  John 138
  Joseph 111
  Joseph Jr. 137
Findlay, James 176
Fisher, (Ferdinand, Ferdd.) 12, 16
Fitchet, Jonathan 180
Fitzpatrick, Alexander 52, 57
  (Edmund, Edmd.) 52, 57
  (John, Jno.) 12, 16
Fleming, Robert 55
Fletchal, _____ 78
Fletchall, _____ 31, 96
  (Col) 6, 69, 147, 172
Fletcher, _____ 42
  (Drury, Drewry) 55, 175
  Saml. 206
Flin, John 18
Flinn, Charles 138
  Florence 138
Floid/Floyd, (Solomon, Soloman) 91, 164, 196
Floyd, Charles 210
  William 171
Forbes (Mr) 29
  Patrick 117, 119, 152
  William 114, 116, 118, 152
Ford, George 111
  George Jr. 111
  John 213
  Thomas 111
Fornea, Andw. 206
Forshaw, Robert 15, 20
Forster, Stephen 42
Fortenor, Charles 158
Foster, John 55
Foust, Caspar 156
  Naomy 156
Foust/Fust, (Burrell, Burwell) 156, 187, 189
  (William, Willm.) 156, 187, 188
Fowler, Daniel 12, 16
Fox, Joseph 38, 157, 192
Frank, Jacob 213
  Stephen 125
Franke, Mi( ) 224
Franklin, Benjamin 38, 157, 192
Frazier, Jacob 40, 141, 159, 194
French, William 37, 153, 190

Frierson, John Jr. 171
Fripp, John Jr. 209
  Paul 210
  Thomas 210
  William Jr. 209
  William Sr. 210
Frits, Henry 155, 187, 188
Frost, Jacob 18
Fry, Henry 12, 16
Fuguey, Henry 13, 18
Fullwood, William 170, 171
Furguson, Wm. 138

-G-

Gadsden, Chris. 86
  Christopher 12, 16
Gage (Gen) 80, 86, 123, 127, 198
Gallher, John 113
Galphin (Mr) 69, 129, 202
  George 42, 134, 135, 140, 183, 185, 186, 200
Gambell, John 170
Gamble, Jehu 12, 19
  Robt. 171
  William 171
Gardner, Isham 60, 143, 149
Garner, Melcher 22, 25, 120
Garner/Gerdner, Jacob 177, 178
Gaston, William 112
Gaston/Garton, Alexander 37, 154, 190
  Hugh 37, 154, 190
  Robert 37, 154, 190
Gatch, John 206
Gather, Thomas 40, 141, 160, 195
Gayle, Caleb 55, 175
  Josiah 175
  Josiah Jr. 55
Gayter, Moses 213
Gee (Mr) 105
  Peter T. F. 52, 57
Geoghagen/Geohagen, James 13, 20
German, Hugh 14, 19
Gibbes,_____, 2, 47, 68, 123, 224
  William 207
Gibson, Benjamin 156, 188, 189
  (Gilbert, Gilberd) 156, 187, 188
  John 156, 187, 188
  Thomas 16
Giessendanner, John (Rev) 156, 165
Gilbank/Gillbank, Jno. 51, 57
Gilbert, John 213
  Robert 213
Giles, Hugh 46
Gill, James 12, 18
  John Jr. 163
Gillespie, John 113
Gillett, Petterson 223
Gillmore, Anthony 14, 20

Gillmore (cont)
  Charles 113
  Thomas 12, 16, 18
Glass, (John, Jno.) 92, 165, 197
  Joshua 92, 165, 197
  Martin 17
Glaze, Jno. 216
Glover,_____112
  (Col) 177
  Jos. Jr. 52
  Joseph 108, 110, 111, 136-138
  Joseph Jr. 111
  Samuel 213
Goddard, John 14, 20
Golding, Reuben 115, 116, 118, 152
Golightly, Reuben 213
Goodwin, Charles 55, 175
  Uriah 153, 201
  William 201
Goodwyn,_____39
  (Capt) 36, 166, 167
  Robert 155, 186-189
  Uriah 36, 190
Gordan, John 181
Gordon, John 18
Gore, Eleazar 66
  John Ashford 66
Gough, John 111
  Richd. 76
Gould, David (Dr) 126, 128
Gowen, James 205
Graham, John 213
  Peter 213
Grainger, Moses 206
Grant, James 113
  John 113
Graves, Frances 216
Gray (Mr) 105
  George 154, 190
  John 153, 190
  Robert 66
Green, Saml. 210
Greenage, (William, Wm.) 52, 57
Greene, Francis Thos. 205
Gregg (Capt) 47
  James 46
  John Jr. 46
Gregory, John 138
Grey, John 37
  (George, Geo.) 37, 51, 56, 57
Griffin, Wm. 38, 193
Griggs, John 52, 57
Gruber, Philip 14. 20
Guerardeau, Peter B. 111
Gulfus, Gustavas 125
Gunter, William 18

-H-

Habersham, Joseph 28
Hagans, James 216
Hagen, Thomas 163
Haig, George 120
Haliday (Mr) 85
Hall, Aaron 216
Hallum, Thomas 98, 161
Hamilton, David 66
  James 75, 221
  John 13, 17, 18

Hammond (Mr) 40
Hanahan, John 138
  Wm. 138
Hanbury, Chars. 16
Hancock (Mr) 129
  (Augustin, Augustine) 40, 141
Hanin, James 66
Hankins, Dennis 222
Hannah/Hanah, Andrew 38, 157, 192
Hannsworth, Henry 55
Hansbury, Chas. 12
Hanshaw, Thomas 163
Harbison, William 99, 162
Harcombe, Thomas 23, 24
Hardee, John 219
Hare, James 14
Haresey, Thomas 17
Harleston (Capt) 220
  John 73, 220
Harlow, John 17
Harmon, Henry 37, 154, 190
Harper, Anthony 115, 116, 118, 152
  Joseph 176
  Robert 224
  Samuel 115, 116, 118, 152
Harrel, Zach. 175
Harris,_____95, 114
  James 176
Harrison, Nathaniel 177, 178
Harrisson, Thos. 219
Harrow, William O. 55
Harvey, Joseph 18
  Thomas 13
  William 206
Harvin, (Richard, Richd.) 55, 175
Harvy, William 223
Hawkins, (James, Jas.) 92, 165, 197
Hawthorn, James 180
Hayne, Isaac 111
Heard, Charles 114, 116, 118, 152
  John 60, 144, 149
Heath, Jno. 176
Heatly/Heatley (Capt) 91, 166, 167
  (Charles, Chs.) 91, 92, 164, 181, 196, 197
Heilsall, William 54
Heir, James 20
Heitman, F. B. 128
Hencock, (Augustin, Augustine) 160, 194
Henderson, Francis 39, 141, 160, 194
  John 39, 141, 159, 194
  William 39, 141, 160, 194
Henry (Mr) 172
Henston, Dennis 38
Hensy, George 12, 16
Hertel, Anne 156
  Henry 156
Heynes, Cornelius 19
Heyward, Thomas Jr. 1
  Thos. Jr. 171
Hickmon, John 213
Hicks, Benjamin 59, 143, 149
Hier, Jacob 125
Hill, Burril 16
  (Edward, Edd.) 55, 175

Hill (cont)
John Jr. 19
John Sr. 17
Joseph 55, 175
Josiah 217
Hilton, Isaac 38, 157, 193
John 39, 158, 193
(William, Wm.) 38, 158, 193
Hindson (Mr) 82
(Capt) 88, 89
Hinson, (Dennis, Denny) 157, 192
Hirde, Isaac 205
Hodge, Benjamin 155, 187, 188
(Edmund, Edmd.) 60, 143, 149
Isham 60, 144, 150
John 60, 143, 149
Hodges, Benjamin 114, 116, 118, 152
Hoit/Hoyt, William 14, 19
Holaday, Elliott 55
Hollen, James 213
Holliday, Alexr. 175
Hollier, Joseph B. 51, 57
Holmes, James 52, 57
Holmes/Holms, David 41, 183, 184, 185
Hoocks, Thos. 77
Hood, (William, Wm.) 158, 193
Hopkins, David 155, 187, 188
Horn, Alexander 52, 57
Horner, Isaac 181
Horry, D. 220
P. 220
House, Elisha 12, 16
Howard, John 52, 57
Howel, Hardy 213
Joseph 213
Howell, Thomas 37, 153, 190
Zachariah 55
Hubard/Hubbard, Michael 13, 17
Hubbard, Peter 60, 144, 150
Hubbard/Hubbar, William 156, 188, 189
Huger (Capt) 220
John 1, 220
Huggins, Andrew 114, 116, 118, 152
James 114, 116, 118, 152
John 114, 116, 118, 152
William 20, 114, 116, 118, 152
Hughes, (William, Wm.) 13, 18
Humphreys, Jno. 23, 24
Ralph 200, 201
Hunter, David 93, 94
Jacob 213
John 162
Saml. 12, 16
Huntsinger, Michael 15, 17
Hutchins, Samuel 51, 57
Hutchinson, Thomas Jr. 111

Hutchison, John 14, 19
Hybart, (John, Jno.) 52, 57
Hyrne, Edmond 14, 15, 19, 21
Henry 111

-I-

Inglis, John 89
Inhoff (Capt) 61
Inman, John 213
Innes (Capt) 80
(Alexander, Alex., Alexr.) 64, 65, 198, 199
Irvine, Hugh 12
Irwin, Hugh 16
Nicholas 16

-J-

Jackson, Basil 54
Isaac 55, 175
John 23, 24, 98, 156, 161, 188, 189
Joseph 14, 20
(Thomas, Thos.) 55, 99, 162, 175
Jacobs, John 40, 141, 159, 195
James, John 55
Jamieson,_____ 95
Janes, John 180
Jenkins, Benjamin 138, 177
John 93, 137, 209, 211
Joseph 137, 209
Micah 138
Reuben 176
Richd. 138
Jennings, Joseph 51, 57
Thomas 211
Jernigan, Alexander 143, 149
Jinnings, Daniel 55
Johnakin, Alexdr. 60
Johnes/Johns, John 155, 187, 188
Johnson,_____ 114
John 52, 57
Johnston, Robert 99, 114, 116, 118, 152, 162
William 19
Jones, David 16
Edmund 125
Ephriam 125
Hugh 14, 19
James 124, 126
John 60, 144, 150, 219
Saml. 205
Thomas Sr. 125
William 125, 218
Jordan, Isaac 163
John 99, 162
Josiah 163
Wm. 51, 57
Jourdon, Henry Jr. 125
Henry Sr. 125
Joyner/Joiner (Capt) 22, 34, 63, 100, 103, 104, 135

Joyner/Joiner (cont)
John 129, 172

-K-

Keating, John 206
Richd. 205
Keeffy/Keefy, Daniel 52, 57
Kelly, Patrick 12
Kendrick, Turner 217
Kennan, Henry 51, 57
Kenneday, Francis 176
John 176
Kennedy, Ceder 223
Erskine 52, 57
James T. 66
Mathew (Dr) 214
Robert 77
Keowin, Thomas 57
Kerby, Richd. 176
Kerr, Malcum 171
Kershaw (Capt) 36, 166, 167, 191
(Mr) 68, 166, 169, 181
Ely 37, 153, 189, 190, 191
Joseph 168, 208
Kierse, George 125
William 125
Killingsworth, Jesse 155, 187, 189
(John, Jno.) 91, 164, 196
Kirk/Kirke, William 13, 18
Kirkland,_____ 39, 68, 70
(Capt) 5-8, 29, 48, 49
Moses 43, 78, 79, 83, 86, 88, 107, 198
Kirkpatrick, (Francis, Fr., Frs.) 112, 113
James 112
Robert 113
Knox, Archd. 16
John 180
Kuhn/Coon, (Conrad, Gunrod) 155, 187, 189

-L-

Lacerty, William 156
Lacey, (Edward, Edwd) 216, 217
Jases. 217
Reuben 217
Ladson, Benja. 209
Robert 120
(Thomas, Thos.) 111, 209
Laferty, John 171
Lamb, Matthew 14, 19
Needon 20
Landy, (William, Willm.) 15, 20
Lane, Edward 55
John 213
Langley, Thomas 14
Larey, Peter 20
Larimore, Thomas 18
Laroch, James 111
John 111
Lassater, William 187, 188

229

Laurens (Col) 1, 64
Henry 1-4, 21, 27, 28,
  31, 33, 35, 53, 59,
  61-63, 66, 67, 69,
  70, 72-74, 77, 78,
  81, 82, 86-88, 90,
  95, 96, 100, 101,
  104, 105, 108, 112,
  123, 124, 129, 130,
  131, 135, 136, 140,
  145, 146, 172, 173,
  177, 182, 184, 185,
  200, 202, 203, 206,
  211, 214, 216, 221
Lavender, Robert 57
Lawrance/Lawrence, John
  93, 94
Leavengston, Robert 52
Lee, David 176
  Drury 176
  Lewis 125
  William 155, 187, 189
Leechmer (Mr) 81
Leeson, (James, Jas.) 52,
  57
Leger, (Edward, Edwd.)
  91, 164, 196
Leigh, Joseph 163
  William 163
Leinard, John 17
Leitch, (Andrew, Andw.)
  22, 24
Lempriere, Clement 26,
  27, 44, 53
Lempriere/Lampriere
  (Capt) 27, 33, 43, 50,
  59, 69, 101
Leonard, Laughlin 114,
  116, 118, 152
Lepeir, Paul 47
Lesur, John 206
Letterling, James 163
Levans, Thos. 171
Lewis, Abel 176
  Benj. 77
  Peter 20
Liddell, Jered 94
Liddle, George 98, 161
Lide, Robert 175, 176
Limmix, Amos 125
  Thomas Jr. 125
  Thomas Sr. 125
  William 125
Linder/Lindor, Lewis 52,
  57
Little (Capt) 88
  Josiah 16
Liveston, John 171
Loadholt, Martin 125
Lockhart, Isaac 60, 144,
  150
Logan (Mr) 95
Long (Mr) 23
  Simon 13, 18
Loocock (Mr) 63, 168
Lott, Willm. 213
Loughrea, Charles 17
Love, Archibald 12, 16
  John 113
  Robert 113
  William 113
Lowndes, Rawlins 1
Lowrey, Isom 138
Loyd, Thos. 223
Loyed, William 223
Lucas/Lucus, William 91,
  164, 196
Lynch, John 163

Lynch (cont)
  (Thomas, Thos.) 12, 15,
  17, 86
Thos. Jr. 21
Lynn, Valuntin 23
Lyons, James 13, 17

-M-

MacDonald, Bartholomew
  19
Mace, Moses 60, 144, 150
Maddock, (Abraham,
  Abram.) 52, 57
Maders, Jacob 125
  John 125
Magness, Peregrine 37,
  153, 190
Maquire, Philip 16
Mains, Thomas 16
Maitland (Capt) 10, 67
Malcolm, Thomas 12, 17
Malkin, John 206
Malone, John 55
Maltby, William 209
Mann, James 163
Manning, Thomas 19
Manton, Thomas 213
Marchant, Samuel 14, 19
Marion (Capt) 220
  Job 76
Marler, James 219
Marque, Anthony 20
Maromet, (John, Jno.)
  51, 57
Marshall, Thos. 205
Martin (Lt) 29
  (Mr) 82
  Francis 55
  James 99, 162
  John 66
  (Robert, Robt.) 36,
   153, 190
  Simon 163
  (William, Wm.) 66, 98,
   161, 171
Mason (Capt) 220
Mathews, Benjamin 111
Matthewes/Matthews,
  Peter 55, 175
Mattison, John 38, 157,
  193
Maxey, Joseph 138
  Robert 138
May, (Benjamin, Benj.)
  40, 141, 159, 194
Mayson,_____ 28
  (Maj) 8, 11, 31, 133,
  139, 140, 166, 179
  (James, Jas.) 7-9, 11,
  31, 94, 149, 167
McAlister, Charles 16
McCalester, Wilm. 66
McCalla, James 171
McCann, Thomas 16
McCarley, Andw. 205
McCartey, Cornelius 206
McCarthy, Mathias 13
McCarty, Cornelias 210
  (Dennis, Denise) 91,
  164, 196
  Jeremiah 16
  Mathias 18
McClain, Jno. 197
McClaughlin, Wm. 111

McCleary, Robert 181
McCleave, (Robert, Robt.)
  13, 18
McClendon, Jesey 213
McCook, Jos. 113
McCool, John 113
McCormack/McCormick,
  (James, Jas.) 55, 175
McCoy, William 171
McCrady,_____ 114
McCrady/McCready, David
  13, 17
McCreight, James 66
McCreon, James 113
McCrieght, David 66
McCullogh, John 77
McDaniel, Daniel 144, 150
  Francis 141, 160
  John 141, 160, 195
McDole, And. 66
McDonald (Capt) 220
  Adam 12, 15, 17, 21
  Brian 12, 16
  Dl. 60
  Francis 40
  John 40
McDowell, James 66
McDowle, Alexr. 66
McElveen, William 171
McElvene, Andrew 165
McElwee, James 99, 161
McGill, John 14, 19
McGilton, John 16
McGilverry (Mr) 42
McGinney,_____ 50
  Charles 38, 192
McGirth, Daniel 114
McGlaham, Lewis 163
McGowan, (James, Jas.)
  13, 18
McGraw, (Benjamin, Benj.)
  40, 141, 159, 194
  Edward 40, 141, 159,
  195
  (William, Wm.) 91, 164,
  196
McGrieff/McGriff, Patrick
  216, 217
McGuire, Hugh 17
McGuire/McGwyer, Merry
  155, 187, 188
McKay (Mr) 89, 90
  Edward 99, 162
McKelvey/McKelvy, Andrew
  92, 197
McKensey/McKenzie, Alexr.
  91, 164
McKewn, James 205
McKinley, James 13, 17
McKinney, Charles 157
McKinney/McKinnie, (Ben.,
  Benjamin) 38, 158, 193
McKinney/McKinnie/McKinny,
  Mordicai 37, 153, 190
McKinnie/McKinney, Roger
  115, 116, 118, 152
  Timothy 115, 116, 118,
  152
McKinnon, William 52, 57
McKinsey, Alexr. 196
McKutchon, James 20
McLain, (John, Jno.) 92,
  165
  Thomas 12
McLean (Mr) 89, 90
  Andrew 89
McLeod, John 138
McLvey, William 66

230

McMahan/McMahen, John Jr. 115, 116, 118, 152
  Peter 98, 161
McMahan/McMahen/McMahon, John 114, 116, 118, 138, 152
McMullen, James 66
McNanamara, John 17
Mcneall, James 216
McNorny, George 138
McPherson, Ulysses 54
Mcquarters, Alex. 66
Mcquoin, James 66
Meckee, Allen 210
  John 210
  William 210
Michau, Jacob 52, 57
Michie, Harry 52
  Henry 57
Middleton (Lt) 5, 7, 43
  (Mr) 63, 81
  Arthur 1
  Henry 86
  Thomas 56, 57
  Thos. Jr. 52
Mikell, William 138
Miles, Allen 22, 111
  Charles 216, 217
  John 217
  Josiah 111
  Robert 22
Millar, Thomas 187, 188
Millen, William 18
Miller, Andrew 93, 94
  (John, Jno.) 92, 165, 180, 197, 210
  Nathan 13, 18
  Robert 93, 94
  Thomas 155
  William 13
Milling (Sarg Maj) 15, 21
  Hugh 12, 16
Mills (Capt) 224
  John 52, 57
  William 223
Mils, Richard 216
Milwee, John 171
  William 171
Mims, Richard 219
Minar, Thomas 14, 20
Miscampbell, James 206
Mitchel, Wm. 213
Mitchell, (Benjamin, Benj.) 40, 141, 159, 194
  Flud 98, 161
  William 155, 187, 188
Mixon, Cornelius 176
  Jessee 176
  Jno. 176
  Michael 176
Moffett, Thos. 55
Monaghan, David 163
Monchell, Charles 17
Mones, Thomas 217
  William 217
Montgomery, Henry 171
  John 154, 190, 217
  William 171
Montgomry, Robert 217
Moor, Michael 18
Moore (Mr) 173
  David 213
  Isham 54-56, 173, 175
  Jethro 163
  John 52, 57
  Samuell 176

Moore (cont)
  Thomas 99, 162, 163
  William 223
Morelli, Frans. 52, 57
Morfet, Thos. 175
Morgan, Michael 38, 158, 193
  Nathl. 138
  (Ormand, Osmand) 92, 165, 197
  (Richard, Richd.) 52, 57
  William 12
Morison, James 66
Morpor, Richard 223
Morrall, Daniel 222
Morris, Charles 125
  James 125
  John 125
  Patrick 99, 162
  W. 144
  (William, Wm.) 60, 150, 163
Morrow, James 217
  John 15, 20
Mosely, William 98, 161
Moshill. Charles 13
Motte (Capt) 220
  (Col) 78-80, 84
  Chas. 220
  Isaac 77
Moultrie, _____ 2, 201
  (Col) 77, 78
  (William, Wm.) 35, 72, 73, 124, 182, 220
Murphey, James 163
  Matthew 176
  Maurice Jr. 176
  Philip 163
Murphy, (Matthew, Matw.) 52, 57
Murque, Anty. 14
Murray, (Alexander, Alexr.) 12, 16
  Jas. 138
  Lawrence 16
  Wm. 206
Murry, David 114, 116, 118, 152
  James 114, 116, 118, 152
Myrick, Turner 206

-N-

Nangle, William 20
Nash, John 12, 17
Nawood, Theophilus 98
Neil, David 175
  Thomas 175
Neill (Col) 5
Nelson, John 171
  Samuel 98, 161
Neufer, _____ 49
Neufville, John 207
Neyle (Col) 68, 69
Nicholls/Nichols, Richard 37, 153
Nickells, Richard 190
Nickels, Alexr. 181
  James 180
Niess, John 12, 16
Noble, John James 12, 16
North, (Edward, Ed.) 51, 57

Norwood, John 219
  Samuel 161
  Samuel Jr. 98
  Theophilus 161
  N__th (Lord) 145
Nunnery, Griffen 176

-O-

Oaks, Daniel 39, 141, 159, 194
Odom, Benjamin 125
  Michael 125
Odum, Abraham 213
O'Kelly, Patrick 17
Omensetter, (Andrew, An.) 14, 19
O'Neall, _____ 115
  (Judge) 114
Orr, William 14, 19
Osborn, Isaac 77
  Thomas 111
Oswald, Joseph 211
Owens, James 39, 141, 159, 194
  John 39, 141, 159, 194
  Joseph 40, 141, 160, 176, 195
  Robert 114, 116, 118, 152
  William 40, 141, 159, 194

-P-

Padget/Paget, Samuel 213, 214
Page, George 18
Paget, Jacb. 224
  Wm. 224
Pardue, Fields 79
Parish, Johnston 38, 157, 193
Parker, Wm. 213, 223
Parks, John 156
Parler, (William, Wm.) 91, 196
Parsons, James 1, 19
Partridge, William 155, 187, 188
Patrick, Charles 181
  John 213
Patterson, George 117, 119
Payn/Payne, (Peter, Petter) 223, 224
Payne, John 37, 153, 190
Pearce, Dixon 60, 144, 150
  Thomas 60, 144, 150
Pearis (Capt) 79, 96
  (Mr) 201
  Richard 202, 203, 204
Pearson, Richard 165
Peeples, Henry 125
Pellum, Edwd. 213
  William 213
Pemble, Thomas 37, 153, 190
Pendergrass (Mrs) 23
Penman (Mr) 90, 199
Penny, William 66

231

Perkins, James 219
Peronneau (Lt) 220
Perry, Edward 111
  Philip 176
  Richard 111
Person, Richd. 92, 197
Peters, Elijah 155, 187, 188
  (Samuel, Saml.) 13, 17
  Solomon 125, 156, 188, 189
Petis, George 213
Pettitt, Joseph 14, 19
Pettypool, Epheram Jr. 55
Peyer im Hoff (Capt) 144, 166, 167
  John Lewis 163
Picket/Pickett, James 39, 141, 159, 194
Pickings, Samuel 125
Pierce,_____ 69
  Thomas 63, 67
  William 75
Piget, Nathaniel 219
Piggot/Pigott, David 12, 16
Pigott, John Jr. 219
  John Sr. 219
Pinckney (Col) 58
  C. C. 15, 21
  Charles 56
  Charles C. 12, 16
  Charles Sr. 1
  Thomas 14, 15, 19, 21
Pitman, Ethelridge 171
Platt, John 171
  Randal 171
Pledger, Joseph 59, 143, 149
Polk,_____ 37, 92
  (Capt) 7, 28, 29, 30, 177
  (Pres) 140
  Ezekiel 62, 138, 139, 172, 173, 178-181
  Thomas 140
  William 180
Ponder, Daniel 177, 178
Pons, William 224
Poole, Ephraim 175
  (William, Wm.) 38, 157, 192
Poole/Pool, Abraham 38, 158, 193
Pooler (Mr) 41
Porter, Josiah 180
  William 164
Post (Capt) 47
  Thos. 46
Postell, Andrew 104, 105
  James 214
Potts, Jonathan 180
Potts, Robt. 66
  Thos. 46
Powe, Thomas 176
Prescott, William 219
Prescotte, John 206
Presler, Peter 213
Prestwood/Preestwood, Augustine 36, 153, 190
Pretter, John 99, 161
Price, John 163
  Samuel 75, 222
Prichard, Thomas 211
Pring, William 19
Prior, Seth 206
Proby, Solo. 12, 16

Proost, John 77
Purkins, Isaac 176
  Jordon 176
Pursor, John 171
Purves (Capt) 4, 7, 30, 31, 166, 167
  John 94, 98, 99, 161, 197

-R-

Rabon, Charles 176
  John 176
Rae (Mr) 41, 42, 129, 183, 184
Rafield, John 171
Ramage (Mr) 23
  (Mrs) 23
Ramsay,_____ 5, 139
Ramsey, Willis 55, 175
Randolph, James 155, 187, 188
Raphel, John 52, 57
Rayford, (Mathew, Matthew) 40, 141, 160, 194
  William 40, 141, 159, 194
Reavs, Daniel 125
  Thomas Jr. 125
  Thomas Sr. 125
Redmond, (Andrew, An.) 14, 19
Reed, David 113
  James 18, 113
  John 13, 18
  Thaddeus 138, 139
Reily, Richard 18
  Robt. 171
Reyly, Milles 223
Reynolds, Benja. 209
  James Jr. 210
  James Sr. 210
  Richard 210
  William 138
  William Sr. 209
Rhodes, William 17
Rian, Jacob 14, 19
Richardson (Capt) 38, 166, 167
  (Col) 68, 69
  E. 39
  (Edward, Edwd.) 157, 192, 193
  George 17
  (Richard, Richd.) 173, 174, 193
  Saml. 77
  Wm. 175
Richman, Jacob 201
Ridgway, Hope 55, 175
Ridley, William 180
Riley, John 13, 16, 17
Rindrick, Palmore 217
Rivers, Stephen 210
  Thos. 77
  William J. (Prof) 177
Robbins/Robins, Daniel 75, 221, 222
Roberts, John 206
  Joseph 13
  Robert 15, 20
  Thomas 111
  William 56
  Wm. H. 51, 57

Robins, James 113
  Thomas 112
Robinson,_____ 79
  (Maj) 5, 11
  Alexdr. 66
  James 98, 161
  (William, Wm.) 13, 18
Robison, Joseph 113, 217
Roche, Thomas 57
Rodgers, Joseph 55
Rogers (Dr) 166
  Alexander (Dr) 58, 167
  Arthur 20
  Clayton 113
  Joseph 175
  (William, Wm.) 38, 113, 157, 193
Roland, Isaac 171
Ross, Daniel 77
  William 19
Roten, Leven 213
Roth, William 14, 20
Rottin/Rotten, John 91, 164, 196
Rowan, Benjamin 180
Rowell, Jerrimiah 176
Rows, Thomas 219
Rudhall, Wm. 51
Rugge, James 23, 24
  William 23, 24
Rumph, Jacob 115
Runnalds/Runnolds, (William, Wm.) 91, 164, 197
Russel, James 99, 162
  John 98, 161
Russell, John 206
  Thomas 17
Russle, Thos. 210
Rutherford, Robert 210
Rutledge (Gov) 115
  Ed. 86
  John 86
Ryan, John 13, 18

-S-

Sabine,_____ 114
Saint, Thomas 66
St. Peirre, Louis D. 8
St. Peirre/St. Perre/
St. Pierre (Lt) 8
Salley,_____ 2, 4, 5, 7, 8, 28, 31, 36, 43, 47, 48, 59, 61, 69, 91, 92, 115, 140, 156, 165
Salley, A. S. Jr. 45, 46, 51, 56, 58, 66, 77, 94, 96, 105, 110, 112, 113, 126, 137, 171, 174, 176, 206, 208, 212, 214, 215, 217, 219, 223
Sams, Charles 210
Sanders, John 111
  Roger 14, 15, 20, 21
  William 111
Sanders/Saunders, James 66
Sandwick, John 14, 19
Sangd., Jas. Miles 217
Savage (Col) 69
Saxon, James 36, 153, 190
Scott, Benjamin 210

Scott (cont)
 David 210
 Gabriel 20
 James 13, 18, 163
 Richard 211
 Robert 46
 Samuel 18
 William 13, 15, 18, 21, 210
Screven, Benjamin 224
Scurry, Thomas 18
Seabrook, John 111
Whitemh. 138
Sessions, Samuel 37, 154, 190
Sexton, Dennis 13, 18
 James 98, 161
Sharborow/Sharburrow, Arthur 99, 162
Shaw (Mr) 81
 Daniel 180
Sheerwood/Sherwood, James 12, 17
Shepheard, Charles 214
Shickels, James 210
Shireman, Michael 210
Siders, John 91, 196
Simmons, Jeremiah 37, 153, 190
 Josiah 16
Simms, (William Gilmore, Wm. Gilmore) 137, 224
Simpson, Hugh 217
 James 213
Sims, William 209
 Willm. 219
Singleton, Bracy 52, 57
 (John, Jno.) 54-56, 175
 Joseph 55
 (Mathew, Matthew) 54-56, 173-175
 (Richard, Richd.) 38, 157, 193
 Ripley 52, 57
Skilling, William 17
Skinner, Thos. 138
 William 98, 161
Skirving, James Jr. 214, 215
 William 111, 120
Slater, John 213
 John Jr. 213
Sloan, Patrick 39
 (William, Wm.) 39, 158, 193
Smellie/Smillie, Patrick 99, 161
Smely, Wm. 111
Smith (Sarg Maj) 166
 Alexander 36, 149
 Andrew 12, 17
 Charles 223
 Henry 213
 Jesse 60, 144, 150
 John 19, 39, 77, 141, 159, 194
 John Carraway 98, 161
 Joseph 38, 157, 193
 Josiah 34, 59
 (Nicholas, Nichs.) 52, 57
 Samuel 114, 116, 118, 152
 Thomas 16, 111
 william 17
 Wm. 206

Smith (cont)
 (William Congdon, Wm. Congdon) 15, 20
Smyly, John 223
Sneling/Snelling, John 155, 187, 188
Snell, Adam 165
Snipes, William Clay 111
Snowden, Joshua 210
 Yates 211
Sojurner, Jacob 213
Solis, Esprit 12, 17
Sommers, John 111
Sowl, Benja. 219
 McKinny 219
Speers, James 213
Spurlock, (Robert, Robt.) 38, 157, 192
Stafford, James 19
Stanaland, Hugh 222
Standley, George 163
Stanley, Benjm. 213
 Joshua 125
 William 125
Stanyarne, Wm. 138
Stapleton, Philip 17
Steel, John 37, 154, 190
Stevens, George 210
Stevenson, James 93, 94
Stiley, John 15, 20
Stinson, Richard 20
Stobo, James 52, 57
Stom, Sabe 55
Stone (Mr) 107
 James 206
 (Prichard, Pritchard) 40, 141, 160, 195
 Sabe 175
 Thos. 206
Stoney, John 206
Storkiff, Thomas 51
Strain, William 18
Stroud, Joshua 176
Stuart (Capt) 183, 184
 (Mr) 63
 Alexr. 180
 Ch. 185
 George 213
 James 223
 John 89, 90
Stubbs/Stubs, John 60, 144, 150
Studavant, Thos. 213
Studdivent, Solomon 176
Willis 176
Sullivan, Daniel 19
Summer (Mr) 49
Summersett, Wm. 17
Sumpter (Mr) 48
Sumter (Gen) 140
Surginor, John 91, 164, 196
Sutherton, Harrod 163
Swan, Stephen 205
Sweat, Nathan 176
 Thomas 176
 William 176
Swilla, John 37, 154, 190
Swinney, John 206
Sykes, Joseph 125

-T-

Tamplett, Elishe 77

Tapley, John 156, 187, 189
Mark 125
Tate/Tatte (Mr) 42, 183, 184
Taylor (Lt) 147
 Abraham 223
 Billington 55
 (Francis, Fras.) 91, 164, 196
 Henry 125
 John 125
 Samuel 114, 116, 118, 151
 William 171
Teabout, 103
Tebout (Mr) 21, 135
Tunes 93, 172
Tedders, John 125
Temple/Temples, Jesse 55, 175
Tennant (Mr) 47, 50
Tennent (Mr) 62, 68, 83
Terry (Maj) 7
Testard, (Robert, Robt.) 52, 57
Thebout (Mr) 63
Theonin, Thomas 52
Theus, John 138
Thomas, James 13, 18
 (Trustum, Tristram) 59, 143, 149
 (William, Wm.) 165, 197
Thomson (Col) 8, 31, 43, 48, 58, 62, 69, 168, 172, 179, 204
 (Lt Col) 133
 Andw. 51, 57
 James 171
 Robt. 171
 William 4, 28, 29, 37, 39, 40, 61, 69, 70, 91, 92, 98, 114, 116, 118, 141, 143, 146-149, 151, 153, 155, 157, 159, 161, 163, 164, 166, 167, 179, 187, 188, 189, 194, 196, 203
Thorpe, Theophilus 12, 17
Tibout (Mr) 45
Tilley, Josiah 205
 Nathl. 205
Tillmon, Eron 223
Timothy, (Peter, Petr.) 1, 4, 134, 145, 216
Tines, Richd. 175
 Robt. 175
Tobias, Jacob 52, 57
Tollemache (Capt) 198
Tonyn (Gov) 8?, 198, 199
 Patrick 1
Toomer, Benjamin 209
 Joshua 210
Touchstone, Andrew 18
 Christopher 213
 Frederick 213
 Henry 213
 John 213
 Jonas 213
Towles, Oliver 114, 116, 118, 151
Townsen, John 176
 Light 176
Travers, Daniel 217
Trescvant, Lockwood 95
Trimble, Richard 13, 17
Trotter, Joseph 92, 165, 197

Troup, John 215
Tucker (Capt) 69
Turbeveal, Isaac 176
Turner, Thomas 14, 19
Tynes, Saml. 55

-U-

Uhrhy, John 163
Ulmer, Phillip 206

-V-

Valantine, William 213
Valentine, Willm. 3
Vance, Moses 157, 192
VanderHorst, Arnoldus 182
Vaughn, Isaac 91, 164, 196
Vergennes (Count) de 1
Verree, Joseph 26
Vertu, John 171

-W-

W_____, Edwd. 206
Wade/Waide, (Benjamin, Benja.) 92, 165, 197
Walker, Gunner 79
Wallis/Wallace, (Micajah, Micajor) 38, 157, 193
Walter (Lt) 77
  John Allen 124
  Richard 216
Ward, James 213
  Joshua 215
Waring, Rich 216
Warley (Lt) 6
  Felix 163
Warnock, John 98, 161
  Michael 98, 161
Warren, John 219
  John Sr. 219
Warrington, William 176
Washon, John 14, 19
Wason/Wasson, Hugh 223, 224
Watkins, William 176
Watson, Nathaniel 18
  Samuel 179, 180
Weatherford/Wetherford, William 37, 154, 191
Webb, Charles 22-25
  John 171
  Theodorick 176
Weight, Isaac 111
Weir, George 213
Welch, Daniel 60, 144, 150
  James 213
Wells, Joseph 155, 187, 189
  Richd. 175
  Robert 58
  Thomas 55
Welsh, Walter 77
Wesberry, Thos. 77
Wescoat, Thomas 138

West, Cato 66
  James 51, 57
  Richd. 206
  William 13, 18, 139
Wethrington, Richd. 213
  Thos. 213
Weyman (Mr) 95
Whaley, Archibald 137
  Thomas 138
Wheeler, Henry 55, 175
Wheet, Josiah 175
White, Arthr. 171
  Ezekiel 38, 157, 192
  Jno. 138
  Robert 37, 154, 190
Whitefield (Capt) 5, 8, 10, 11
  Geoe. 115, 117, 119
  Geor. 8
  George (Rev) 5
Whittington, Ephraim 176
  Francis Jr. 176
  Owent 176
  Richard 176
Wiggins, John 223
Wiles (Mr) 4
Wilkinson (Mr) 123, 129, 140, 147, 186, 201, 203, 204
  Edward 135, 202, 203
  Morton 111
  Will, Philip 44, 136
Williams, Burgess 60, 143, 149
  Gardner 155, 187, 189
  Henry 117, 118
  Jas. G. 51, 57
  John 19
  Joseph 91, 164, 196, 210
  William 17, 55
  Wm. 217
Williamson, Andrew 2, 3, 69
  William 1
Wills, Rich 55
Willson, Henry 115, 152
Wilson (Capt) 123
  Daniel 51, 57
  John 111, 138, 144
  Robert (Dr) 58
  Samuel 180
  William 39, 138, 141, 159, 177, 178, 195
  Willm. 66
Wimpee, John 171
Wimpey, Henry 40, 141, 159, 194
Winds, Abijah 17
Winingham/Winningham, William 156, 188, 189
Winn, R. 188
  (Richard, Richd.) 141, 159, 189, 194, 195
Winningham, Thomas 40, 160, 195
Wisdom, James 18
Wise, _____ 37
  (Capt) 60, 61, 148, 166, 167
  Ezekiel 138
  (Samuel, Saml.) 59, 132, 133, 143, 144, 149
Withers (Mr) 33
Witt, Samuel D. 55
Wofford (Col) 96
Wolf, Isaac 176

Wood, Charles 19
  Thomas 36, 153, 191
  William 125
  Wm. 38
Woods, Andrew 113
  James 171
  John 171
Woodward (Capt) 39, 166, 167, 168
  John 39, 141, 159, 194
  Thomas 40, 141, 142, 159, 194, 195
  William 206
Wooley, Lazarus 19
Wootan, John 91, 164, 196
Wootan/Wooton, (Daniel, Danl.) 91, 164, 196
Wournell, William 125
Wright, James (Sir) 183
  John 37, 153, 191
Wyley/Wyly, Henry 60, 144, 150, 155, 187, 188
Wynne, Richd. 39

-Y-

Yancey, Hezekiah 115, 117, 119, 152
Young, Daniel 60, 144, 150
  Wm. 66
Yutzy, Conrad 165
  Magdalen 165

-Z-

Zachry, Thomas 213
Zubly (Mr) 40

www.ingramcontent.com/pod-product-compliance
Lightning Source LLC
Chambersburg PA
CBHW070249230426
43664CB00014B/2464